SON OF A FARMER,
CHILD OF THE EARTH

A Path to Agriculture's
Higher Consciousness

ERIC HERM

son of a Farmer

child of the Earth

**A Path
to Agriculture's
Higher
Consciousness**

dreamriver
press

Dreamriver Press LLC
www.dreamriverpress.com
or contact at:
388 Altantic Avenue
Brooklyn, NY 11217
U.S.A.

First Dreamriver Press edition, 2010

ISBN-13: 978-0-9797908-9-8
ISBN-10: 0-9797908-9-1

Library of Congress Control Number: 2010928701

1. NAT011000-NATURE / Environmental Conservation & Protection
2. NAT038000-NATURE / Natural Resources
3. GAR016000-GARDENING / Organic

About the front cover:
This picture was taken on the homestead of the author's
great-grandparents. The land has been in his family
for almost 100 years. The author is pictured along with his son
(in the background), who is the fifth generation to live on this land.
Photo by Alison Herm.

Designed by George D. Matthiopoulos

This book is printed on 100% recycled paper.

Preserving our environment
Dreamriver Press chose Legacy TB Natural
100% post-consumer recycled paper for
the pages of this book printed by Webcom Inc.

Mixed Sources
Product group from well-managed
forests, controlled sources and
recycled wood or fiber
FSC   www.fsc.org Cert no. SW-COC-002358
© 1996 Forest Stewardship Council

Printed and bound in Canada

Dedicated to my two sons
and future generations everywhere

What people are saying about *Son of a Farmer, Child of the Earth*

"Please put this book on your must read list. Eric Herm's *Son of a Farmer, Child of the Earth* puts it all together with all the backup facts, connected dots, and heartfelt prose. I can now recommend this one book to my students instead of the usual 20 or so that have been necessary to adequately describe the current state of our culture, governance, and environment. It is indeed impressive that a young farmer from West Texas has overcome his regional and occupational bias to write such a brilliant book and done so with such integrity and openness. Perhaps *Son of a Farmer, Child of the Earth* will instill within its readers the courage to become the warriors of our uncertain future."

Scott Pittman
Director and Founder with Bill Mollison of the Permaculture Institute

"The food we eat and the farms on which it is grown are taken for granted by the majority of our population. Eric Herm is qualified to tell the real story about farm life that today is dominated by a few gigantic, multinational corporations that have infiltrated our federal agencies and paid Congress to vote in their best interest. This book uncovers the deceptions of the elite group of agribusinesses that control agriculture's seed, feed and fertilizer all the way to the dinner plate. This is an invaluable source for anyone wishing to learn the secrets of American agriculture and should be used as a textbook in our schools and colleges. Most Americans have little understanding of our agricultural heritage; Eric's book is a must read for those wishing to understand our nation's food system."

Derry Brownfield
Legendary rancher and national radio talk show host

"With erudition, poetry, and a profound love for his parched West Texas landscape, Eric Herm reawakens 'the farmer in all of us', showing how we can free our food system from corporate control while recovering our deepest humanity. Herm offers a deeply engaging mix of personal insight, scientific knowledge, populist rage, and a quest to regain a true partnership with the rest of nature."

Brian Tokar
Author of Earth for Sale, The Green Alternative, *and* Toward Climate Justice: Getting to the Roots of the Climate Crisis

"One way or another, a whole bunch more people will be taking up farming as a life's work in the next few years. The challenges they will face will be the greatest since the first plows cut the Fertile Crescent because the speed of changing climate now is unprecedented. Our next generation of farmers will have to scratch a living and rebalance the carbon cycle. With good-natured humor and humility, Eric Herm shows the way forward."

Albert Bates
Director of the Global Village Institute for Appropriate Technology and author of The Biochar Solution: Carbon Farming and Climate

Contents

Acknowledgements

A big thanks to my wife, Ali, for your calming smile, selflessness, and tolerating all my crazy tangents, ideas, and experiments...and for tolerating West Texas. You stand strong and graceful through the most difficult of times. Thank you for never giving up on our love.

This book was inspired mostly by the birth of my son, Wyatt. Your laughter and energy inspire me to do as much as I can each day to make the world a better place. May you direct your energy in future years to help create a better world. And to my child-to-be—may you grow up in a healthy, harmonious environment.

Mom and Dad, you've practiced unconditional love and patience throughout my lifetime. Thank you for keeping things in perspective for your children and grandchildren. Dad, thanks for being open-minded and keeping me grounded through all the wild ideas I've thrown your way and for being the best farmer I know. Mom, thank you so much for always being there to lend a hand or your heart, no matter the situation or hour.

And, of course, my granddad, Donnie. Your sense of humor, friendship, and wisdom have helped me more than you will ever know throughout the years. Thanks for being a wonderful teacher.

Thanks to: Shirley and Richard, for your literary and editorial guidance; Jim, for your passion in organics; J., for your computer wizardry; Beverly, Kay, and Jill, for your healing abilities; and Lynn L., for making sure I kept writing.

Last, but not least, a big token of gratitude to so many brilliant minds—pioneers of innovation and truth such as Philip Callahan, George Washington Carver, Rudolph Steiner, Nikola Tesla, William Albrecht, Charles Walters, Mike Ruppert, Joel Salatin, and many others who refused to let the lies of the system detour their desires, talents, and pursuit of the truth. Your work continues to inspire me.

And to countless other family members and friends who have helped open my mind and encouraged me to do, see, read, and say more than I ever would have on my own.

Foreword

Eric Herm is a youthful member of an endangered species—the American farmer. And his passionate manifesto deserves to be read by everyone of his generation; by all Americans, in fact.

Herm has left us a trail of breadcrumbs on his personal journey of discovery, and it makes for a disturbing read. How have we humans managed to turn the act of growing food into a process of killing the soil, robbing other species, and poisoning ourselves—a process so unrewarding that millions of farmers have simply given up? How have just a few chemical companies come close to owning the very basis of our global food system? Fortunately, a spate of recent books—led by Michael Pollan's *In Defense of Food* and Eric Schlosser's *Fast Food Nation*—has educated millions of readers to the perils of the modern industrial food system. But it is where they leave off that Herm begins; where they state the problem, he has staked his future on a solution.

America needs enormous numbers of new farmers to follow in Herm's footsteps. The 20th century saw the replacement of farmers with machines running on oil, and with chemicals made from fossil fuels. In this century, as oil and other resources dwindle, we will need generations of *children of the Earth* to take up once again the venerable occupation that feeds us all. That means we require a revival not just of the many skills that farmers need, but a renewal of rural farming culture, and the creation of an economic system that rewards what really matters—healthy food and healthy planet—more than it does speculation in imaginary claims on ill-defined wealth.

Herm is a radical in the true sense: he wants to get to the root of problems. And he reveals ecological farming to be perhaps the most radical act that any young person can engage in. The era we have entered upon—this century of changing climate, depleting resources, and disappearing species—calls for radicalism of exactly this sort.

If there is hope for the future, it is here.

Richard Heinberg
Senior Fellow, Post Carbon Institute
Author, Peak Everything

We still talk in terms of conquest. We still haven't become mature enough to think of ourselves as only a tiny part of a vast and incredible universe. Man's attitude toward nature is today critically important simply because we have now acquired a fateful power to alter and destroy nature. But man is a part of nature and his war against nature is inevitably a war against himself...Now I truly believe that we in this generation must come to terms with nature, and I think we're challenged as mankind has never been challenged before to prove our maturity and our mastery, not of nature, but of ourselves.

RACHEL CARSON, April 1963

We can't solve problems by using the same kind of thinking we used when we created them.

ALBERT EINSTEIN

What it lies in our power to do, it lies in our own power not to do.

ARISTOTLE

Prologue

THE PROVERBIAL FORK IN THE ROAD
A Road Less Traveled

> *The key to change is to let go of fear.*
> ROSEANNE CASH

> *I do not feel obligated to believe*
> *that the same god who has endowed us*
> *with sense, reason and intellect*
> *has intended us to forgo their use.*
> GALILEO GALILEI

Point of Recognition

Before I begin, you must know this—I don't know all the answers. What I do have are ideas in the form of a new direction that will better serve us, our purpose, and our posterity. This book is about trying to provide some healthy solutions to many problems we are currently faced with not only in agriculture, but also in life in general. Hopefully the content will stimulate your conscience regarding the unthinkable challenges our children will be faced with in the years to come if we continue our current destructive methods.

Unfortunately, over these next few years a significant portion of commercial farmers will suffer or fail along with consumer retail, fiat currency, the automobile industry, commercial real estate, affordable fuel, and inefficient urban living. Shortly after the Civil War, farmers represented 67% of America's population—145 years later we are less than 1%. In 1935, the U.S. peaked at more than 6.8 million farms and 30 million farmers out of 127 million American citizens.[1] In 2009, there were approximately 960,000 farmers out of 300 million American people.[2] Of the 2,064,700 remaining American farms, only 38.2% are financially profitable.

Farm Type	Number of Farms	Percent of Farms
Non-family farms	42,300	2.0
Farming sales > $500,000	61,300	3.0
$250,000 - $499,999	91,900	4.5
Limited resource	150,300	7.3
$100,000 - $249,999	171,500	8.3
Retirement	290,900	14.1
Farming sales < $100,000	422,200	20.4
Residential/Lifestyle	834,300	40.4
TOTAL	2,064,700	100.0

(Statistics according to the Federal Department of Agriculture)

This vanishing act of farmers isn't happening solely in America, it is a global issue. In 1985 there were more than 28,000 dairy farmers in England and Wales, and only 11,551 in November of 2009.[3] In January of 2010, farmers in Greece continued to hold up traffic on major roads for more than one month straight with blockades, protesting higher tax rates and demanding more subsidies to survive economically. Thousands of farmers barricaded

1. http://www.epa.gov.
2. *Ibid.*
3. Olga Craig, "The Dairy Farmer Reduced to Tears", *The Telegraph*, http://www.telegraph.co.uk/earth/agriculture/farming/6958013/The-dairy-farmer-reduced-to-tears.html. January 9, 2010.

some 23 highway junctions across northern and central Greece with their tractors, losing more than $25 million a day for the Greek economy.[4] With Indian farmers continuing to diminish at their current rate, there will be 400 million "agriculture refugees" in that country alone by 2020.[5]

If we persist in following the model of commercial agriculture, we are destined to fail. Perhaps commercial farming, as designed, must die in order for Nature and humanity to fully recover and *real* farming to begin anew. Most likely the only method of farming that will survive is the one focused on a healthy, organic operation supporting local families, friends, communities, towns, and cities. The era of the 3,000+ acre family farm will soon be a thing of the past. Will we choose eradication because we blindly refuse to change or will we survive by evolving into a smaller, stronger, and healthier vocation that the rest of humanity and all living creatures can depend upon? Now is the time to answer that question as we stand at the proverbial fork in the road.

By 2007, there were more prisoners in this country than farmers. So, I write this with full awareness that I am an endangered species—a young farmer. I'm fully aware of the tenacity which exists in a man, particularly the breed that are farmers. Despite our stubbornness, we can no longer deny the inevitable—we are in the final days of a broken system. The statistics, research, and analysis within this book form a story that must be told to ensure we know not only what we've become but where we are headed. Our ability to survive relies solely on our ability to change and our ability to unite. We're going to need more farmers...and fast to feed and clothe this world.

---

4. Helena Smith, "Greek Economy Worsens with Farmers Refusing to Back Down", *The Guardian*, http://www.guardian.co.uk/business/2010/jan/31/greek-farmers-blockade-impasse, January 31, 2010.
5. Devinder Sharma, "Displacing Farmers: India Will Have 400 Million Agricultural Refugees", Share the World's Resources, http://www.stwr.org/food-security-agriculture/displacing-farmers-india-will-have-400-million-agricultural-refugees.html, June 22, 2007.

It is time for a new breed of farmer to step forward. I believe many young people are looking to return to the land, to work with Nature and all living things. I sense a movement which will return young men and women with their families back to country living from metropolitan and suburban lifestyles. Perhaps it is the young farmer, the novice, the rural revolutionary, the re-beginners who will hear the truth and walk the path we must follow in order to create a healthier world.

As farmers, we've transformed into part of the problem rather than the solution. Without immediate and radical changes in our mentality and agricultural practices, nobody should pity us. Fueled by desire, we are fully capable of getting ourselves out of the mess we've helped create. Our problems cannot all be blamed on governments and corporations. We have allowed this hostile takeover. Without a change in direction toward an organic, sustainable agricultural system based on a local economy and fair trade we will perish along with the banking and automobile industries. Food and clothing (which we produce) are much more of a necessity than money and cars. Herein lies our conundrum as a nation of corporate co-dependents.

Know this. I am not some "liberal tree hugger". I was born a country boy with a hankerin' for independence and a disdain for authority. I am not a scientist or geneticist. I do not have a Ph.D. in physics, botany, ecology, geology, or biology. While I have no special degree in regards to science, I do possess a very strong connection to Nature. I am a fourth-generation farmer. I am a naturalist and a survivalist. I am redneck and hippie. I am cowboy and Indian. This is my dichotomy. This is the battle waged within me daily, allowing a balanced existence. The redneck tries to kick the hippy's ass. The Indian calmly brings the wild cowboy back to center...when possible. In Nature, I am often in total harmony. With humanity, I am frequently at war. While I'm not currently an organic farmer in our commercial operation, I play one at home—continually experimenting with various projects dealing with making the Earth a better place. Those healthy experiments spill over into our commercial operation, giving me hope that I'll one day buck the entire system of commercial agriculture.

Undeniably, we've followed the wrong lead for too long. The Powers That Be epitomize what ails Mother Earth. We've fallen for the entire pyramid scheme of paper money, basing most of our thoughts, dreams, and goals around scraps of paper with numbers and dead presidents on them.

Not much remains in Nature from what was once there centuries ago. Many resources have been wasted in the last century thanks to deforestation, oil-influenced transportation, increasing populations, and a disregarding attitude of superiority. Not enough minds seem to acknowledge that many of our current agricultural methods involving "modern technology" are simply based on methods destructive to Mother Earth. Our procrastination is inexcusable, and we must begin a healthy transformation. We must change the rules and, if necessary, change the game entirely. Catherine Austin Fitts once said, "Those who win in a rigged game get stupid." Improving should be our goal, not winning.

I am hopeful we will fully recognize the dangers of our current methods and alter our lives accordingly. I am hopeful we will educate ourselves rather than plug our ears and cover our eyes, pretending our destructive practices are harmless. I am hopeful we will unite in purpose before it is too late.

To farmers, may the content inspire you to break free from trends ripping us apart. We must lead an awakening to solve most of these problems if agriculture is to survive. Are there enough farmers remaining? Will our own children or grandchildren ever know the freedoms we once knew? It is my hope they will. But, if we walk farther down the current path we now tread grudgingly upon, I am fearful few of Nature's purities or our Constitution's freedoms will survive. Decades, perhaps centuries from now, Nature will recover. We will not. To younger generations, please learn from the sins of our plundering.

To those who eat food, drink water, and breathe air (which should cover pretty much everybody), may this book motivate you to be farmers in your own right, or in the very least give you reason to learn how to provide for your family in a healthy manner by becoming less dependent on corporations and government for your survival. There is a farmer in each of us. That is to say there exists a portion of us which is connected to all of Nature, a part craving a primordial connection and a kindred relationship with the Earth. May the content educate you on some of the many challenges that farmers face and that prevent agriculture from being as pure as it should be.

Turning blind eyes and deaf ears to our crimes against Nature will not erase them. Pursuing old, tired paths will all but surely seal our doomed fate. This is not an exaggeration. Now is the time for our species to unite and for us to empower ourselves with knowledge and liberate our souls with action. Not later. Now. If we wait, it will be much too late. If we pretend everything is okay, all will be lost. Now is the time for action. It has been said that there are three things you can't hide forever—the sun, the moon, and the truth. Let the truth now rise above these dark, muddied waters. This is no time for egos. This is no time to wait for government bailouts. It is sink or swim. Will we chose life? Or is death too tempting to ignore? It is my hope, plea, and prayer we chose life.

Gone are the dinosaurs that once ruled this Earth. Gone are the Vikings and conquistadors, cowboys and Indians. Gone are generation after generation of heroes and villains, kings and queens, peasants and surfs, and numerous leaders and followers. Gone are so many creatures and kingdoms once plentiful and strong, but they are all now nothing more than historically precious and poetically romantic characters in a very compelling story.

In our quest for conquering more, we cross large oceans in tiny boats to find what? We build walls to protect us from whom? We construct roads and bridges to take us where? We explore the heavens to find why we are here, what we should do, and who we should become. Yet, after centuries of performing such heroic measures, what have we discovered? Our spiritual destination is determined by our current path of thoughts and actions whether spiritual in concept or not. What have you truly discerned about your own existence?

Now, I hope you will join me...at least in thought, if not also in action. Then, perhaps we can solve some of the many issues at hand. After all, this is the only planet we have, the only soil our feet will walk, the only air our lungs will breathe, the only food our bellies will digest, and the only water to quench our thirst. Let us begin a path to agriculture's higher consciousness.

The Road Back Home

Harvest season was over...finally. Here it was February of 2005, and I could still hear the roar of cotton strippers echoing along the horizon like mechanical herds grazing the prairie's last supper to the bone. Clouds swam slowly and lowly overhead. Winds whispered a stillness the likes of which only the calm of dusk can bring.

I had little, almost nothing to do with the crop until the end —filling in for one worker here and there. Ending a long-term relationship and tired of bouncing from one hapless job to another, I was certain drastic change was needed in my life. This change had to be accompanied with purpose. Through all my days of traveling and philosophizing, the most dominant thoughts which plagued my mind were:

"What a twisted version of life we insisted was the norm."

"What a strange time to ignore our problems."

"Why is everything about money?"

"Why does religion build walls rather than bridges?"

"Why are we trying so hard to mess up a perfectly good planet?"

I was 31 years old, and for the first time in my life there resided a sick feeling deep in my gut. I was seriously questioning why I was not a part of the family farm. It had been my decision nine years previous to remove myself from that way of life, to get as far away as possible from West Texas, from John Deere tractors, bloody knuckles, grease-stained blue jeans, sweat-soaked t-shirts, empty prairie, and flat horizons full of nothing but wind, sandstorm, drought and unfulfilled youth. But now, now life felt...different. Vibrant. I felt reborn. The Earth spun to a new rhythm, desperately needing me to be a part of her song and dance.

I'd finished painting the trim on my parent's house, grabbed a beer from the fridge, stepped outside, and strode across the backyard to fully embrace the late evening sky. Yellows gave birth to oranges, oranges to reds, reds to violets, and violets to blues. It was yet another masterpiece. For some strange reason I remembered a line in a movie where some crazy character at an extravagant New York City party was asking the age-old question, "Does life imitate art or does art imitate life?" My question was, and still is, "What's the difference?"

My legs wound me in and out of naked cotton stalks. I could hear their thoughts focused on where their children were going. "Don't worry," I laughed. "They're off to clothe the world." I wasn't certain my response comforted them or not as I was focused on being careful not to break web-stitchings of various spiders from one stalk to another. Lost in thought, I sat crosslegged in the rows. Listening. Watching. Feeling. Waiting for a moment of brilliance.

Along the county road, telephone poles bent southward from several years of strong northerners pushing against their splintery flesh. I felt dizzy, as if the Earth's rotation was explaining itself in full detail to my skull. Laying flat on my back, I began to cover my legs with sandy soil, baptizing my body into the Earth's spirit. Buried up to my chest, I continued to lie perfectly still, focused on nothing but my next breath. I thought to myself, "Now is the time to return. Come back home. This is where you are needed."

But then I thought, "Are you kidding me? I don't want to come back to this place...do I?"

But home was calling me back. I could feel the Earth speaking through me, into me, whispering to my spirit. At first, I shrugged off the notion of returning to the very place which stole my youth. Why would any sane person return to the heart of West Texas? I mean, I knew whole-heartedly this was where the desert gave birth to the prairie, where bone met rock, south met west, brown met orange, and forever met never again. On top of all that, why would I want to enter a profession designed to break most men? It just didn't make any sense. But, not much did.

The soil smelt like dirt—the crumbling, cracking dry grains of Earth thirsting for more. The air smelt like long days of sweat and isolation. A smell that slowed my heart and panicked my spirit. One part longed for such emotion, the other wished it never existed. "Here I am again," I thought. Like an animal who senses danger, I had returned home instinctively. This time it felt different. This time there existed a mutual agreement between myself and the same land that drove me insane years ago with thoughts of mediocrity. Rising upward, uncovering my numbed body, I grinned and realized I hadn't been sane in years. Naturally, when crazy meets insane, everything makes perfect sense.

Back in Lubbock I spent days and nights contemplating not just who I was but what I wanted to do and accepting what I needed to do. I broke up with my girlfriend of two years as she was not prepared for such a transformation. What I needed to do was clear. What I wanted to do could wait. A few days later I packed everything I had into my 1973 Oldsmobile Delta 88 convertible and headed south down Highway 87, humming Mac Davis' *Lubbock, Texas, In My Rearview Mirror*. I was off to be not just a son of a farmer any longer, but a new breed of farmer hell-bent on changing my life and Life (as a whole) for the better.

And the vision was gettin' clearer in my dreams.

Chapter 1

PLANTING TINY SEEDS
Altering Our Point of View

Think small. Planting tiny seeds
in the small space given
you can change the whole world or,
at the very least, your view of it.
LINUS MUNDY

Fear not that thy life shall come to an end,
but rather fear that it shall never have a beginning.
JOHN HENRY CARDINAL

All Dreams Reach for the Sun

We are all children of the Earth. No matter where we are from, what we do or what we believe, each one of us is part of the soil, rivers, mountains, trees, plants, prairies, deserts, and oceans. Every particle is connected to the next, with each life-form depending upon the existence of so many other fascinating creatures.

As one of the most influential species, we have an obligation to the rest of the planet. Time and money represent the greatest barriers in fulfilling this obligation, and they are nothing more than illusions in this world. Our minds are more powerful than our bodies if we simply free our imaginations; free them from the boundaries and barriers of the expected. Right there—where our minds break free and our unified spirit travels across the cosmic prairie—is a new Life. It is where seedlings break through the surface, stretching for the sun, and dreams transform into the everlasting warmth of reality.

As farmers, we must accept our role as guardians of the Earth whole-heartedly, refusing to sell ourselves and the land into slavery. Until now we've tangled our minds into the wreckage of a corporation-led mentality, where Nature's bounty is merely another tradable commodity. Our philosophies are financially motivated rather than spiritually, and our purpose is lost in meaningless goals. Following corporate agriculture's persuasion, we've accepted a leading role as assassin, carrying out the morbid execution of Nature in exchange for a briefcase full of money. Until we accept Nature as part of our true being, we will change nothing.

I stare into this horizon of things to come. Not completely certain what the future might bring, I continue to gaze into the blaze that is the setting sun. My vision blurred, I stumble. My purpose confirmed, I continue in the direction in which I remember warmth's embrace. From this prairie-like desert I witness a collage of mirages. In the blistering heat, distant images appear which make me question the legitimacy of our existence and meaning. The heat boils my brain. Sweat turns to blood. Thoughts melt into wild hallucinations. This requires meditation in the shielding shade for a spell. Rest will aid in gathering energy and information, but I must be careful how long I relax in the solace of shadows, for there is much work to be done.

The Fruit of Life Becomes the Root of Disaster

Everything in Nature begins and ends with the seed. Just as in life all things begin and end with a dream. The trick is knowing what is vital and what is detrimental in between. Without seeds, life on Earth would be impossible for us. Hobby gardeners and commercial farmers know you can't have a healthy crop without healthy seeds. It's simple genetics. From these tiny little flakes of matter spring forth all living things including the largest of trees. Yet, here, early into the 21st century, very little focus is placed on healthy, natural seeds. To put it bluntly, much of our indigenous seed supply is in great peril.

An extreme threat exists, encompassing the potential to obliterate the laws of Nature and therefore obliterate all of us in the process. No, it is not weapons of mass destruction, terrorists from another country, nuclear wars; neither is it melting polar icecaps, peak oil, economic turmoil nor an airborne virus transforming us into zombies. The very things assuring certain death for humanity and Nature are tiny seeds. Ironically, some of the tiniest and most recognized symbols of life could one day be what prevents Life as we know it from surviving in a healthy manner. These seeds do not come from a remote South American jungle or antediluvian times. They were created in a laboratory in St. Louis, Missouri. They are commonly known as genetically modified organisms or GMOs. Farmers know them as Roundup Ready seeds.

When I moved back to our family farm in West Texas in 2005, I thought Roundup Ready cotton was an excellent answer to our high fuel and labor expenses. Short-term, it is an excellent remedy for those problems, but I was unaware of the countless other long-term problems it would create. Thinking this method would solve many of our financial issues, I talked my father into planting more than 1,000 acres of Roundup Ready cotton in 2005 and just under 1,000 acres in 2006. Doing absolutely no research beforehand, I had no idea what I was doing to the ecosystem. One afternoon while I was planting cotton, a couple of old friends from the city came out to witness cotton farming first hand, taking some photos of me on the trusty ol' John Deere tractor. They were fascinated by the warning labels on the bags of Roundup Ready cotton seed on the trailer. My friend Shirley read aloud the warnings on the side I'd conveniently ignored. Her husband J. took some snapshots.

"Frightening," he said, shaking his head in disbelief.

I simply laughed, thinking, "Yeah, big deal."

When you grow up with chemicals as an extension of your farming practices, more warnings with skulls and crossbones draw little attention to what crimes you are committing against

Nature. When I was a child and young adult, chemicals were always around during each planting season. It was simply a part of the process. I hated them. They irritated my skin. Once in a while my eyes would burn. Once inhaled, you could feel certain chemicals literally pulsate through your lungs and head. I had no idea farming was possible without these products, let alone how dangerous they were to my own health and the environment. Away from farming, I had refused to use chemicals in my own home or on my lawn, but strangely on the farm it was acceptable.

The Roundup Ready seed variety allows farmers to spray Roundup herbicide over small, young plants in the early stages without causing damage to the crop. Roundup Ready 2 or Flex allows farmers to spray Roundup herbicide throughout the growing stages of the plant without causing damage to the crop. Bollguard I and II contain built-in worm control (the gene of *Bacillus theringetus* or Bt) minimizing the use of insecticides. I'm sure part III is soon on the way. Bollworms are already building a resistance to this particular seed.

A study by the University of Wisconsin discovered that the Bt toxin, when mixed with naturally occurring antibiotics, becomes even more deadly to vital pollinating insects such as honeybees, flies, etc.[1] Monsanto announced Bollguard I would no longer be sold as of January 1, 2010 due to the bollworm's evolved resistance to its genetic makeup. There are no known signs of pollinating insects building up a resistance to Bt. These seed varieties have their equal in other crops such as canola, corn, and soybeans, as well as other corporations' versions.

After researching these seeds and Monsanto, I realized that their use was a huge mistake on my part. I discovered a vast amount of literature documenting the potential and definite dangers of GMOs and also revealing Monsanto's intentions of

---

1. George Gallepp, "Scientists Find Compound that Makes Bt Pesticide More Effective", College of Agriculture and Life Sciences, University of Wisconsin, May 21, 2001, http://www.cals.wisc.edu/media/news/05_01/zwitter_Bt.html.

cornering the market in virtually every vital seed necessary for food production. I read of countless lawsuits filed by Monsanto against individual farmers and realized I was supporting a company that would do anything in its power to generate more profit even if it had to chew up and spit out every last farmer and every other living creature walking the Earth. Through years of in-depth research, it has become evident to me that Monsanto and other companies producing genetically modified seed inflict further damage on the planet rather than help agriculture or humanity. It is greed in its purest form.

Edward Bernays was the nephew of world-renowned psychoanalyst Sigmund Freud. He put his uncle's theories to action in the world of advertising, creating jingles for radio and television in the first half of the 20th century. He's known as the "Father of Spin". And Americans swallowed the bait—hook, line, and sinker. In short, he messed around with our brains, convincing us to buy much more than we needed, but because it was delivered with a song, jingle, and dance, we ate it up like a Thanksgiving dinner. His early clients included Monsanto and DuPont, and they have no doubt employed his methods to support their greedy ambitions to manipulate and control all of humanity and, in essence, all of Life on this planet. I'm also often reminded of the quote by Henry Kissinger over 20 years ago in a letter promoting the Trilateral Commission: "Control oil and you can control continents. Control food and you control the people." Let those words marinate for a moment, chilling the marrow in your bones.

Corporations like Monsanto, Dow Chemical, DuPont, and Bayer Crop Science have raided our seed supply, genetically altering DNA so that they may pimp Life's beginnings to not only farmers, but all humans, catastrophically accelerating much of Nature's ruin. Smaller seed companies are being bought, chewed up, and spat out like sugarless gum, and, nine times out of ten, Monsanto is the one handing over the checks in return for more power and control. Year after year, delinting plants, cotton gins, grain mills, and other seed manufacturing plants are going out of business because the American farmer has turned away from conventional seed from Mother Nature and become increasingly addicted to Monsanto's mentality.

Genetically modified (GM) seeds are quickly wiping out our natural seed supply. Those genetically modified versions pollinate our conventional seed, committing a hostile takeover, and then officials from a company like Monsanto waltz into any farmer's field or seed delinting plant, take samples, and file a multi-million dollar lawsuit against the farmer for stealing their seed when he is actually saving his own seed (a method practiced by farmers since the beginning of agriculture). Indigenous seed will be compromised by genetically modified seed, which is patented, as the genetically modified genes invade those of Nature. The corporation's plan? Basically to own every seed on the planet. Sound too much like a horror movie? Am I exaggerating? Perhaps paranoia has taken me over and I've lost my mind? I'm afraid I haven't…not yet anyway. According to the U.S. Department of Agriculture (USDA), the U.S. genetically modified food harvest in 1999 showed significant percentages of GMOs:

GM Crops in 1999	
Soybeans	57%
Corn	38%
Cotton	65%
Potatoes	4%
Canola	50%

How fast and easily have GMO crops multiplied? Fast forward just a few years, and we see how GM versions of these few commodity crops, which are the "bread and butter" of our entire food chain, have spread across America like a hellish brushfire. Jeffrey Smith, author of *Seeds of Deception* (an excellent book on Monsanto, GMOs, and the downfalls they bring), sheds more light on this subject than anyone else in America. Smith's research has revealed alarming statistics of the percentages of commercial crop seeds that are, as of June of 2007, genetically modified:

GM Crops in 2007	
Soy	89% (an increase of 51% from 1999)
Cotton	83% (up 19%)
Canola	75% (up 25%)
Corn	61% (up 23%)
Hawaiian papaya	50%
Alfalfa, zucchini and yellow squash	(small amount)
Tobacco (Quest® brand)	

(Courtesy of www.seedsofdeception.com)

And that's just to name a few crops. Experimental plots have already begun in wheat and rice. Can you imagine if wheat, rice, corn, and soy crops were completely genetically modified? It is very close to happening. By 2012, this catastrophic event will probably be a reality. Genetically modified alfalfa is being pushed as well. If Monsanto is allowed to continue the manufacturing and distribution of Roundup Ready soy, wheat, and rice, then very soon almost all our food will be contaminated and compromised. We will be attempting to nourish our bodies and minds with the cloned illusions of genetically modified food—and, believe me, this is not a promising career choice. In less than eight years, these crops have risen by 20-50% in GMO productions. I shudder to think what these figures will be in another eight years.

"But, surely this is high-tech stuff we're dealing with here. This is the evolution of man at his finest. We're so smart to come up with this stuff," you may insist, trying your best to ignore your higher conscience.

Really? Perhaps you've already become yet another victim of the brain-staining of Monsanto's advertising, which assures us they are here "to help feed the starving world". Yeah, and I've got some lovely oceanfront property here in West Texas I'd like to make you a sweet deal on too.

The main problem here is not really Monsanto or similar corporations. It is the farmer. We've been buying this nonsense and never really seem to question its place in Nature. We never find ourselves asking, "Is this what is best for the soil, the plants, the community, agriculture, or my children?" As long as we make a profit, everything else be damned. And that's exactly what we're doing—damning all things. Why must we wait for post-mortem mandatory announcements by the Environmental Protection Agency or the USDA warning us of the uses and abuses of toxic products used increasingly in commercial agriculture?

Any Way the Wind Blows

Some of you may be asking, "What's the big deal? It's just a little ol' seed. What should we be scared of?"

Well, I'm so glad you asked. 'Cause dear ol' Mother Nature likes to sing her song on occasion—meaning the wind doth blow. With those winds comes pollination and seed scattering. In fact, the wind is one of the most frustrating things about farming. Yes sir, you can be the best farmer in the world, but seeds from your neighbor's weeds can wreak all kinds of havoc on your fields. Tiny little seeds can easily be blown up to one mile away, especially here in West Texas. Likewise, genetically modified seeds get tossed around just as easily. Let's say you are a farmer trying to grow and save your conventional certified cotton, canola or corn seed to supply yourself with a respective cash crop for two years or more. And your friendly neighbor across the turning row is growing Monsanto's or Bayer Crop Science's latest version of genetically modified cotton, canola, or corn, and, guess what, the wind is blowing across his field to yours during the pollinating or harvesting process. You've got a serious mess on your hands because GMOs have crossed with your all-natural, indigenous seed.

So, what happens next? Well, the respective corporation will most likely file a multi-million dollar lawsuit against you for violating their "patent"...unless you beat them to the punch with environmental issues, defamation of character, etc. Even if you do win, their lawyers will appeal and appeal until they are blue in the face and you are hollow in the pocket.

It's eerily similar to the likes of an Exxon Valdez oil spill. You remember that disaster, don't you? The tanker from Exxon that spilled 257,000 barrels of oil into the bay of Prince William Sound along the pristine fishing coastline of remote Alaska in 1989? It killed fishing in that area, along with the entire ecosystem consisting of seals, whales, herring, salmon, crab, lobster, and virtually every other species in the North Arctic waters. Yes, the fishermen and townspeople of Valdez and Cordova won a $5 billion lawsuit in court. Did they receive that check? Not a dime. Fisherman, local businesses, canneries, etc., went belly up while Exxon continued to rake in over $5 billion each quarter. Twenty years later, and they are still waiting. Appeal after appeal, Exxon refused to admit fault and thumbed their nose at the law. In 2007, the Supreme Court upheld the case, but the compensation was cut in half to $2.5 billion. Yet, not one dollar has been received. Exxon, in its arrogance, ignored the Supreme Court and didn't even get a slap on the wrist. Imagine if you or I did the same. We'd be marched straight off to the nearest federal facility.

Monsanto and the others are in their own way causing even more damage than Exxon could ever dream about. Over decades, oil will slowly dissipate through Nature. Genetic engineering by contrast dominates, invades, and destroys Nature. It takes between five and ten generations for that indigenous seed to return to its native genetic makeup. That means it can take up to one decade for the GMOs to be flushed out of seeds' molecular structure.

The most infamous case of Monsanto vs. Farmer involves Percy Schmeiser of Bruno, Saskatchewan, Canada. He spent 40 years developing canola seed resistant to various diseases and blights. That is until 1996 when wind spilled genetically modified canola onto his farm from neighboring fields. Monsanto filed a lawsuit against Schmeiser for violating their patent laws, after he caught the seed from his canola crop, just as he had been doing for four decades. Monsanto sought between $15 and $37 per acre. In the end, Schmeiser was forced to destroy his canola seed supply contaminated by Monsanto's GM seed. The legal battle lasted until 2004—typical of Monsanto's legal dealings. But Schmeiser never quit. He never backed down from the corporate giant. He lost the lawsuit, but was not forced to pay the $400,000 Monsanto was seeking since he did not use the seed for financial gain. Schmeiser won a moral victory in the case as the Canadian Supreme Court ruled Monsanto liable for contamination and pollution of a farmer's field.

A quote on Schmeiser's personal website sums up this ambiguous battle of Monsanto vs. Farmer. "In my case, I never had anything to do with Monsanto, outside of buying chemicals. I never signed a contract. If I would go to St. Louis and contaminate their plots—destroy what they have worked on for 40 years—I think I would be put in jail and the key thrown away."

The story of this brave Canadian farmer spread across the entire world. In 2000, Schmeiser was awarded the Mahatma Gandhi Award in India, in recognition of his working for the betterment and good of mankind in a non-violent way. His refusal to coward to a corporate giant like Monsanto sent shockwaves throughout the agriculture world. His heroic stand will not soon be forgotten.

Let's head south to visit our Mexican neighbors, where corn began with the Mayans. Genetically modified corn started showing up in Mexico between 1998 and 2001, even in the extremely remote areas of the sierras in Oaxaca and Puebla, where the cultivation of corn began thousands of years ago. GM corn is finding its way into tortillas, taco shells, chips, and many other forms of Mexican food. Half of the corn-growing regions in Mexico discovered contamination readings as high as 60% in 2002 during a government study. Much of the precious varieties that took two to three thousand years to become resistant to various diseases, drought, and insects are being contaminated by cross-pollination with genetically modified corn varieties. This is an irreversible compromise of one of our greatest staple foods.

The Mexican Government was forced to step in and enforce prohibitions against genetically modified corn, but larger farmers still sneak in planting of the laboratory seeds to please companies such as Cargill and Archer Daniels Midland (ADM), who now control between 60-80% of the corn flour and tortilla market. In 2006, taco shells milled and confected by Gruma and marketed by Kraft were found to contain Starlink corn, not yet authorized for human consumption, resulting in the largest call-back of any transgenically contaminated product in U.S. history.[2]

Wind aids in the cross-pollination between Nature's seed and the laboratory "test tube" seed, not to mention the drifting of the Roundup herbicide used in pre-planting and post-emergence stages of the respective crops. This is the basis of another war being waged right now along turning rows across the world.

Through the years Dad and I have had hundreds of acres of cotton killed or severely set back due to Roundup drift from neighbors. We've been fortunate enough in some cases to receive compensation from the flying service that damaged our crops. A relative was not so fortunate in 2007 (a bumper crop year for our area). They had about 40 acres of a 160-acre field unable to produce due to Roundup damage. Surrounded on three sides by

---

2. John Ross, "Big Biotech is Forcing Farmers to Buy GMO Seeds: The Plot Against Mexican Corn", *Counterpunch*, http://www.counterpunch.org/ross02142007.html. February 14, 2007.

Roundup farmers, the outer perimeters were knocked back by the careless methods of fellow farmers and lifelong neighbors. They received zero compensation. Each farmer will usually hitch their wagon to the good ol' boy routine, "Well, I wouldn't do that to you." No, but the chemical would. Often, people want to shut their eyes and consciences by pretending they are not part of the problem. And it is getting worse each season. Most Roundup farmers are not careless with their chemical application, but it only takes one nearby to ruin your conventional crops.

In May of 2009, my neighbor had his Roundup Ready cotton sprayed by Helena Chemical Company less than 40 yards from my home garden. The Roundup herbicide drifted and wiped out over 800 garlic bulbs, and all of my tomato, pepper, potato, bean, and corn plants. Within 48 hours every single plant in my garden curled up into a fetal position. Leaves curled upward, cupped around the edges, and the plants showed visible signs of suffering. For three or four days I couldn't figure out what had happened until I discovered my neighbor had sprayed Roundup a few days previous. I flew into a rage yet maintained my cool talking to Helena company officials. They were very courteous yet proceeded to blame a plane spraying half a mile away to the southwest. I wasn't buying that. I told the company reps I was going to do a tissue sample testing for Roundup.

The local store manager replied, "You can't test for Roundup."

"Really?" I replied, knowing full-well Glyphosate (the key plant-killing ingredient in Roundup) was easily detectable.

The lab tests came back positive for Glyphosate. After informing him of the results, he replied, "Well, I don't think we did it."

That's how these chemical companies work. Did I receive the $4,000 in damages? Take a wild guess. They put their lawyer against yours, and these chemical companies have a lot more money to spend on attorney fees than an individual farmer. Thanks to my neighbor and Helena Chemical Company, I lost an entire season of garlic, tomatoes, peppers, potatoes, beans and corn as months of hard work spiraled down the drain.

Tomato, pepper, onion, garlic, and potato plants are extremely sensitive to Roundup. One whiff and their leaves curl upward and they are unable to produce healthy, normal-sized fruit. Very frustrating when you begin an entire garden from seed. Money cannot replace healthy food. What will happen as more careless neighbors continue this practice? How will money alone nourish a hungry belly? With a global food crisis looming, the widespread usage of such destructive herbicides should be used with extreme caution. As long as we continue to think Roundup Ready crops are the only answer, agriculture is doomed.

I've seen trees, grass, and all green living things transformed into a brown haze overnight from aerial application. A neighbor's oak tree that was over 200 years old was nearly destroyed by a careless crop duster pilot spraying 2-4D (the modern version of Agent Orange), a very nasty herbicide banned in most countries. Whether it is from crop dusters, gigantic spray rigs, or small spray rigs, just a breath of Roundup can wreak havoc on an individual or family. It's what we can't see that kills us. There will be blood spilled all across the country as these battles continue along turning rows. We are creating a war zone in rural fields. Roundup farmers have sprayed this poison for so many years it is becoming second nature. The spray boom is the 21st century's version of the plow. But even as nasty as the Dust Bowl was, ceaseless sandstorms have nothing on the worldwide disease and sickness caused by these chemicals and crops that contaminate our soil, water, and air. The companies who make money from their sales couldn't care less who suffers in the process. It is up to the farmer to stop this calamity.

In 2005, Macon County, Georgia, became the gloomy example of what Roundup Ready farming could possibly create nationwide. This area of the country once boasted of being the Genetically Modified Crop Mecca of the entire United States. Now, there are no boasts. More than 7,000 acres of farmland were lost that season due to the abuses of Roundup application. Weeds such as pigweed (*Amaranthus* or careless weed) and horseweed

(Mayer's tail) took over fields as they developed a resistance to the Roundup herbicide. What was once easily controlled with one or two annual applications of Roundup now had to be eradicated the old-fashioned way—the hoe or some other herbicide. The Macon County Extension Service said it took two years after the 2005 season to get those fields back into shape. But apparently the lesson wasn't learned as these farmers switched genetically modified seed companies, planting Liberty Link (another genetically modified seed company owned by Bayer Crop Science) varieties, which is simply another verse to the same song.

With the Roundup Flex seed varieties, farmers can spray as many times as they see fit. It is not uncommon now for farmers to spray Roundup three or four times during a growing season. Locally, I see the effects of this in the irrigated fields of farmers who have used Roundup religiously for several years. They now have weeds they can't get rid of. Roundup hardly phases the weeds. Other farmers' fields are showing signs of excessive toxins as well. The poison accumulates over time, resulting in more weed pressure and lower yields. The land becomes sick and uses much of its energy to fight off the symptoms that result from it being poisoned over and over again. Ultimately, these farmers will one day have land that can no longer produce anything but weeds. Much like an extreme drug addict or alcoholic who can no longer stomach solid foods, these patches of earth will become too sick to function normally. Rehab is the only thing that will heal. Who knows how much money and time that will take? Apparently, it is a risk many are willing to take. Perhaps they feel like it will be a problem for someone else to deal with. Maybe even their own children or grandchildren. This truly baffles me. In a nutshell, chemical agriculture is much like drug or alcohol abuse in that the more you use, the more it takes for the drug to do its job.

The Perverse Marriage of Our Government and Monsanto

"But, our government wouldn't allow this to happen if it was really so harmful to everything!" With fear creeping in, you look to the highest form of authority to verify that they are watching out for us.

Well, I hate to be the one to tell you that our beloved government is as much a part of the problem as these giant corporations. Yes, those so-called leaders in D.C. who vote themselves a pay raise each year are doing nothing to stop this gravy train. In fact, they often seem to be adding more grease to the wheels.

How can a company patent over 11,000 different plants or seeds identical to the ones naturally produced by Mother Nature? Let's ask our government. They are part owners of the terminator seed patent. Ask former Secretary of Defense, Donald Rumsfeld. He is a former President of a Monsanto sister company. Ask Supreme Court Justice, Clarence Thomas, a former legal defender of Monsanto. Ask Linda Fisher, head of the Environmental Protection Agency during the Bush administration, and a former Executive Vice President of Monsanto. Hell, ask dozens of other former Bush or Clinton appointees once employed by the Monsanto oligarchy. In this respect Monsanto is to the agriculture world what Goldman Sachs is to the economic world.

Monsanto's reign in genetic engineering planted its political seed in the early 1980s during the Ronald Reagan administration. His Vice President (and soon to be the next President), George Herbert Bush, met with Monsanto executives behind closed doors in 1986 to discuss the "deregulation" of the genetic engineering industry's rapid growth. Many companies were jockeying for position to be the leader in genetic engineering, but Monsanto had the fast track with the White House. Monsanto did business with the U.S. Government and the CIA (which Bush was head of from 1970 to 1980) during the Vietnam War, when they created the infamous herbicide Agent Orange to defoliate the Vietnamese jungles. After winning the 1992 Presidential Election, Bush Sr. wasted little time ensuring that Monsanto marched unmolested to the front of the line of GMO producers. On May 26, 1992 Vice President Dan Quayle boasted of the administration's agenda on genetically modified food to a group of executives and reporters in D.C., stating, "The reforms we announce today will speed up and simplify the process of bringing better agricultural products, developed through biotech, to consumers, food processors and farmers. We will ensure that biotech products will receive the same oversight as other products, instead of being hampered by unnecessary regulation." He added, "We will not compromise safety one bit."[3]

Our own President and Vice President gave complete and total authority to a corporation whose primary goal was and is higher sales and larger revenues. This industry was intent on altering DNA in living organisms and selling these manipulated goods (seeds, food, etc.) to the unsuspecting and uneducated public, and it could not be restricted by a pesky little thing like regulation. Why? Well, the Reagan administration prided themselves on the deregulation of everything—business, banking, so why not biogenetics as well? So, basically, our beloved EPA, FDA, and USDA were told to stay put—no need to worry because Monsanto would do the honorable thing and police itself. Oh, yeah?

Bush pushed the boulder over the cliff when he signed an Executive Order in 1993, ruling that GMO plants and foods were "substantially equivalent" to the same species of plants in Nature, i.e. corn, cotton, canola, or whatever. The doctrine of "substantial equivalence" allowed the GMO era to truly blossom, with nothing standing in its way. No regulation. No laws. No strict testing enforced to determine short- or long-term effects on humans or Mother Nature. Nothing. Why? It all goes back to Kissinger's chilling remarks—complete and total control of the people.

To allow a company the right to add foreign genes to various

---

3. Kurt Eichenwald, "Biotechnology Food: From the Lab to a Debacle", *The New York Times*, January 25, 2001.

plants and allow them to patent such a plant is at best ludicrous. Over hundreds of thousands of years, farmers and seed companies have worked on plant breeding, developing stronger seeds and plants to overcome diseases through a natural process of cross-pollination. This process of genetic engineering (GE) forcefully disrupts the organism's DNA, as the foreign genes are incorporated into its makeup.

The contradiction of the "substantial equivalence" doctrine was evident once the ruling was upheld by the United States Supreme Court (along with Clarence Thomas) that GMOs were now to be treated as "natural food additives" and consequently could not be subjected to any special tests. So, the staple of our food supply was then considered "additives". How convenient for Monsanto. Especially when you consider 26 years later approximately 70% of our natural food supply has been compromised by the likes of Monsanto, Bayer Crop Science, and the rest of the GMO industry. That percentage is growing each year.

The entire "Change We Can Believe In" campaign by President Barack Obama must be seriously questioned after his appointment of Michael Taylor as advisor to the FDA in July of 2009. Taylor was the Vice President of Public Policy at Monsanto from 1998 to 2001. He served as a private attorney for King & Spalding in the 1980s, representing Monsanto. While serving as the FDA's Deputy Commissioner for Policy from 1991 to 1994, they approved of Monsanto's Polisac, a controversial growth hormone for dairy cows.

In case you need a little more proof of the revolving door between a major corporation like Monsanto and our U.S. Government agencies such as the FDA (Federal Drug Administration), the EPA (Environmental Protection Agency), and the USDA (United States Department of Agriculture), here is a handy list of some of those linking the two forces:

Donald Rumsfeld: Secretary of Defense in the President George W. Bush administration; former CEO of Monsanto subsidiary G. D. Searle, which produces the GMO-based artificial sweetener Aspartame.

Clarence Thomas: current U.S. Supreme Court Judge; former defense attorney who helped defend Monsanto in several lawsuits.

Linda J. Fisher: former Administrator of the EPA's Office of Prevention, Pesticides, and Toxic Substances; current Monsanto Vice President of Public Affairs.

Michael A. Friedman, M.D.: former Acting Director of the FDA; Senior Vice President of Clinical Affairs for Monsanto's pharmaceutical division G. D. Searle.

William D. Ruckelshaus: former head of the EPA under President Nixon and President Reagan; currently on Monsanto's Board of Directors.

Mickey Kantor: former U.S. Trade Rep. and lawyer to President Clinton; currently on Monsanto's Board of Directors.

Hugh Grant: current CEO of Monsanto and member of the President's Advisory Group of CropLife International and of Civic Progress in St. Louis. He makes over $16 million a year in salary, bonuses, and stock options.

Michael Taylor: current top advisor of the FDA; private attorney for King & Spalding in the 1980s, representing Monsanto; FDA's Deputy Commissioner for Policy from 1991 to 1994; Vice President of Public Policy at Monsanto from 1998 to 2001.

For decades, legislation has been and continues to be written by campaign-contributing corporations. Our politicians don't have the courage to stand up for America anymore because they are too busy subordinating themselves to receive their "contributions". Let's not kid ourselves. America, and particularly the American farmer, is being slaughtered by companies like Monsanto, Bayer, DuPont, and several others with dear ol' Uncle Sam rooting them on. The worst part is that most of us don't even realize it...yet. It is very difficult for me to trust or believe any study the EPA, FDA or USDA comes out with involving genetically modified seed, food, or crops because of the numerous ties between Monsanto and these governing agencies.

With President Obama's appointment of biotech and GMO enthusiast Tom Vilsack as Secretary of Agriculture, I'm not optimistic about this administration's "change" in policy or attitude toward Monsanto and the rest of the GMO corporations. I hope I am wrong. But Ronnie Cummins, Executive Director of Organic Consumers Association, wasn't enthused either, along with many in the organic and sustainable agriculture movements. Cummins said in a statement in January of 2009:

> Vilsack's nomination sends the message that dangerous, untested, unlabeled genetically engineered crops will be the norm in the Obama Administration…Our nation's future depends on crafting a forward-thinking strategy to promote organic and sustainable food and farming, and address the related crises of climate change, diminishing energy supplies, deteriorating public health, and economic depression. Obama's choice for Secretary of Agriculture points to the continuation of agribusiness as usual, the failed policies of chemical- and energy-intensive, genetically engineered industrial agriculture. Americans were promised "change", not just another shill for Monsanto and corporate agribusiness. Considering the challenges we collectively face as a nation, from climate change and rising energy costs to food insecurity, we need an administration that moves beyond "business as usual" to fundamental change—before it's too late.

Vilsack, the former Governor of Iowa, was named Governor of the Year by the biggest biotechnology industry group, the Biotechnology Industry Organization. He is also the founder and former chair of the Governor's Biotechnology Partnership. Needless to say, it is evident Vilsack will do everything he can to ensure that "test tube" foods and crops continue to dominate the marketplace.

Monsanto continues to fight against farmers' rights to protect their company and crops against GMOs. On April 27th, 2010, while this book is being sent to press, the U.S. Supreme Court will be ruling on the ban against the sale of Monsanto's genetically modified alfalfa. A federal judge ruled against Monsanto's sale of their genetically modified sugar beets, as well. The Supreme Court's ruling will have a monumental and significant impact on the safety of our food. Depending on this judgment, Monsanto will or will not have free reign on our future food supply, opening or closing the door to the sale of any and all genetically modified crops.

Our Future State of the Present

A video documentary, *The Future of Food*, presents the case against GMOs in a visual fashion. It deals in large with Monsanto and their Roundup Ready seeds or GMOs. I won't go into much detail, but, by and large, it covers the in-your-face truths of the politician-buying corporation Monsanto developing a monopoly and attempting to corner the world seed market in certain crops like cotton, soybeans, canola, corn, wheat and rice. Without regulation, who knows what else they are contriving in their laboratory minds?

The whole idea of a cash crop plant being resistant to herbicides and insects has many farmers salivating at the possibility of saving time, labor, and fuel, which should translate into saving money. Right? Undoubtedly in the short-term it reduces the wear and tear on tractors and equipment, since less tillage is required. Without question it requires less labor to work these crops, eliminating the need for hoeing and seasonal labor. And yes, it saves fuel, but this comes with a heavy price tag of decimating the quality of Life as a whole.

Let's examine the other side of the coin. In the two years during which Roundup Ready cotton was planted on our farm, we noticed firsthand that the conventional plant from Mother Nature will out-produce the laboratory plant every single season, hands down. Any farmer who has planted both will tell you the exact same thing. Also, as farmers reduce or eliminate tillage of the soil while planting exactly the same genetically modified crop year after year, soil erosion magnifies intensely. We've witnessed this with some of our neighbors who only spray Roundup on their weeds instead of plowing. Their barren fields create sandstorms in heavy winds, significantly more so than plowed fields with organic matter or cover crops.

But back to the documentary. After having viewed this film I was inspired to immediate action in my community. I sent copies of the documentary to 16 farmers I knew who were planting Roundup Ready cotton extensively. Of those farmers, only one phoned. He was the only one who even wanted to speak with me on this matter, and yes, as a father and grandfather he was concerned about what he was doing. For you mathematicians, that is a whopping 6.25% who gave enough thought to the impact he was having on Life to actually verify it with a conversation. The rest, who are also fathers and grandfathers, never said a word to confirm they even watched it.

"How is this possible?" you scream, pounding your fists.

Plain and simple. It's all about the Mighty Dollar.

When pressed on the issue of GMO crops, farmers will explain their rationale in a variety of one-sentence shrugs:

"Yeah, but I gotta make a livin.'"

"Well, I gotta make my landlords happy."

"I can't make a crop otherwise."

"There's nothing wrong with it."

"Roundup doesn't hurt anything." (My personal favorite)

Without remorse, each passing year it is easier for many farmers to feel like GMO crops are becoming second nature. Until we are able to re-evaluate our concept of currency, we are going to continue getting into a deeper mess. As long as 93.75% of our species places more value on pieces of paper with dead presidents on them than the food we eat, the water we drink, and the air we breathe, we are doomed.

The biggest gain in Nature with the planting of GMOs is the reduction in fuel consumption as tillage is minimized or eliminated altogether. While that is a compelling argument, it is the equivalent of having stronger arms after amputating both your legs. With the Bollguard and Bt seed varieties, Monsanto and Monsanto farmers will boast they are helping the environment because they are minimizing or eliminating insecticide use. That is true. But what Monsanto won't tell you and what these farmers don't want to realize is the deadly impact this seed has on insects, birds, and other wildlife attempting to digest genetically altered food on a daily basis.

We are already witnessing a die-off of various vital species, from honeybees and butterflies to bats and frogs. This is not coincidental. All things are connected. All things are one. We're still sacrificing much more than we are gaining. We're pumping much higher amounts of toxins into the air, soil, and underground water supply. While it is a short-term victory for the farmer, it is a long-term disaster for the entire ecosystem on Mother Earth, particularly humans.

Making Sense of the Dollars and Cents

In 2009, one 50-pound bag of Roundup Ready cotton cost $250, Roundup Ready Flex $280, Roundup Ready Flex Bt $310, and Roundup Ready Flex Bt 2 $330 on average in the U.S. A 50-pound bag of conventional cotton seed, after considering the certified planting, delinting and bagging costs, runs at roughly $20-$25 per bag. Just a tad difference in pricing. Many farmers still convince themselves they are spending and risking less with Roundup Ready seed. Part of the "contract" agreement in buying Roundup Ready seed is that the farmer must also purchase the Roundup herbicide to treat the crop.

If the average cotton farm is 2,000 acres, then the farmer puts roughly $160,000 ($80/acre) into his cotton crop with seed and herbicide alone, and the great majority of that money is going to Monsanto. In an average year, a dry-land cotton farmer doing this is not going to spend money in any other area. Not only are organic fertilizers forgotten, but so too are other products that might enhance the soil or plants. If one million farmers (averaging 2,000 acres per operation) across the world use this model then you quickly see where $160 billion is spent in agriculture. And we wonder why we have problems in this industry or why our profits are diminishing.

Each season, Monsanto continues to raise its prices, charging farmers a "technology fee", since they have the patent on the respective seed. What a deal. More fittingly, what a clever scam. And each year, more and more farmers fall victim to this scam, pursuing the path of least resistance. No doubt it is an easier way to farm. But no farmer can convince me this saves money over a five-year period when factoring in lower yields. Never mind the soil degradation as toxins overwhelm healthy soil life, and various weeds transmutate, developing a resistance to the herbicide over time. On top of all this, farmers who plant GMOs are sacrificing the freedoms of a natural seed supply by purchasing seeds each growing year from a company which is in complete control of pricing and seed breeding.

Monsanto is faring far better than the average farmer planting their crops. Following record sales in 2006 and 2007, Monsanto more than doubled its profits in 2008. Net income rose from $689 million to $2.024 billion in the three-year time period. The chart on page 46 shows the numbers on a steady rise from 2006-2008.

In relation to land, just how many acres are we talking about? In 2008, genetically modified corn was planted across 29 million acres in this country alone. But this isn't just happening in the USA. This is a global mission. And they prepared enough of the Roundup Ready 2 Soybean to plant on 45-55 million acres around the world in 2009. Over 4.5 million acres of genetically modified

Monsanto Profits			
	2006	2007	2008
Net income	$689 million	$993 million	$2.024 billion
Net sales	$7 billion	$8.3 billion	$11.36 billion

cotton (76% of all cotton acres) in India were planted in 2008—more than tripled from the previous year. Total cotton production is dropping in America with just under 10 million acres planted in 2008, surrendering over 8 million acres (80%) to genetically modified cotton. This equates to more than 93 million acres of farmland, which is more than 145,000 square miles of GMO crops and about the size of the State of Montana. These figures do not even include countries like China, Pakistan, Mexico, Australia, Brazil, or Japan.

Other GMO Corporations

Bayer Crop Science is becoming more competitive with Monsanto in the GMO world. The world's fourth-largest pharmaceutical company offers farmers herbicide-resistant crops with their Liberty Link varieties in cotton, corn, canola, and soybean. In 2007, the company raked in more than $6 billion in global sales and enjoyed a 9.5% increase in sales in 2008. Bayer Crop Science has focused on expanding their operations and advertising in Europe and South America, allowing the corporation to grow at a faster rate than the rest of the top ten GMO corporations. Their sales in America rank third. DuPont and Switzerland's Syngenta remain a steady second and third globally.

Bayer Crop Science's FiberMax seed varieties are arguably

some of the best developed conventional cotton seed varieties. Dad started planting FiberMax conventional varieties in 2001, confessing he'd never seen any other variety as productive. But Bayer Crop Science no longer offers the conventional varieties, focusing solely on their GMOs. It is becoming more and more of a problem for farmers to find high-quality conventional seeds, conveniently increasing sales in GMO crops.

Do you see how fast the GMO ball is rolling downhill? Do you see how large it is getting? Do you see how easily it is gaining momentum? Guess who is sitting quietly at the bottom of that hill? That's right—you, me, and most certainly our children and grandchildren.

While the "test tube" seeds of Monsanto and the likes of Bayer Crop Science, Syngenta, and Deltapine (Monsanto) have met little to no resistance in America, some farmers are taking a stand in India, led by Dr. Vandana Shiva. A physicist and ecologist who is a recipient of the Alternative Nobel Peace Prize, Shiva traveled with some Monsanto executives over 20 years ago and expressed her concerns about GM seeds. She opened up about this journey in the documentary *The World According to Monsanto*:

> And they [Monsanto] said "To us it doesn't matter if the crops don't do well. They'll still come back for more of our seeds." The farmer gets wiped out, the land gets wiped out, the company's markets grow. That, I think is the real tragedy of genetic engineering—that the failure of agriculture is a mark of success for the corporations.

Many farmers turned to Monsanto's Bollgard variety, thanks in large to some excellent marketing by Monsanto. The commercials show great fortune and luck befalling Indian farmers who choose the Bollgard seed. The commercial bogusly guaranteed higher yields and more income despite the fact that the seed cost the farmers four times more than the conventional seed. Yet, the cotton crops experienced various diseases and were attacked by aphids, thrips, and, yes, even bollworms. The farmers did not experience higher yields; consequently many did not have the money to pay their debts off at their banks—the money they needed to buy the GE seed.

In India, you have two options as a farmer when you cannot pay off your bank loans—sell land or commit suicide. Many chose suicide. From 1997-2005 more than 25,000 Indian farmers committed suicide, accounting for 15% of all suicides of the country's 1.2 billion population.[4] Shiva and many other activists blame Monsanto and the early failures of the GMO crops for adding to farmers' economic stress. In July and August of 2009 alone, at least 76 Indian farmers committed suicide.[5] And news spread quickly across the globe that more than 1,500 Indian farmers committed suicide in 2009 through the month of September.

Here in America, suicides among farmers are not talked about. News focuses on farms, not the farmers. In America, the bollworm is already building resistance to the genetically altered seed. This should not prove to be a surprise to Monsanto or Monsanto farmers, as insects have historically built up a resistance to most pesticides produced. Insects are capable of mutating and adjusting their DNA to overcome the negative side-effects of pesticides over time.

But Monsanto shows no signs of slowing down or questioning the direction in which it is heading. On its website, the company boasts of its research and development constantly seeking more plant life manipulations. The company also invests in discovering and delivering new fruit and vegetable products:

> We spend approximately $2.6 million per day to drive our
> R&D engine. We are now in one of the most productive and

---

4. Chad Heeter's *Seeds of Suicide: India's Desperate Farmers* documentary.
5. Devinder Sharma, "I Know Why Farmers Kill Themselves", http://www.devinder-sharma.blogspot.com/2009/08/i-know-now-why-farmers-kill-themselves.html, August 2009.

exciting periods of our R&D pipeline, which can help us widen the competitive gap. We're poised to launch four game-changing technology platforms that will rewrite productivity per acre and create compelling growth for our shareowners well into the next decade.

Gulp. And they have more "high-tech" stuff being launched in the near future. Enter Smartstax Corn, "which combines eight modes of action in multiple traits and provides season-long yield protection in three areas: above- *and* below-ground insect protection as well as our most comprehensive weed-control package." It's going to get scarier each planting season. Soon, they'll have a seed that will jump out of the bag, hop to the field, plant itself, and offer you coffee and doughnuts each morning when you drive by. Where will this assault on Nature stop? Can we not see the horrors? Are we this out of touch? Is money that important?

Corporate America isn't stopping with our global seed supply. On top of all the GMO crops introduced in the past 20 years, American company Aqua Bounty Farms has successfully engineered genetically modified salmon to grow much faster and larger than regular salmon. Research performed at Purdue University has already found that releasing transgenic fish into the wild could damage native populations to the point of extinction.[6] The transgenic fish become extremely hostile to native fish of the same species. And most recently, two corporate giants, International Paper and MeadWestvaco, were planning genetically modified forests for the Southeastern United States by replacing native pine trees with genetically engineered eucalyptus trees.[7] This would have devastating ecological effects.

---

6. William M. Muir and Richard D. Howard, "Possible Ecological Risks of Transgenic Organism Release when Transgenes Affect Mating Success: Sexual Selection and the Trojan Gene Hypothesis", Department of Animal Sciences and Department of Biological Sciences, Purdue University, May 19, 1991.
7. Paul Voosen, "Genetically Modified Forest Planned for American Southeast", *Scientific American*, January 29, 2010.

Terminator Seed Puts the *T* in Travesty

Let's not forget about Iraq. Remember that country? There was the whole war thing, the weapons of mass destruction, and the "temporary" occupation of the oil-rich nation that has been ongoing for seven years. Yes, that Iraq. You know, the place we're spreading democracy, right? Well, we aren't doing any favors for their farmers. As part of the new "Constitution" of Iraq's heralded democracy, Order #81 in the draft Constitution states that farmers can no longer save their own seed, but they must purchase their seed from one of five companies (this was later cleverly revised as part of a new patent law). Guess who is at the top of that list. Monsanto! And since Monsanto just bought out Deltapine for $1.5 billion in 2007, technically they are one of four companies. With the purchase of Deltapine, Monsanto is now the proud owner of the terminator seed. And what is the terminator seed, you ask? A seed which produces a sterile plant, therefore eliminating the possibility of a plant continuing Nature's precious and vital cycle by reproducing via seed season after season.

It Does the Body Bad

For all the specific studies of GMO-related diseases and illnesses, I strongly recommend the writings of Jeffrey M. Smith. There have been countless tests on rats and mice in which these rodents ended up with stomach lesions, bleeding digestive tracts, cancerous tumors, and undeniable signs of potentially fatal diseases after just 30-90 days of a steady diet of "test tube" corn, potatoes or tomatoes. Many tend to have a "who cares about rodents anyway" mentality, so let us move on to reactions of larger species, shall we?

Perhaps you'd be interested to know about the severe allergic reactions of Indian farmers, who harvest Bt cotton by hand. Workers developed mild to severe allergic reactions which included "itching, swollen, red eyes; solid- or fluid-filled raised lesions on their faces and hands, feet, backs, necks, and abdomens; nasal discharge and/or excessive sneezing".[8] The studies also noted that the workers had never experienced these reactions to cotton in past seasons and that they only occurred when Bt cotton arrived in their fields.

Fatality rates of livestock also escalated with the arrival of Bt cotton in India. Beginning in 2005, "among 29 herds with 2,168 sheep, 549 animals (25%) died...Visits to two other villages yielded similar reports, with deaths sometimes occurring within four days of initial grazing. Farmers estimated that the deaths in the region were 10,000."[9] These same farmers also stated that they had never experienced this with normal conventional cotton before GMO crops arrived. Those who returned to conventional seed said the problems went away. In these examples if the animals had a choice between genetically modified corn and natural corn, livestock chose the natural corn first.

Some might argue, "But India is so far away from America that it really doesn't have any relevance to us here."

Perhaps you should be informed of entire villages in the Philippines...oh wait, still very, very far away from us. Statistics involving children always hit close to home. What long-term effects this will have on future generations who have grow up exposed to GMOs from birth is frightfully unknown.

Numerous studies have unveiled that when proteins attach to sugar chains (glycosylation) the proteins can turn into dangerous allergens.[10] This process happens in all genetically engineered foods. Is it simply coincidental that so many more children have developed allergies to peanuts, wheat, soy, milk, and other

---

8. Jeffrey M. Smith, *Genetic Roulette: The Documented Health Risks of Genetically Engineered Foods* (Yes! Books, 2007), p. 31.
9. *Ibid.*
10. FIFRA Scientific Advisory Panel, "Mammalian Toxicity Assessment Guidelines for Protein Plant Pesticides", SAP Report No. 2000-03B: 23, http://www.epa.gov/scipoly/sap/2000/june/finbtmamtox.pdf.

vital crops derived from commercial agriculture in the past 20 years? According to Universal Food Allergy Awareness (UFAA), there has been a 400% increase in food allergies among children in the past two decades, a 300% increase in asthma, a 300% increase in ADHD, and a 1,500% increase in autism. We are poisoning our kids with infected foods laced with tons of herbicides, pesticides, and fungicides in a genetically modified toxic blender. As we continue to buy toxic foods from a compromised food and agriculture system, more money is needed for the mounting medical costs of keeping our children healthy.

Perhaps you should be informed of the milk-enhancing wonder drug that Monsanto genetically modified for an already overflowing dairy market. Yes, Monsanto saw fit to introduce rBGH (recombinant bovine growth hormone,) labeled Posilac in its marketing schemes, to increase a cow's milk production by 20%. In 1993, Monsanto proudly rushed the growth hormone onto the scene, guaranteeing dairy farmers higher productivity, which would bring higher incomes. They failed to inform dairy farmers of the potentially high-risks for not only the cows but anyone who consumed dairy products from these cows. According to the Center for Food Safety's website:

> In addition to hormones used to increase milk production (see rBGH/rBST), there are six hormones approved for use in beef cattle. Two of these hormones, estradiol and zeranol, are likely to have negative human health effects when their residues are present in meat, including cancer and impacts on child development. Concerns about these potential health impacts have left many scientists doubtful of the safety of hormone use in meat production.
>
> The negative environmental impact of hormones entering waterways from livestock feedlots also is cause for alarm. Researchers have found that fish can exhibit significant effects from this pollution, e.g. females begin to exhibit male characteristics, and vice versa, in areas of high hormone concentrations.

A company wouldn't be so cynical as to peddle a product simply for financial gain and then try to cover it up once they know it is lethal or at least detrimental to people's health and the ecosystem, would they? Perhaps you should be informed of the citizens living in Anniston, Alabama. One leading scientist has labeled Anniston as "the most contaminated place on earth". And the 30,000 people living there have Monsanto to thank for that tragic label.

Polychlorinated byphenyls (PCBs) are a class of organic compounds with one to 10 chlorine atoms attached to biphenyl, a molecule composed of two benzene rings with each containing six carbon atoms. They were used as dielectric fluids in transformers and capacitors, coolants, lubricants, stabilizing additives in flexible PVC coatings of electrical wiring and electronic components, pesticide extenders, cutting oil, flame retardants, hydraulic fluids, sealants, adhesives, wood floor finishes, paints, de-dusting agents, and in carbonless copy paper. Proven to be a serious cancer-causing agent, PCBs were banned in 1976 with the signing of the Toxic Substances Control Act. Yet citizens of Anniston continue to suffer from chronic symptoms caused by the toxins found in their drinking water due to drainage from the old plant Monsanto operated. Who knows if that area of the state will ever recover from decades of toxins endlessly flooding rivers and creeks, and seeping into the earth around it?

Informative and entertaining documentaries such as *King Corn* and *Food Inc.* shed much light on corn crops and our food industry's morbid links to low-quality products. Much of that relates directly to genetically modified seeds producing inferior plants and fruits. What most people do not think about in terms of genetically modified cotton is that the clothing products derived from it can also damage our health. Our clothing drapes our skin, becoming a part of our body. Over time, microscopic cells from "test tube" cotton permeate our flesh and are absorbed into our bloodstream. How many more children and adults experience skin rashes now than 20 years ago? New skin diseases such as Morgellons Disease are popping up across the globe. The fiber crops we grow become the very fabric of our lives, and here we are producing harmful fabric for an entire world.

Analysts estimate that approximately 60-75% of processed foods commonly found on supermarket shelves or in restaurants are genetically engineered.[11] But, that percentage is growing each year. Monsanto and these other corporate giants specializing in genetic engineering have turned the entire planet into one large test plot for their laboratory creations. The escalating production and sales of GMOs is nothing short of a deranged experiment with humanity and Nature as the guinea pigs, and time is the only accurate measurement of the side effects' severity.

Mummification of Mainstream Media and Universities

Why should we not trust Monsanto? Well, I don't know...perhaps I'll make a stab in the dark here. They are the same company who manufactured DDT and Agent Orange, assuring us their usage would have no dangerous effects on man or Nature. How did that work out?

Let us find out how much money Monsanto contributes to key agricultural universities such as Texas A&M University. These institutes are key influences not only on what farmers do or don't, but also play a major role in seed breeding. They also train young farmers, entomologists, agronomists, biologists, and other scientists, influencing young minds in the agriculture and food industries.

As far as university research goes, corruption runs deep. Simply follow the money. In March 2009, Monsanto announced on their website they had awarded a $10 million grant to Texas A&M University:

...which will help identify and support young scientists in-

---

11. According to http://www.seedsofdeception.com.

terested in improving research and production in rice and wheat, two of the world's most important staple crops, through plant breeding techniques. Monsanto is funding the program, which will be administered by Texas AgriLife Research, an agency of the Texas A&M University System, for the next five years.

That is one grant contributing $2 million per year to one American university. Do you really think Texas A&M professors and researchers are going to denounce genetically modified crops when their generous salaries and department funding are bought and paid for by the very company that is the world's leading manufacturer of such a product?

Let's take a look at the media's part in this. The Federal Communications Commission (FCC) is more monopolistic or at least oligarchic than it is democratic, particularly after President Bill Clinton passed the ruinous Telecom Act of 1996, which did away with previous laws prohibiting businesses from owning an excessive number of media companies.

Having been a broadcast journalism major in college and with more than six years of experience in print, radio, and television, I can attest firsthand to the biased corruption of our mainstream media. In radio, Clear Channel owns more than 1,000 radio stations across the country. The "big boys" buy the local "mom and pop" radio stations that play good music. They then transition them into their robotic format of either pop music's best of the "80s, 90s and today", a generic country format or their droning classic rock format. (I was an employee of Clear Channel for about six months.) The second largest radio group owners are Cumulus Broadcasting Inc., with approximately 250 stations across the nation.

The television industry has been plundered by the entertainment industry, trading in hardcore journalism for brain-numbing stories about Britney Spears, Lindsay Lohan, Angelina Jolie, and Brad Pitt. Perhaps the largest is Time Warner, which merged with AOL. Time Warner owns CNN, *Time* magazine, and TBS, and controls a large portion of web advertising thanks to its AOL merger. Rupert Murdoch, an infamous neo-conservative, owns Fox News Channel and 26 television stations outright.

The three major television networks are just as intertwined. CBS is now owned by Viacom, which also owns UPN, MTV, MTV2, VH1, Nickelodeon, the Movie Channel, TNN, CMT, BET, and 50% of Comedy Central, not to mention Paramount Pictures and Infinity Broadcasting (radio ownership of 184 stations). ABC was bought out by Disney, as was the sports broadcasting company ESPN. General Electric still owns NBC, as well as MSNBC.

These stations receive millions of dollars in advertising from the agro-chemical companies, which spare no expense in brainwashing anyone whether they farm 10,000 acres or simply want to get rid of a pesky weed in their driveway. Monsanto, DuPont, and Dow Chemical spent more than $50 million over a three-year time period alone to ease fears about genetically modified crops and foods in the U.S. and Canada. Do you think a handful of corporations are going to turn down that kind of advertising? Better yet, do you think they're going to run a story exposing the devastating effects of genetically modified seed, Roundup, or any other Monsanto, DuPont, or Dow Chemical product?

Yes, this is deep. And it's going to get even deeper if we do nothing.

Turning the Ship Around Before It's too Late

I guess we could all run away to live in a hippie commune somewhere, but that won't make this problem any less real, nor will it safeguard us against the long-term effects of the genetic modification of our food products. Surprisingly, there are more practical solutions.

In the last decade many serious gardeners and small-scale organic farmers savvy to the whole GMO debacle have turned their attention to saving our natural seed supply. If you grow your own food and haven't started practicing the art of saving seeds, you might consider seriously beginning to do so. And if you haven't started growing your own food, even on an extremely small scale, I advise you to do so. The ability to grow your own food is one of the greatest freedoms we've forgotten about.

Why would we put all our power and trust into the hands of companies who seem to be determined to destroy the essence of life? Several organic seed suppliers across the nation have done a fantastic job of preserving many types of seed. Bountiful Gardens, Plants of the Southwest, and Horizon Herbs come to mind. But it is vital that many more farmers and gardeners step up to the plate and take a swing, as well. We shouldn't dismiss the significance of our seed supply and expect the obligation to preserve it to rest only on seed companies. We are responsible adults who really ought to educate ourselves.

As farmers, ranchers, gardeners, and naturalists, we can boycott Monsanto products altogether. Why purchase a jug of Roundup when heavy mulching, compost, used vegetable oil or an old-fashioned hoe can reduce or eliminate unwanted plant growth around your home or garden? Refuse to buy GM seed of any sort. Ensure your local delinting plants and grain elevators stay in business by giving them your business and money instead of manipulative corporations like Monsanto and Bayer Crop Science. For gardeners, plant fruits and vegetables closer together, and use mulch and compost to keep away most weeds. Raised beds are another excellent way to keep out unwanted plants, also making it easier on the back muscles to pull weeds. We can create an environment that weeds will not thrive in by balancing our soil with the sufficient minerals, maintaining healthy energy and sugar levels in our topsoil.

We *must* protect our seed supply. As commercial farmers, the best way to do that is to boycott Monsanto altogether. Refuse to purchase Roundup Ready seed. Refuse to buy Roundup. Refuse to purchase any genetically modified crop from any company including the likes of Bayer Crop Science, DuPont, and Syngenta or any other soulless corporation out to pillage Mother Nature and the farmer for a buck.

The ETC Group released global seed company statistics in 2007. Monsanto alone accounted for 23% of all seed sales. Along with DuPont, Syngenta, and Bayer Crop Science, the four companies controlled 49% of the world's seed sales. The following ten corporations had power over 67% of the entire seed market:

2007 Global Seed Sales		
1. Monsanto (US)	$4.9 billion	23%
2. DuPont (US)	$3.3 billion	15%
3. Syngenta (Switzerland)	$2.0 billion	9%
4. Groupe Limagrain (France)	$1.2 billion	6%
5. Land O'Lakes (US)	$917 million	4%
6. KWS AG (Germany)	$702 million	3%
7. Bayer Crop Science (Germany)	$524 million	2%
8. Sakata (Japan)	$396 million	2%
9. DLF-Trifolium (Denmark)	$391 million	2%
10. Takii (Japan)	$347 million	2%

There are rumored to be at least a handful of seed vaults scattered around the globe. The most important and recent one, snug in the Norwegian countryside, was completed in 2008:

> The Svalbard Global Seed Vault is a secure seedbank located on the Norwegian island of Spitsbergen near the town of Longyearbyen in the remote Arctic Svalbard archipelago. The facility was established to preserve a wide variety of plant seeds from locations worldwide in an underground cavern. The seed vault holds duplicate samples, or "spare"

copies, of seeds held in genebanks worldwide. The seed vault will provide insurance against the loss of seeds in gene-banks, as well as a refuge for seeds in the case of large-scale regional or global crises. The island of Spitsbergen is about 1,300 kilometers (8010 mil) from the North Pole.[12]

The question is who will control the sale or release of such seeds if a global catastrophe were ever to occur?

The major financial contributor to this seed vault is the Bill & Melinda Gates Foundation. That's right, BFFs of the Rockefeller Foundation. Point is, each family should have their own seed vault. Do not ever depend on governments or corporations to have our interests in mind if and when there is a major global crisis.

Old refrigerators or closets on an inside wall make wonderful storage places for seed. Gun safes are another excellent storage place. Seeds need to be kept out of the sun in a cool, dry environment. I do not recommend plastic baggies, as moisture is likely to occur. Old glass jars such as baby food jars, mason jars and other clean food jars with airtight lids make excellent seed containers. Most seeds will last up to three or four years, if taken care of properly. Many will last even longer if frozen or in airtight storage.

If we hope for the best, prepare for the worst, and expect somewhere in between, there will be no real need to panic in such a dire situation. The best thing to have in a hopeless situation is hope. And that is attained by being prepared, keeping your cool, and allowing your mind and body to work in a diligent manner instead of being consumed with fear and panic because you've done nothing to ready yourself or your family for such an event.

Back to the corporations and GMOs. In a nutshell, we are growing "a cancer". Sure, it looks like a plant. It acts like a plant. And, it even smells like a plant. But this is merely an illusion—it is

---

12. This information comes via Wikipedia.

"cancer" on a stick. We've been lied to. We've been manipulated. We've been sold a forest full of rotten fruit. Yet we continue to buy the seed, grow the plant, harvest the fruit, and sell the "cancer" to the first bidder. Merely complaining about the price we pay isn't enough. Talk is cheap. Action is the only proper reaction.

We should, for example, demand tougher laws and restrictions against all genetically modified organisms. We should also revolt against governing agencies who continue to allow the patenting of living organisms. The intention of genetic engineering is not to solve world hunger, end war, or cure diseases. It will create more hunger, more wars, and more diseases. Any sincere intentions of good in the beginning have long since been disrupted and completely invaded by the temptations of those yearning to control Life and manipulate humanity for their own gain.

History either repeats itself or at least rhymes, but we cannot afford to either repeat or rhyme this time. Our seed supply is of much greater importance than the current panic regarding oil prices and supply, Wall Street or the irresponsible behavior of those running the banking industry and this country. Forget crude. Without seed there is no energy. Forget money. Without food, what good will paper currency, gold, or silver do you? We are talking life and death here. If we sit idly by, not only watching, but contributing to these companies like Monsanto, we are accomplices in the destruction of Mother Nature. By allowing corporations and our government to patent plants, seeds, and all forms of life, we stand no chance of surviving. Forget sustainability. Forget health. Forget harmony. Forget profits. Forget grandchildren. All will be lost if we do nothing. All will be ruined if we simply pursue our current path. I cannot put enough emphasis or energy into this point. We must save our seed supply! We must rid ourselves of a genetically modified life in agriculture! Only Nature knows what is perfect. Not men in white coats motivated by shareholders and profits. Only Nature can cleanse away our toxic habits. No seed reaches the sun without water. Without uncontaminated water, Life is impossible. Without water, all the seeds in the world will not save us from hunger.

Helpful Sources

It is possible a simple email or phone call to your representative or senator will do little to no good, in which case harassing companies such as those listed below might be more effective. If that doesn't work, boycotting is the best medicine against corporate organizations that turn a deaf ear to consumers.

Board of Directors
Monsanto Company
800 North Lindbergh Boulevard
St. Louis, MO 63167
c/o Charles W. Burson, Secretary
Phone: 314-694-1000

The Rockefeller Foundation
420 Fifth Avenue
New York, NY 10018
Phone: 212-869-8500
          800-645-1133
Fax: 212-764-3468

The Dow Chemical Company
2030 Dow Center
Midland, MI 48674
Phone: 800-422-8193
          (U.S. and Canada)
          989-636-1463
Fax: 989-636-1830

DuPont Company
1007 Market Street, D-11036A
Wilmington, DE 19898
Phone: 302-774-4249
Fax: 302-774-2093

Wal-Mart
702 Southwest Eighth Street
Bentonville, AR 72716-8611
Phone: 502-731-4000

Albertson's
250 Parkcenter Boulevard
Boise, ID 83706
Phone: 877-932-7948

H-E-B
Attention:
Customer Relations Department
P.O. Box 839999
San Antonio, TX 78282-3999
Phone: 210-938-8357
          800-432-3113

IGA Inc.
8725 W. Higgins Rd.
Chicago, IL 60631
Phone: 773-693-4520

Kroger
(America's largest
retail grocery store.
2008 sales: $76 billion)
1014 Vine Street
Cincinnati, OH 45202
Phone: 800-689-4609

Stop & Shop
1385 Hancock Street
Quincy, MA 02169
Phone: 800-767-7772

"Safe" Seed Companies

These companies have taken the safe seed pledge, stating they have no links to genetically modified plants—courtesy of www.earthlypursuits.com:

Territorial Seed Company
London Springs, OR
territorial-seed.com

Nichols Garden Nursery
Salem, OR
nicholsgardennursery.com

Peters Seed and Research
Myrtle Creek, OR
pioneer-net.com/psr/homepage.html

Seeds of Change
Sante Fe, NM
seedsofchange.com

Native Seeds
Tucson, AZ
nativeseeds.org

Seed Savers Exchange
Decorah, IA
seedsavers.org

Abundant Life Seeds
Saginaw, OR
abundantlifeseeds.com

The Thyme Garden
Alsea, OR
thymegarden.com

John Sheeper's Kitchen Garden Seeds
Bantam, CT
kitchengardenseeds.com

Johnny's Seeds
Albion, ME
johnnyseeds.com

Wood Prairie Farm
Bridgewater, ME
woodprairie.com

Some of the Possible Sources of GMOs:

The following information is compliments of the kind folks at www.seedsofdeception.com:

- Dairy products from cows injected with rBGH.
- Food additives, enzymes, flavorings, and processing agents, including the sweetener aspartame (NutraSweet®) and rennet used to make hard cheeses.
- Meat, eggs, and dairy products from animals that have eaten GM feed.

- Honey and bee pollen that may have GM sources of pollen.
- Contamination or pollination caused by GM seeds or pollen.

Some Ingredients That May Be Genetically Modified:

- Vegetable oil, vegetable fat and margarines (made with soy, corn, cottonseed, and/or canola).
- Ingredients derived from soybeans: soy flour, soy protein, soy isolates, soy isoflavones, soy lecithin, vegetable proteins, textured vegetable protein (TVP), tofu, tamari, tempeh, and soy protein supplements.
- Ingredients derived from corn: corn flour, corn gluten, corn masa, corn starch, corn syrup, cornmeal, and high-fructose corn syrup (HFCS).

Some Food Additives May Also Be Derived from GMO Sources (This list may change as we encounter new information):

ascorbic acid/ascorbate (vitamin C), cellulose, citric acid, cobalamin (vitamin B12), cyclodextrin, cystein, dextrin, dextrose, diacetyl, fructose (especially crystalline fructose), glucose, glutamate, glutamic acid, gluten, glycerides (mono- and diglycerides), glycerol, glycerine, glycine, hemicellulose, hydrogenated starch hydrolates, hydrolyzed vegetable protein or starch, inositol, invert sugar or inverse syrup (also may be listed as inversol or colorose), lactic acid, lactoflavin, lecithin, leucine, lysine, maltose, maltitol, maltodextrin, mannitol, methylcellulose, milo starch, modified food starch, monooleate, mono- and diglycerides, monosodium glutamate (MSG), oleic acid, phenylalanine, phytic acid, riboflavin (vitamin B2), sorbitol, stearic acid, threonine, tocopherol (vitamin E), trehalose, xanthan gum, and zein.

Processed Foods That May Contain GMO Ingredients:

Infant formula
Salad dressing
Bread
Cereal
Hamburgers
Hot dogs
Mayonnaise
Crackers
Cookies
Chocolate
Candy
Fried food
Chips
Veggie burgers
Meat substitutes
Ice cream
Frozen yogurt
Tamari
Soy sauce
Soy cheese

Tomato sauce
Protein powder
Baking powder
(sometimes contains
 corn starch)
Powdered/Confectioner's
sugar (often contains
corn starch)
Confectioner's glaze
Alcohol
Vanilla
Peanut butter
Enriched flour
Vanilla extract
(sometimes contains
corn syrup)
Pasta
Malt
White vinegar

Non-Food Items That May Contain GMO Ingredients:

Cosmetics
Soaps
Detergents
Shampoo
Bubble bath
Clothing
Pharmaceuticals
Nutrient supplements

Resources

BOOKS
Genetic Modification by William F. Engdahl
Genetic Roulette by Jeffrey M. Smith
Seeds of Deception by Jeffrey M. Smith
Seeds of Destruction: The Hidden Agenda of Seed to Seed by Susan Ashworthe

WEBSITES
allredfarmandgardens.com
www.avaaz.org
bountifulgardens.org
centerforfoodsafety.com
etcgroup.org
everlastingseeds.com
geneticroulette.com
gmwatch.org
horizonherbs.com
organicconsumers.org
percyschmeiser.com
plantsofthesouthwest.com
responsibletechnology.org
saynotogmos.com
seedalliance.org
seedsofdeception.com
seedsofdestruction.com
seedsavers.org
truefoodnow.org
wholefoodsmarket.com

VIDEOS
Food Inc.
The Future of Food
The World According to Monsanto

Chapter 2

RAIN AND CLEAN WATER
Purifying the Mind, Cleansing the Body

> *There will be a rain dance Friday night,*
> *weather permitting.*
> GEORGE CARLIN

> *It is the calm and silent water*
> *that drowns a man.*
> GHANAIAN PROVERB

Whine(ing) into Water

West Texas is just how it looks to the naked eye—raw, imperfect, and unforgiving in its vast stubbornness of prickly pear, mesquite trees, rattlesnakes, and horned toads. Water avoids the landscape like the white man did until the turn of the 20th century. Miles and miles of waterless earth roll into the horizon in search of long-lost playas that have gone dry. This barren bulge of earth rests silent like an old man only wanting to be left alone and strikes with the vengeance of a young fool when bothered. West Texas is a batch of jalapeno cornbread served on a lonesome gravel road with not a glass of water in sight. But it is always dished with a polite grin and sympathetic eyes, convincing us that if we stay for a spell, we'll understand everything and expect nothing else in return.

Summer's horizon sizzles. The earth sweats, almost sobbing at noon and comes to a high boil of uncontrollable weeping by mid-afternoon. Here, gentle summer rains that last all day come along as often as a good dog you never trained—they are few, far between and always leave you wanting more of the good times.

As a child growing up in West Texas very few of my play days were ever "ruined" by rain. Into my adolescence, I became more aware of this dryness as I spent summers hoeing cotton. I begged distant clouds for shade and drizzling drops to cool my tired body or halt the workday completely with a soaking rain. Jackrabbits clung to their shadows for comfort as if their sweaty silhouettes were a glimpse of night's heroic arrival. No creature dared brave the summer sun and scorching winds, fearing the hounds of hell would soon appear and take them deeper into the fiery abyss below.

In retrospect I don't recall a single day of hoeing missed due to rain. Rarely, if ever, were our August, two-a-day football practices interrupted by rain. Only the baking sun and a few dilapidated clouds mocking us. In the early 1990s, a decade-long drought began in West Texas. It was maddening for all farmers in the area. Furthermore, millions of American farmers would not continue farming into the 21st century, as failed crops trumped economic growth throughout the country.

It is a helpless and lonely feeling to endure droughts as a farmer or any creature dependent upon rain for survival. Droughts are physically, emotionally, and spiritually demoralizing. Much like the soil, crops, and native vegetation, we thirst for rain and it's purification to energize us. We wait and wait—hoping, praying, begging, pleading for relief in the form of moisture. Rain is Nature's greatest comfort, the tranquility of tiny drops falling from high above, speaking the language our soul longs for. It is like a mother calming a frightened child, holding us against her bosom and whispering, "Everything will be alright." Rain washes away our greatest fears, phobias, regrets, and paranoia. Rain reminds us how quickly bad evolves to good and doubt transcends to belief. A good rain is like a lover kissing us all over, sending chills to our core. It is a safe zone, just the tranquil beauty of water falling from the heavens.

It is difficult to understand what we can't control. Anger often follows the confusion, then pessimism consumes us like a vindictive drug. We find ourselves continually asking, "Why?" while expecting nothing but the emptiness of the void to continue. Even the most optimistic lose faith in prolonged droughts when everything is on the line. We begin to question ourselves, our occupation, our religion, or any deity proclaimed by our ancestors. At times, our minds pull our souls to the darkest edge of existence. Each thought haunts our movement, paralyzing progression. Perhaps we feel God is punishing us. Perhaps we simply feel insignificant. Perhaps we are so numb we feel nothing at all. Despite our paralysis, we never forget what those heavenly drops feel like dancing upon our flesh, or sound like tapping on our rooftop, or look like soaking into the Earth's own skin.

I firmly believe that there is a reason for everything. If a problem exists, so too does a solution. Somewhere a response awaits our curiosity. We are our own creators and must accept our responsibility in some way for the creation of the situation in which we find ourselves. If we create thoughts of rain, can we not also create rain to surround our form? Is there not a Medicine Man living within each one of us? Are there not thunderclouds in our hearts? Is there not lightning in our minds? So, where then is the next rain we so desperately seek if not on the tips of our tongues?

Perhaps one of the most painful aspects we fail to accept in Nature is that the soil must rest. Just as our bodies and minds must have ample time to recuperate, so too must the Earth. We see the plants growing each season, yet we do not feel the extreme amount of energy the soil must provide for millions and millions of plants to grow and mature. Sometimes drought is a way for the land to rest. That concept is difficult to accept, particularly when your occupation depends on rain in order for you to support your family.

From the summer of 2008 to the summer of 2009, much of the southern U.S. was in the midst of a severe drought. In our area, we didn't receive a single inch of rain in over four months from December 2008 to March 2009. From California to South Carolina, droughts consumed many crops. China and Australia also reported their worst droughts in decades. Southern California was hit badly and the feds stepped in, cutting off irrigation to California's desert-like Central Valley, destroying their crops.

Cynical thoughts have drugged my mind into the depths of uncertainty and disbelief. I've fallen into severe depression during drought. I have tried to fight despair, but after the severity of drought lulls on for more than one year, it gets to a farmer. Lots of stress and worry over nothing—just ask my wife. Negative thoughts, ideas, and emotions are no help. They affect your mind, body, and spirit in a disparaging fashion. Depressing thoughts breed harmful actions and reactions. Despite Dad's, Mom's, and my grandfather Donnie's attempts to assure me everything would be okay, I allowed the negativity to wrap itself around my inner being. Old farmers have seen just about everything Mother Nature has to offer. Most have told me it doesn't get any easier to experience, and that accepting it and knowing that it too shall pass is the key to persevering.

We must not allow the gloom of drought to consume us or lead us down a cynical path. We must learn from such challenges and search for alternative methods to overcome them. For those of you with a job not dependent on Mother Nature, you may not fully understand. But imagine living somewhere with no electricity, no water faucet, no hoses of any sort. The only way your plants or trees can be irrigated is from the Heavens. It is an extremely humbling and vulnerable position to find oneself in.

The parallels shared between the Earth as a whole and the human body are undeniable. The Earth is about 70% water with rivers, creeks, and streams pulsing into lakes before flowing out to sea. Our bodies are about 70% water, as well. So, in the great words of comedian Tom Green, "Then only 30% of me has to swim across this river." So true, so true indeed. Like the rivers, creeks, and streams, our bodies contain miles and miles of arteries and veins transporting blood to and from our hearts, which pump life through our bodies. The oceans are this planet's heart, pumping water back into the air, circulating it throughout our ecosystem, recycling our most precious resource for all living creatures to absorb. We are one and the same. Without water, nothing is possible in this life. Through realizing the vital nature of this resource, we will not only recognize the importance of conserving and protecting our water supply, but also focus on cultivating our relationship with water so that we strengthen that primordial bond.

Draining the Fountain of Life

Here in America, we take water for granted...for now. Turn on a faucet in our homes and there it flows. It's easy to convince ourselves it is in abundance. Whether for baths, showers, cooking, gardening, and landscaping or livestock and crop irrigation, water flows from underneath the soil to the surface with a little electricity and a simple turning of a valve. As we continue to exhaust below-ground aquifers, streams, and lakes, we will soon be faced with a need for other means to draw our water.

We now know that less than 3% of the world water supply is fresh water, since 97% is salt water. Much of that is frozen or out of our reach. Scientists claim our drinking water supply is closer to 1% of the entire water on the planet.

Today, the Nile, Colorado, and Yellow Rivers no longer flow to the ocean. The longest river in the world (the Nile) can no longer find its way to the ocean! And yet, we continue as if all is well with our water supply. Where creeks and streams once ran full of life, there are now only dried veins stitched into the Earth's flesh.

Yes, we are feeding and clothing the world, but as irrigation systems continue to pump and pump and pump, we are depleting our future water supply. If agriculture truly consumes 80-85% of this nation's fresh water for crops and livestock, and the Ogallala aquifer (stretching from South Dakota to Texas) really is being depleted at a rate 160% greater than its recharge rate, we are heading irrevocably into a natural disaster.[1] We are creating the unthinkable—complete destruction of our fresh water supply.

---

1. Dale Allen Pfeiffer, "Eating Fossil Fuels", From the Wilderness, http://www.fromthewilderness.com/free/ww3/100303_eating_oil.html, October 2003.

How much water is enough to irrigate cotton, corn, wheat, or any other crop? How much money is enough to stuff in our pockets? This isn't robbing Peter to pay Paul, but rather killing our children so we might live in luxury. By maximizing per acre profits with excessive irrigation we are sucking dry the blood within our own bodies, draining our children's futures. In the case of water usage, excess does not lead to the palace of wisdom. It leads to a derelict world of decay.

Some experts have already suggested we abandon irrigation altogether in areas with little rainfall in order to preserve the water supply. I disagree with this principle. Moderation is the only answer, for now. If farmers cannot comply with that, then regulation is inevitable. I detest excessive amounts of laws and regulations, but when it comes to protecting our dwindling water supply, I'm all for them—particularly when it is overwhelmingly evident that man is looking no farther than his own pocketbook. As mentioned earlier, the U.S. government shut off irrigation to parts of the California Central Valley, destroying crops in this desert region. This water prohibition was advertised as being imposed to save protected fish. Not much was mentioned of California's receding water supply. The farming towns involved will vanish over the next few years. Where will the people go? What will they do for work? And how will we replace this vast source of food? This area grew almost 10% of America's entire food supply with over 250 different crops. It also represented over 16% of the country's irrigated land relying on the second largest aquifer.

In 1949, about 4,300 wells irrigated 550,000 acres in Texas. Fifty years later, as many as 8 million acres rely on irrigation systems in Texas. The southern High Plains (my neighborhood) accounts for roughly 68% of all irrigation in Texas. Why? Because it has the driest climate in the state. To the west of Lubbock lies Gaines County. This is some of the most desert-like territory in the state, yet it produces more peanuts and cotton than anywhere in the country due to an excessive number of irrigation circles. More than 400,000 acres of irrigated farmland is found here with less than 15,000 residents.[2]

---

2. *The Handbook of Texas Online.*

It is not only farmers abusing our water supply. Living in urban areas such as Lubbock, Texas, I've witnessed extremely wasteful practices of water usage. Businesses irrigating huge grass lawns with sprinkler systems in the heat of the day during summer; the flooding of streets by opening fire hydrants (why?); and inefficient rain drainage/runoff along streets and sidewalks are classic examples. Many urban areas simply drain the rainwater from several blocks into one large area commonly designated as one of the city parks, which then serves as nothing more than a huge bowl to absorb the quasi-floods caused by miles of concrete and pavement.

City planners give little to no thought concerning Mother Nature when laying down miles and miles of hardened earth. To feed a deranged sense of comfort in modern suburbia, humanity has instead focused on building as many over-sized cookie-cutter houses as possible per block with as little grass (backyard) area as possible. I get hot flashes, breaking into a sweat, every time I drive around these neighborhoods. Where does the rainwater go? It is wasted in low intersections and flattened streets. Why is there not more civic planning to widen streets with grass areas to catch the runoff or create slopes to run water into people's yards or onto trees along hot summer sidewalks? And somewhere Joni Mitchell is singing, "They paved paradise, and put up a parking lot."

But the depletion of our water supply from agricultural and urban methods of abuse has nothing on that from corporate America. Bottled water companies are taking full advantage of a $400 billion industry in today's tinfoil economy. Despite the fact that the water of 33% of bottled water brands is no safer than tap water, we continue to purchase tiny plastic bottles of water priced more than three times higher than gasoline (December 2009: gasoline less than $3 per gallon, while bottled water equated to $10 per gallon). Incidentally, it takes two to seven barrels of water to produce one barrel of oil. Corporations have yet again figured out a way to profit from us on a daily basis from the most essential element for our lives, and we continue to overpay them rather than spend the money to secure our own supply of "safe" drinking water.

Water in the Well

Not long ago, it was easy to believe our underground water was completely healthy to drink, bathe our bodies in, wash our faces with, and brush our teeth with. That couldn't now be further from the truth. According to the March 2009 issue of *Acres U.S.A.*, "over 50% of the nation's drinking water wells contained detectable amounts of nitrate and 7% have detectable amounts of pesticides."[3]

For the past century agriculture has done more than its share to contaminate our underground water table by combining excessive usage of pesticides, herbicides, and petroleum fertilizers. In some areas fish have such high levels of the pesticide atrazine that it is genetically altering the males, transforming them into females. Atrazine is used on approximately 65% of the U.S. corn crop and has been sprayed for the past 35 years. Interesting how its use is still widespread here when it has been banned not only in the European Union but also the very country (Switzerland) in which it is made. For some strange reason, the EPA ruled in 2006 that there are no severe risks or dangers in the usage of atrazine. We use 80 million pounds of atrazine each year on our corn crops in America.

Syngenta, the company which manufactures atrazine, hired the University of California at Berkeley to conduct a study of the potential dangers of their product. The university discovered that atrazine "demasculates or chemically castrates" male frogs, other amphibians, and fish. Males (with traces of atrazine) grow ovaries and lay eggs.[4] Could this affect the human species as well? Are men becoming emasculated via chemical invasion?

---

3. Mike Amaranthus, Ph.D., Jeff Anderson and John Marler, "Degraded Soils, Food Shortages and Eating Oil: Restoring Soil Life Through Biological Agriculture", *Acres U.S.A.*, March 2009.

4. Robert Sanders, "Pesticide Atrazine Can Turn Male Frogs into Females", UCBerkeleyNews,http://berkeley.edu/news/media/releases/2010/03/01_frogs.shtml, March 1, 2010.

According to the Agency for Toxic Substances and Disease Registry's website (www.atsdr.cdc.gov), atrazine is "the most heavily used pre- and post-emergence herbicide in the United States." The website also states that:

> In humans, atrazine exposure has been associated with increased pre-term delivery, miscarriage, and various birth defects. However, the lack of information on exposure levels and the simultaneous exposure to other pesticides makes these studies inadequate to assess whether these effects are attributable to atrazine exposure.
>
> There is evidence that atrazine disrupts the normal function of the endocrine system. Several animal studies have shown that atrazine exposure disrupts estrus cyclicity and alters plasma hormone levels; these effects appear to be mediated by changes in the gonadal-hypothalamic-pituitary axis (feedback or communication system between reproductive organs and the brain) and lead to premature reproductive aging.
>
> Developmental effects have been observed following pre-gestational, gestational, and lactational exposure of rat and rabbit females or post-weaning exposure of rat pups to atrazine. The observed effects included post-implantation losses, decreases in fetal body weight, incomplete bone formation, neurodevelopmental effects, delayed puberty, and impaired development of the reproductive system.
>
> Epidemiological studies that included cohorts at triazine manufacturing facilities, case-control studies of farmers, and ecological studies of populations living in areas with atrazine-contaminated drinking water, collectively, provide suggestive evidence of an association between atrazine exposure and several cancers including non-Hodgkin's lymphoma, prostrate, brain, testicular, breast, and ovarian.

Tests across the country of our nation's drinking water show an even more disturbing invasion of our water supply—pharmaceuticals. As the majority of Americans are entranced by some type of anti-depressant or other chemical, they are flushed into the water table via sewers and other underground water pipes and enter our streams and rivers. So they are eventually recycled back into our water supply once again.

Factory farms are another key polluter of our water supply. Nitrates from animal waste seep into the ground, along with the toxic antibiotics pumped into their bodies. When thousands of animals are confined to a small area in feedlots, dairies, etc., their waste overwhelms any local water supply whether above or below ground.

Oil field activity is another destroyer of well water. Old lines are often not capped properly, and they begin to seep either salt water or other toxic elements from old gas or oil lines buried and forgotten. For the past five years, oil activity has increased all around us in West Texas. Oil well sites are a common place to find hundreds of thousands of gallons of water being pumped away into a small pond or lake area to scrape up a few barrels of oil here and there. That water soon evaporates and is gone.

Whether it is in urban or rural areas, not enough attention is focused on our water supply. We can't allow apathy or disbelief to keep us from facing the dire consequences of our gluttonous habits. Without water, we are nothing. We cease to exist. Rather than all our focus remaining on energy in the form of oil or electricity, water should be at the top of the list.

Global Weirding

Whether you believe in "global warming" or not, it is undeniable that the Earth is changing. She is experiencing a radical transformation in rushed fashion, thanks to our gluttonous population of six billion and growing. Droughts and flooding are becoming more and more extreme around the globe. I liken what is happening to our Mother Earth to a woman going through birthing pains and menopause at the exact same time. Not exactly a thrilling ride for anyone around. We can argue all day whether it is another ice age coming or a fatal heat wave, but that's equivalent to a small group on a tiny wooden boat in violent seas, arguing why the large vessel sank when they are headed straight for a rocky shore. The bickering must end. The only solution is swift and proper action.

Scientists are now saying the Arctic ice melt is occurring even faster than the worst pessimists anticipated.[5] Recent models suggest the Arctic will be ice-free in the summer months as early as 2013.[6] The consequent rapid cooling of the Atlantic waters will drastically alter weather patterns not only in Great Britain and Europe, but perhaps the entire world. As the Atlantic conveyor belt, which is pushed by warm waters from the Gulf of Mexico, will be shut down by slushy fresh waters, predictions vary from a miniature ice age for the northern hemisphere to major droughts elsewhere. Unfortunately, we are about to find out. With hundreds of millions of barrels spewing into the Gulf of Mexico waters from BP's Deepwater Horizon oil rig explosion, who knows how polluted and/or damaged the entire Gulf Coast and the Atlantic Ocean will be once that oil is carried up the Atlantic coast.

We've seen our share of neurotic weather in West Texas for the past several years, some might say for the past 80 years. West Texas is about as extreme as it comes in terms of the highs and lows of Mother Nature. For instance, in 2005 we had about 17 inches of rain on our farm, which is average for this area of West Texas. In 2006, less than 11 inches fell. In 2007, we witnessed a record of more than 40 inches! But the very next year, 2008, was as dry as it gets with less than 9 inches recorded. Floods and droughts con-

---

5. Stephanie Dearing, "Arctic Ice Melt Faster than Thought: Ecosystem in Peril", Digital Journal, http://digitaljournal.com/article/287158, February 6, 2009.

6. Rod Nickel, "Arctic Climate Changing Faster Than Expected", ABC News, http://abcnews.go.com/Technology/wireStory?id= 9762170, February 5, 2010.

vulse across the country like a drunken donkey crossing a frozen lake. Whether this is man-made or not, the fact is that neurotic weather patterns are becoming more and more common.

All studies of the near and distant future predict more mayhem, greatly affecting our rivers, lakes, and underground water tables. The Intergovernmental Panel on Climate Change predicts more than 200 million people will not have enough water in Latin America, Asia, and Africa in less than 10 years. Their long-term predictions are for nothing short of a disaster.[7]

If you're like most people, you read statistical predictions that may or may not happen in 40 or 90 years, and think, "It doesn't matter. I'll be long gone." And most of us will be, but our offspring will be here long after us. I believe those occurrences are more like 4-9 years away rather than 40-90.

Most foreign countries, particularly those in Africa and Asia have been heavily dependent upon America's vast wheat and corn crops. As water tables drop and the prices to bring that water to the surface greatly increase, we will not grow those crops as plentifully as we have the past 40-50 years with the aid of plentiful irrigation and low-priced commercial fertilizers. Those days of vast abundance are gone.

We're kidding ourselves if we think we can continue to abuse our water supply any longer without global repercussions. Many areas throughout the United States, such as California, New Mexico, Arizona, Nevada, and Texas, are already witnessing dry wells and underground aquifers. As corporations in the drinking water industry drain pure mountain springs and other natural streams throughout the country, above-ground water is rapidly vanishing before our very eyes. This has nothing to do with global warming, but has everything to do with the excessive habits of corporations fueled by profits, not by what is best for Mother Nature.

---

7. Lisa Friedman, "Coming Soon: Mass Migrations Spurred by Climate Change", *The New York Times,* March 2, 2009.

Which corporations? Nestlé, Coca-Cola, and Pepsi are the big ones. They lead a $400 billion industry sucking dry once healthy flowing creeks and rivers in states such as Michigan, Tennessee, and Pennsylvania. These money-making moguls think nothing of destroying a rural community or a beautiful piece of Earth, digging their claws into Mother Nature for the sheer sake of profits for their companies and shareholders. With no laws in place to limit them, they place a pump into any natural body of water, sucking out over 400 gallons of water every minute.

Coca-Cola and Nestlé head the list of American corporations which have turned the essence of life into an economic product. Nestlé was thrown out of the state of Wisconsin as they tried to pump water from the Great Lakes for their bottled water. They moved next door to Michigan, where they continue to fight citizens over water rights. Coca-Cola's Dasani water brand is sold in remote African countries, causing poverty-stricken villagers to pay more for water than a Coke. They have no alternative, as their rivers and lakes are often polluted or full of bacteria causing such disorders as dysentery.

We are paying more than three times as much per gallon for bottled water as we are gasoline, which is shipped primarily from the Middle East (2,000-miles away), carried by railroads and trucks across the country, and refined through a delicate process before it is trucked to the gas station in its ready form. With water, all we really need is to install a carbon filtration system with an ultraviolet light, costing less than $1,000, to safely filter our home water supply. (Download a free guideline for installing the proper water filtration system for your own home or business at www.foodandwaterwatch.org/water/pubs/water-guides/filtration-guide/water-filtration-guide.)

The amount of plastic necessary for bottled water creates a gravely serious environmental impact. Food and Water Watch estimates bottled water creates about 1.5 million tons of waste each year. As much as 47 million gallons of oil is required to manufacture all that plastic annually. Although recycling might ease our anxiety about the waste we produce a little, the majority of bottles are simply tossed after use. As we continue to find more "plastic islands" floating in our oceans like the Great Pacific Garbage Patch (twice the size of Texas), we should minimize our reliance on plastics in all purchases and packaging, particularly water.

Plastics are petroleum-based products. They contain several hazardous compounds in their chemical makeup. Bisphenol A (BPA) appears in all plastic water bottles, linings of cans, and other plastic containers. A report by the FDA in 2010 warns of exposing pregnant mothers, infants, and young children to plastics because of the high amounts of BPA.[8] Midwives and doctors are reporting unusual physical abnormalities in newborn babies. Many believe this is directly related to excessive usage of plastic water bottles. Stainless steel, glass, and Nalgene products remain much healthier options for water and food storage.

Water corporations like Suez (United Water) and Veolia (Vivenda) are involved in marketing privatized water across the world, including many third world countries, forcing people to pay for water from their own taps at home. Often water pumps are only turned on once a week, but the villagers do not know when, so they are essentially being charged for keeping taps open, though only air flows.

American cities have also privatized their water to these corporations. New York City, Las Vegas, Houston, and Atlanta have all privatized their water to Suez. Chicago has privatized its water system to Veolia. Many of these companies' highest-ranking board members and CEOs have direct ties to the World Bank. Suez, Veolia, Coca-Cola, and Nestlé are to water what Monsanto, Bayer, and DuPont are to seeds.

At our current rate of consumption, we will witness wars over water right here at home in the next decade, much like we are witnessing wars over oil in the Middle East right now. Only these

---

8. "Update on Bisphenol A for Use in Food Contact Applications: January 2010", U.S. Food and Drug Administration, http://www.fda.gov/newsevnts/publichealthfocus/ucm197739.htm, January 2010.

wars will not pit America's armed forces versus some far-off foreign terrorists. These wars will pit neighbors versus neighbors; farmers versus urban dwellers; countrymen versus countrymen; and citizens versus corporations.

Mother, Mother Ocean

While writing this book, I began reading *The World Is Blue* by scientist, explorer, and oceanographer Sylvia A. Earle. Through this valuable work, Earle brings into the open many of the startling facts and statistics of ocean life degradation and other destructive changes, and I felt compelled to include some of this vital information here. The general temptation to consider that the oceans are so vast and infinite that we can do no harm to them is both thoughtless and reckless. Many fish species are disappearing due to our overwhelming indulgence in taking more than we give. And what we do give back to the ocean is pollutant in nature. We must realize that much of what we put into our soil and water eventually reaches the ocean. No matter how microscopic its traces may be, consider that there are almost seven billion of us contributing. It has taken us less than a century to wreak serious havoc on the oceans. Many have lived without love, money, or fame, but not a single one of us can make it without healthy oceans.

From commercial fertilizer runoff to illegal dumping of toxic chemicals and plastics, our excessive tendencies are overwhelming our most precious bodies of water, from lakes and rivers to the vast blue oceans connecting one continent to another. As a young man, I witnessed firsthand the excessive nature of commercial fishing while working on salmon seiner boats off Kodiak Island in Alaska. It is extremely hard work, and I respect what these fishermen do in putting their lives on the line in dangerous elements. Commercial fishing is essentially farming the ocean, harvesting Nature's bounty. The more fish, the more money—hence, the more successful a fisherman is. It is yet another industry taking more than it gives. While we feed humanity with tasty meals, we destroy fish populations at such an accelerated rate that they cannot naturally reproduce fast enough to restock what we take. We upset the delicate balance of ecosystems involving endless numbers of species, including ones needed to maintain healthy phytoplankton and ocean life.

Earle writes:

> Earth's life-support system—the ocean—is failing. But who is paying attention? Throughout our history, the mostly blue natural world has been regarded as something to be vanquished, tamed, or otherwise used for purposes that seemed to make sense at the time. Deeply rooted in human culture is the attitude that the ocean is so vast, so resilient, it shouldn't matter how much we take out of—or put into—it. But two things changed in the 20th century that may jolt us into a new way of thinking.
>
> First, more was discovered about the nature of the ocean and its relevance to the way the world works than during all preceding history. Second, during the same narrow slice of time, human actions caused more destruction to ocean systems than during all preceding history. And the pace is picking up.

Earle backs up these passionate words with disturbing statistics:

- Since the middle of the 20th century, hundreds of millions of tons of ocean wildlife have been removed from the sea, while hundreds of millions of tons of wastes have been poured into it.
- 90% of many once common fish have been extracted since the 1950s; 95% of some species, including bluefin tuna, Atlantic cod, American eel, and certain sharks have been killed. And taking them is still allowed. Destructive fishing techniques—trawls, longlines, rock-

hopping dredges—not only continue to take too much, they have destroyed habitats and killed millions of tons of animals that are simply discarded. Every year industrial fishing wantonly kills hundreds of thousands of marine mammals, seabirds, and sea turtles, hundreds of millions of fish, and invertebrate animals.

- Half of the shallow coral reefs globally are gone or are in a state of serious decline since the 1950s; in much of the Caribbean, 80% are dead.

- Deep coral reefs are being destroyed by new deep trawling technologies aimed at capturing fish that are decades, even centuries, old. The destroyed corals are thousands of years old.

- More than 400 "dead zones" have formed in coastal areas in recent decades, and the number is increasing and accelerating, reflecting changes in ocean chemistry.

- The ocean's pH—the measure of alkalinity or acidity—is changing, owing to increased carbon dioxide that in turn becomes carbonic acid. Consequences are likely to be most obvious for coral reefs, mollusks, and plankton housed in carbonate shells, but the changes touch all forms of life in the sea.

- Most troubling, perhaps, is the profound, widespread ignorance about the ocean and its vital importance to everyone, everywhere, all the time. It is not just the fact that less than 5% of the ocean has been seen, let alone explored. Even what is known to scientists is not widely appreciated by the public, and certainly not by most policymakers.

There is much more provided by Earle in this vital read. Each page is another tidal wave of passionate pleas and relentless observations of reality. She informs us why the ocean matters to us as a species:

But most of all, it matters that the world is blue because our lives depend on the living ocean—not just the rocks and water, but stable, resilient, diverse living systems that hold the world on a steady course favorable to humankind. The big question is, what can we do to take care of the blue world that takes care of us?

Constructing and Re-constructing Rainforests

Worldwide there exist less than 10 billion acres (4 billion hectares) of forests, which is roughly 30% of total land space. Sounds like a lot of real estate. But those numbers are shrinking rapidly. From 2000 to 2005, more than 18 million acres of forest were destroyed globally. Ancient rainforests, both tropical and temperate, are responsible for about 28% of the Earth's oxygen turnover through photosynthesis. These vital regions also help keep excessive amounts of carbon dioxide balanced, acting as a colossal living filtration system for the entire planet. The World Wide Fund for Nature (WWF) released a report stating that deforestation will destroy 60% of the entire Amazonian Rainforest by 2030.[9] Brazil and other countries have already declared deforestation as a state of emergency.

Despite these warnings, more rainforest is destroyed each year so ranchers may graze more cattle and farmers plant more soybeans. The destruction of rainforests and forests alike also eliminates thousands or even millions of other species. From ancient trees and medicinal plants to birds, insects, and other wildlife, these jewels of Nature are home to all walks and flights of precious creatures.

The Bush family is rumored to have purchased more than 273,000

---

9. Alison Benjamin and agencies, "More than Half of Amazon will be Lost by 2030, report Warns", *The Guardian*, http://www.guardian.co.uk/environment/2007/dec/06/conservation.endangeredhabitats, December 6, 2007.

acres of forest in Paraguay, along the Brazilian border (George H. Bush reportedly owns 173,000 acres, and George W. purchased 100,000 acres).[10] This happens to be next door to some of the most abundant waterways in the world and sits atop the Guarani Reservoir, the world's largest aquifer. Another interesting footnote is that the Bush's South American Ranch is just a few miles away from the U.S. Mariscal Estigarribia Military Base. The most devoted Bush supporters might suggest the prestigious family is moving there to protect such a vital water supply, but given their environmental track record it is highly unlikely. As several powerful governments, corporations, and families jockey for position to profit from and plunder our remaining water resources, we must continue to encourage and improve our water situation by reviving Nature.

In his book *Science in Agriculture*, Arden Anderson describes the vital role of trees in Nature:

> Trees serve as highly directional capacitors, altering the electrical tension in the atmosphere and thus the weather. Wilhelm Reich found that he could simulate this function with metal tubes grounded in water. He demonstrated that clouds, atmospheric pressure and storm fronts, and ultimately the weather could be altered with such devices. Many scientists have replicated Reich's experiments and confirmed his results. Trees are nature's weather regulators. It is well known that trees improve the atmosphere of an area and that massive clear-cutting alters the rainfall of that same region. This is simply nature at work, applying the laws of physics that man has ignored, denied, or exploited. There are no accidents in nature. Every cause has its effect. Scientists like Callahan and Reams have realized this and been able to see the perfect divine order in all things. Plant

---

10. CP News Wire, "Hideout or Water Raid: Bush's Paraguay Land Grab", Counterpunch, http://www.counterpunch.org/cp10202006.html, October 20, 2006.

function, like the function of every living system, is a marvel. It is much more sophisticated than any man-made system, yet it is no less straightforward in its principles of operation and design. The principles of nature are valid throughout; they apply equally to a living cell and to a semiconductor or a microchip used by NASA.

Anderson affirms the idea that knowledge without action is useless, stating, "Understanding these principles and laws does not in itself raise good crops or regenerate soils. It does, however, give you a blueprint by which to grow good crops and regenerate poverty soils. You must read the blueprint and then assemble the necessary materials to carry out the plan."

Through studying Nature it is easy to conclude that rainfall is heavier in forested areas. The entire American Midwest receives between 24-46 inches of rain annually, compared to the 114 inches of the Amazon Rainforest. Rocky Mountain areas in the United States receive 60-80 inches of rain each year. In one year, a 100-foot tree can take up over 5,000,000 gallons of water from the soil and transpire it into the air, retaining 350 gallons of water (2,900 lbs.) and exhaling 6,000 pounds of oxygen.[11] In desolate areas such as West Texas, mesquite trees are one of the few trees to grow, but they are relatively new trees to the region (less than 100 years old), brought up with grazing cattle from Mexico in the early 20th century. Our average rainfall is 17 inches.

By planting more trees, we are encouraging the natural cycles of Nature. Trees breathe in and exhale moisture, recycling water from their roots up to their leaves. This moisture evaporates, encouraging cloud formations, some of which build into rain and thunderclouds. Thus, trees help create a wonderfully natural water system. They also help filter the air for us, not to mention putting out sufficient amounts of healthy oxygen for us to breathe.

---

11. Northwest Territories: Tree Managment Division, http://forestmanagement.enr.gov.nt.ca/forest_education/amazing_tree_facts.html.

Why would we continue to cut off our nose to spite our face? Why destroy healthy air for money? How much clean air can money buy? How many sets of lungs?

We could create our own miniature rainforests all around us. If each county, city, town, or community dedicated a weekend or two each year to planting 100 mature trees, think how much we could strengthen our environment, our air, and our rainfall. We have the power and ability to increase the rains, if we are willing to put in the hard work. If each American farming family planted 100 trees over the coming years, that is 100 million more trees. Imagine if another 50 million Americans (16% of the population) planted 20 trees each. We would have then replaced more than one billion trees in this country alone. Multiply that around the world, and we begin to rapidly improve the health of our environment.

Certain groups and organizations have done incredible work in reforestation. One of the most well-known groups is Men of The Trees in Western Australia. Since 1979, this determined group has planted more than 7 million trees and continues to plant as many as 800,000 trees each year. This is remarkable. Men of The Trees was founded in 1924 by Richard St. Barbe Baker in England. This group is the perfect example of what can be accomplished by our species if we put our minds and muscle to it.

Man-made Reservoirs

Most ranchers create a pond or tank to help water their livestock that range across vast amounts of land. In drier regions, this is often the only way to water grazing herds. Windmills are an extremely efficient method of pumping underground water into concrete or metal tanks for livestock on large ranches and pasture land. But if instead we create a small or large pond, we are also creating a healthy environment for Nature to thrive.

Sloped, hilly landscape provides plenty of watershed in most areas. Old creeks and streambeds are visible, stemming from a time when moving waters were much more common. Following the trails of these dried waterways during a good rain, it is easy to track an ideal place to build a pond.

A large backhoe is ideal for this task. Yes, it takes several hours of labor performed by a very expensive piece of equipment, but leasing this machine can be quite affordable in the long run. Even if you don't have a neighbor to hire for this job, the local National Resource Conservation Service (NRCS) office can help find you a local contractor. A couple of days of hired labor ($2,000 more or less) will build an adequate pond to last a lifetime. Rather than paying an expensive electric bill for water wells each month, your money is spent up front. The NRCS will also provide vital information about drilling a test-hole and determining if your soil type will hold water or not. Some sandy soils are too porous to seal properly and make an efficient water-holding structure. Bentonite clay, or sodium bentonite, can be added to seal these soils. It is very effective and environmentally safe.

These ponds harness Mother Nature's offerings for generations to come and help preserve precious topsoil. If grass is not already established leading up to the reservoir, it is a good idea to allow grass to re-establish itself. This prevents topsoil from washing away and serves as an excellent filtering system of contaminants washing in from nearby roads or highways. Building a protective fence around the watering hole prevents livestock from contaminating their water source with high levels of fecal matter. A 12-volt battery-operated pump can fill a nearby metal or plastic tank for the herd. Birds and other wildlife will be extremely thankful for such a creation. Once the pond fills with water and vegetation grows, stocking it with fish will provide a healthy aquatic ecosystem, keeping the water filtered naturally. This also can double as a recreation area for the family. Planting trees around the pond will also help prevent evaporation and provide shade for fishing, reading, bird watching, or whatever tickles your fancy.

These methods are not to be confused with damming up natural flowing rivers and streams with mega-ton concrete dams. Damming up wild, untamed rivers such as the Colorado, Mississippi, or China's Nu River causes many problems within the ecosystems along riverbanks. Water becomes stagnant. Various fish species cannot complete their migration patterns, causing large die-offs. The natural mineralization process is interrupted as well, due to snowmelts, mudslides, etc., being held up in one large area rather than depositing much needed life all along the watery path of streams, lakes, creeks, and finally the ocean. Our attempts to manipulate Nature's lifelines with skyscraper concrete slabs are clogging up the main arteries of her heart.

Harvesting Rainwater

There is another good way we can recycle the rain Mother Nature sends our way. The next time it rains, watch carefully how

Water Use Statistics		
Use	Gallons per capita	Total daily use
Showers	11.6	16.8%
Clothes washers	15.0	21.7%
Dishwashers	1.0	1.4%
Toilets	18.5	26.7%
Baths	1.2	1.7%
Leaks	9.5	13.7%
Faucets	10.9	15.7%
Other domestic uses	1.6	2.2%

much water falls from the roof of your house. Most people don't give it a second thought. Imagine collecting every last drop from your roof so that nothing goes wasted, and somehow guiding that rainfall to trees and other plant life instead of causing unnecessary soil erosion or flooding downhill. Imagine then not only homes but businesses in towns and cities, farms, and communities worldwide installing rainwater harvesting systems so that their gardens and landscaping flourish without ever wasting any of the precious water beneath our feet.

The average American family currently uses about 69 gallons of water per day. According to Amy Vickers' *Handbook of Water Use and Conservation,* daily indoor per capita water use in the typical single family home is 69.3 gallons (see the chart on page 89).

By installing more efficient water fixtures and regularly checking for leaks, households can reduce daily per capita water use by about 35% to about 45.2 gallons per day. Here's how it breaks down for households using conservation measures:

Water Use Statistics		
Use	Gallons per capita	Total daily use
Showers	8.8	19.5%
Clothes washers	10.0	22.1%
Dishwashers	8.2	18.0%
Toilets	0.7	1.5%
Baths	1.2	2.7%
Leaks	4.0	8.8%
Faucets	10.8	23.9%
Other domestic uses	1.6	3.4%

If we use these statistics as a model for our current lifestyle, we can figure that the average family needs about 25,550 gallons of water to operate its home each year. For anyone with a sizable garden, that amount could easily double. This is where rainwater harvesting steps into play.

Just how much can one save or collect off the roof of one's home, barn or other structure? The formula is 0.62 gallons of rainwater per square foot per one inch of rain. So, let's say you have a 40 feet x 50 feet roof structure (2,000 total square feet) and you receive one inch of rain. You will collect approximately 1,240 gallons of rainwater. If your average annual rainfall is 20 inches, one household can collect about 24,800 gallons of rainwater each year. This averages out to almost 250,000 gallons of water in a ten-year period! If we were to cut out leaks and install certain handy devices to prevent wasteful use, most homes could satisfy their entire water demands with rainwater alone.

Our barn on the family farm is currently 40 feet × 100 feet in dimensions. Our annual rainfall is about 17.5 inches in this part of West Texas. But this one structure allows us to harvest over 40,000 gallons of rainwater each year. We will have harvested over half a million gallons in 12 years off this one structure. Now, multiply this across the country, and our water supply is now sustainable. By harvesting rainwater, we allow ourselves the self-sufficient power to provide our own healthy water supply without depleting our underground source.

Building a Rainwater Harvesting System

While rainwater is as pure as it gets, the water can be contaminated with bird droppings, leaves, dirt, and other debris. There are many ways to maintain a healthy rainwater harvesting system to avoid contaminants. I first used black poly tanks purchased locally from a plumbing store for catching rainwater off our house and made use of two used 3,000 gallon tanks (once used for commercial fertilizer) for the barn rainwater. The laws of gravity take hold in rainwater harvesting. I drilled holes with a hole-saw into each lid, securing cloth screen with baling wire around the downspouts. I highly recommend screens along the gutters to keep out tree branches, mice, and other unwanted debris. Occasionally, you'll want to clean the screen or whatever filter you find necessary. In the case of the smaller tanks, I plumbed them into a garden hose attachment, which I ran directly to trees and garden plants. A small 12-volt pump and battery ($150-$200) can be used to give you more pressure uphill if necessary. On the larger tanks, I used two-inch valves I could hook up to our portable water tanks used for foliar sprays and sub-soil fertilizing. By using the rainwater, the pH remained neutral as opposed to our highly alkaline well water. A steady application of rainwater helps lower our soil's pH just a hair rather than keeping it in the high 7.8-8.2 area. Rainwater will also help balance out acidic soils. Plant absorption is maximized with rainwater in foliar applications as leaf and flower molecular structures open fully with the presence of rainwater.

Make certain the tanks have a spill-hole, which gives the water a place to go once the tank is full. If there is no spill-hole, the tank will explode from the excessive pressure built up inside. Before placing tanks, make sure the ground is level and the tanks are secure from high winds. (I've retrieved empty 3,000 gallon tanks three miles away after persistent winds. Once these things get rolling, they are capable of causing serious damage, and they don't stop until the laws of inertia are affirmed.) Also keep in mind how and where you want to use most of the rainwater. Whether it is for drinking water or strictly outdoor usage for gardens, trees, etc., you want to make it as user-friendly as possible. For the 3,000 gallon tanks, I first built a large stand, placing each tank three and a half feet above ground, allowing gravity to flow the water into the portable tank. This worked well until the tanks evened out with about 750 gallons remaining in the storage tanks. I later placed these tanks on the ground and used a small 2.5 horsepower motor and pump to extract every gallon of water.

Much more elaborate systems can be built as more companies or individuals are specializing in rainwater harvesting systems for private and commercial use. I hired Eddie Craig with Texas Rain Catchers in Clyde, Texas, to plumb two buildings into a 10,000 gallon tank from Pioneer Water Tanks. By using proper downspout adapters fitted into four-inch PVC pipe from the gutter to the tank, with first-catch filters, it is a much more efficient system than I could have ever built myself. Plus, I learned a great deal by asking many questions. We also had a 16,000 gallon tank on one end of our barn, so we didn't have so many black poly tanks scattered around.

If the rainwater is to be used for drinking water, make certain you do the proper research. A metal tank is needed instead of a poly tank. Drinking water stored in these plastic tanks is not recommended and can be dangerous. Companies like Blue Scope Water and Pioneer specialize in water storage tanks for drinking water. A filtration system is also much more important to eliminate bacteria and other contaminants such as herbicides, pesticides, and pharmaceuticals. This can be achieved with a carbon filter and an ultraviolet light, which can add up to some serious bucks. If cash is limited, certain alternative inexpensive systems have proven effective. A glass tube exposing rainwater to sunlight will help, along with a Berkey water filter or some other carbon-based water filter. If you're interested in finding out more information on rainwater harvesting, the *Texas Manual on Rainwater Harvesting* can be downloaded for free online. It provides excellent and easy-to-use information on what one needs to build an efficient rainwater harvesting system.

Rise of Permaculture

Nature creates a vital cycle where water exists. It doesn't take a Henry David Thoreau to realize that much more life exists around water. Whether it be an ocean, lake, river, creek, or pond, the presence of water attracts all forms of creatures. Remember that precious graph in science class depicting the cycle of water from the ocean to sky to trees to Earth and back to the ocean? This forms the whole basis of permaculture, which is a term coined by two Aussies, Bill Mollison and David Holmgren.

Permaculture also encompasses the philosophy of creating "food forests". This is achieved with native vegetation, maximizing the potential of the natural landscape, and building swales to catch water runoff for plants and trees. By creating a water-friendly ecosystem, we are copying Mother Nature in a very flattering manner.

Imagine how much rainwater is wasted through excessive runoff when there is no natural way to guide it toward trees or other vegetation that so desperately need it. By creating landscaping that invites rainwater rather than detours it away, our trees, plants, and shrubs will thrive even more and require less irrigation and labor. Digging deeper wells for trees rather than the customary building up of borders around the base of their trunks is a classic example of how doing things in the ways we have been programmed to do them is not always best. By creating a sponge-like environment with composting and mulching, we can also absorb more water instead of losing much of it to evaporation or run-off.

The same rules apply to farming. Much farmland is not table-flat prairie where the rain is distributed evenly across its acres. Most farmers build terraces or swales to prevent hard rains from creating huge erosion issues. Dad has built huge terraces on several of our fields through the years. Often, I cursed the huge mounds as I crossed them on tractors with large tillage equipment, but after a four-inch rain in 2007, I saw firsthand how important they were in preventing soil erosion and directing water towards a draw at the bottom of the hill. The usage of contour rows rather than straight rows also helps with this issue by preventing water from running off the land too quickly and not seeping into the soil. We use special dikers on our pre-planting tillage equipment, which help create miniature levees along the row prior to planting.

For experienced farmers and gardeners, I am aware I am preaching to the choir, but for those of you who are novice farmers, gardeners, and fellow stewards of the Earth, this is sound advice.

One man who has devoted much of his time to the necessity and beauty of rainwater harvesting and utilizing permaculture techniques in creating a more water-friendly environment is Brad Lancaster of Tucson, Arizona. He is the author of *Rainwater Harvesting for Drylands and Beyond* (3 volumes). I highly recommend these books as they offer detailed drawings, pictures, and pages of proven methods backed by over a decade of experience.

For instance, Lancaster points out that for every inch of rainfall...

- A 10-foot wide paved street will drain 27,800 gallons of runoff per mile.
- A 30-foot wide paved street will drain 83,500 gallons of runoff per mile

For every 100 mm of rainfall...

- A 3-m wide paved street will drain 300,000 liters of runoff per kilometer.
- A 9-m wide paved street will drain 900,000 liters of runoff per kilometer.

Lancaster continues to tour the country, educating everyone from city planners to Nature lovers. His methods encourage planting native trees and other vegetation to endure local climates easily. Trees planted along city streets provide shade in the summer heat. These trees are also to be planted with large tree wells to hold massive amounts of water.

The year before I read Lancaster's books, I had planted several fruit trees in our backyard. They were suffering greatly in a year-long drought. Careful not to destroy established roots, I dug circled trenches about one-foot deep around each tree. I filled each one half full with rich compost. Although we endured another severe drought the following summer, the trees grew significantly. By utilizing my rainwater catchment system, each tree could hold up to 30 gallons per watering. The water soaked in slowly and evenly up to two feet away from the tree's base, encouraging a healthier root system. During rain and snowfall, these trees are capable of accessing 20 times the amount of water. Rather than building up a bed around these trees, preventing rainwater from entering, the deep compost trenches invite rain into the heart of the tree's root zone. This prevents runoff, which also causes soil erosion. Efficiency in water utilization (particularly in dry regions) is the key. For everything I plant by hand now, I use this method.

Toby Hemenway is another author with significant experience in rainwater harvesting and permaculture techniques. In his workshop during the 2009 Fredericksburg, Texas, Renewable Energy Roundup, he endorsed the eight steps of rainwater harvesting:

1. Observe.
2. Start at the top.
3. Start small.
4. Slow it, spread it, sink it.
5. Always give water somewhere to go.
6. Plant a living sponge.
7. Stack functions.
8. Evaluate, reassess.

Hemenway's book, *Gaia's Garden*, is an extremely detailed book on permaculture with many colorful photos and wonderful illustrations to help plan, design, and create "food forests" by making the most of rainfall. With swales, terraces, and many other Earth-friendly techniques, permaculture may very well be the most efficient manner in which to feed ourselves. But perhaps permaculture's greatest focus is creating a permanent ecosystem beneficial for all walks and flights of Nature. Hemenway writes in *Gaia's Garden*:

> Ecological gardens also blend many garden styles together which gives the gardener enough leeway to emphasize the qualities—food, flowers, herbs, crafts, and so on—he or she likes most. Some ecological gardening finds its roots in edible landscaping, which in a creative melding, frees food plants from their vegetable-patch prison and lets them mix with the respectable front-yard society of ornamentals. Ecological landscapes also share trails with wildlife gardens, they provide habitat for the more-than-human world. And since local florae get prominent billing in these gardens, it has much in common with native-plant gardens.
>
> But these landscapes aren't just a simple lumping together of other garden styles. They take their cues from the way nature works. Some gardens look like natural landscapes, but that's as far as the resemblance goes. I've seen native-plant gardens that require mountains of fertilizer because they're in unsuitable soil and herbicides to quell the vigorous grasses and weeds that happily rampage among the slow-growing natives. That's hardly natural. An ecological garden both looks and works the way nature does. It does this by building strong connections among the plants, soil life, beneficial insects and other animals, and the gardener, to weave a resilient natural webwork. Each organism is tied to many others. It's this interconnectedness that gives nature strength. Think of a net or web: snip one thread, and the net still functions because all the other connections are holding it together.

For us to begin such a reconstruction of our farms, gardens, backyards, and neighborhoods, a transformation must begin within us first. Think of it as a mental baptism of sorts, cleansing us of past transgressions against Nature. Let us welcome the blessing of water into our homes, our gardens, our soil, and our lives. Simply by copying Nature, we can create a fully functioning ecosystem in our own backyard. Once we begin creating such vibrant small plots of Life, they will give birth to something magnificent—something that will last. How can this not be contagious?

Organic Matter: Nature's Sponge

Lifeless soil compacted by heavy tractors and equipment and weakened with extreme amounts of chemicals will not retain water in an efficient manner. Hardened soil will lose a high percentage of rain due to evaporation as it cannot seep through the surface. Loose sandy soil cannot hold water in the root zone of plants long enough as water sinks through the subsoil out of the reach of a young plant's root zone.

The most natural way in large-scale farming to accumulate organic matter is by rotating forage crops such as haygraizer, wheat, maize, etc., to increase substance or life in the soil. Composting is a key function in most small-scale farming and gardening operations. Compost recipes can consist of manure (cow, chicken, rabbit, etc.), leaves, grass clippings, kitchen scraps, green manure (baled alfalfa, peas, mung beans, etc.), as well as trace minerals or other organic fertilizers. For those without access to significant amounts of alfalfa, other legume hay, livestock manure, or used coffee grounds are excellent sources of organic nitrogen, as well as our own urine. That's right. Human urine is a great source of organic nitrogen. Compost piles must have plenty of time and heat to germinate any grass, weed, or other plant seeds before being mixed into your garden or farm. Turning the mixture every few days also allows proper mixing of the ingredients to form one marvelous concoction.

A compost recipe I've found to be extremely effective is one used by world-record tomato grower Charles H. Wilber, whom I discuss further in the next chapter. Wilber recommends the following mix in a wire caged area about four-foot-wide. Place a three-inch layer of hay on the bottom. (He used kudzu, but I substitute alfalfa. Any baled legumes or organic nitrogen-fixing plant will work fine.) Dampen the hay with water. Then add either two inches of cow manure or one inch of chicken manure. Next, Wilber added one-quarter inch of garden soil sprinkled with colloidal clay and granite dust or hardwood ashes. This mix is repeated until it is rounded above the top of the wire cage to drain properly.

Wilber cautions growers to never let it rain on the compost, so covering with a small tarp is ideal. He says to turn the heap every three days (five times) with a pitchfork, after that once a week until the compost pile maintains a strong humus (degraded organic material) dark color. Reaching an optimal temperature of 160° for two days helps the compost pile activate and the manure and hay to properly digest. Keep the compost damp and store in bags or containers until ready to spread in the garden.

Soils with plenty of organic matter or compost also have more air space within the soil, aiding in the aeration process. This will also help in soils flooded with heavy rains, allowing the water to soak in beneath the soil surface, rather than creating muddy swamp clay drowning out plants or causing root disease. Organic matter also helps balance out the soil's pH level. A pH of 6.5 is considered optimal, while acidic soils are lower than 7.0, and alkaline soils register higher. Soil samples from our area have registered as high as 7.8, with calcium and magnesium levels way out of balance and extremely low organic matter of 0.8%.

Studies show that healthy soil with 2% organic matter has irrigation necessity reduced by 75% in comparison with unhealthy soil with less than 1% organic matter.[12] Healthy earth with suf-

---

12. Toby Hemenway, *Gaia's Garden*, 2nd edition (Chelsea Green Publishing, 2009), p. 98.

ficient composting or rich humus content will absorb rainfall and hold it longer in the root zone of the soil for the plant or tree to access for a longer period of time. This is crucial particularly in areas where drought is common and irrigation not feasible. So, in theory, a field with healthy top soil could maximize its plants' production with just 2.25 inches of rain rather than three inches. This is significant, particularly in dry agriculture regions such as the Southwest. Taking it one step farther, one inch of rain on a 100-acre field with 2% organic matter will soak up 202,554 more gallons of rainwater than 100 acres of depleted soil, which would lose as much as 232,446 gallons to evaporation and run-off. Factor in a three-inch rain, and a farm is misplacing 7,000 gallons of water per acre. A rich soil soaks in more water, maximizing yields, therefore creating healthier plant life.

Resources

BOOKS

Blue Gold by Maude Barlow
Gaia's Garden by Toby Hemenway
Handbook of Water Use and Conservation by Amy Vickers
Holy Order of Water by William E. Marks
Rainwater Harvesting for Drylands and Beyond
(3 volumes) by Brad Lancaster
The End of the Line by Charles Clover
The Silent World: A Story of Undersea Discovery and Adventure
by Jacques Cousteau
The World is Blue by Sylvia A. Earle
Water Consciousness by Tara Lohan
When the Rivers Run Dry by Fred Pierce
Wizard of Sun City by Gary Jenkins

WEBSITES

bluescopewater.com

ecosutra.com
eden-foundation.org/project/semmoroc.html
endoftheline.com
greeningthedesert.com
harvestingrainwater.com
menofthetrees.com.au
oasisdesign.net
oceanconservancy.org
patternliteracy.com
permaculture.biz
permaculture.org
permacultureportal.com
pioneertanks.com/au
texrca.org
http://www.twdb.state.tx.us/publications/reports/Rainwater-HarvestingManual_3rdedition.pdf

VIDEOS
An Inconvenient Truth
Blue Gold
Flow
The End of the Line
Thirst

Chapter 3

RESTRUCTURING THE SOIL
Spiritual Growth

Each footstep alters the earth.
CHRIS OFFUTT

*So long as one feeds on food from unhealthy soil,
the spirit will lack the stamina to free itself
from the prison of the body.*
RUDOLF STEINER

The Lost Art of Healthy Soil, Food and Body

Strong soil is this Earth's bountiful kitchen. Healthy seeds and plentiful rains are key ingredients in bringing forth our daily nourishment. Fruits and vegetables grow from the Earth, bringing out each vitamin and mineral we need to fuel healthy minds, bodies, and spirits. As farmers and gardeners, we are the chefs, making sure the necessary ingredients are added for the best meal possible.

Throughout my twenties, I never paid much attention to what I put into my body. Whether indulging in fast-food consumption or excessive partying, I was able to convince myself the human body was invincible. All food was simply fuel for the tank. Soon, my body convinced my mind otherwise. Gravity and common sense prove to be equal party crashers over time. The body, much like the Earth, cannot continually perform at a high-level with minimal input. A full tank does not guarantee optimum performance along Life's highway. Though we are mortal, it is up to us to maximize our potential, and that requires the highest grade fuel possible.

If we truly are what we eat, should we not be much more in tune with what enters our body and becomes part of our whole? In the same manner, as farmers, we put ourselves into the Earth and our crops. Should our consciousness be absent from such vital labor? In a sense, we become part of everything we produce. Our harvest not only rewards us personally but all who partake in what is harvested. If we bless our crops with proper minerals, nutrients, and love while Mother Nature adds her blessings of rain and sunshine, how much more fulfilling is our purpose?

Rather than focusing on more product for less price, we must focus on replenishing the soil. The weakening of our nation's soil contributes to an unavoidable chain reaction leading to the destruction of energy and Life as we know it. A depleted soil begets our food's lack of nutrients. Food without proper mineralization begets bodies lacking the energy and minds lacking the clarity to live a fulfilling life. Perhaps we've deprived our bodies of crucial vitamins and minerals for so long, our minds are unwilling to accept the obvious as truth. Instead, we will believe much of what the talking heads on television say, or take advice that will affect our entire lives from a complete stranger with a white coat and a paper certificate on their office wall.

Statistics from the USDA reveal that today's food has 30-70% less nutritional value than food 50 years ago. We can talk all we want about freedom or power, but a nation is only as strong and healthy as its own soil and food supply. A nation that can neither feed nor clothe itself is powerless and frail. The collapse of any society or empire throughout history can be linked to its diminished resources. This is the greatest lesson we've refused to learn in our times of high-tech gadgets and gotta-have-it-now philosophies. We continue to gorge ourselves with an excessive amount of soulless food, leading our bodies down the path of obesity, diabetes, and other severe health problems. While our bellies are full, we're starving to death. We're malnourished yet severely overweight. This starts with our soil. By talking about our soil, we are literally getting to the root of many of our problems.

Undisturbed topsoil has thousands and thousands, millions and millions of years worth of natural goodies mixed into its vast richness, thanks to volcanic eruptions, glacier meltings, free-ranging animal herds (like the buffalo), and cosmic dust. That combination of Nature's brilliant recipe bestowed us with the gift of completely healthy soil. The plow and chemical farming destroyed most of that precious resource by the mid-1900s. As more and more pristine forest, prairie, and pasture is turned under, we destroy the magnetic properties of the soil along with Nature's wondrous recipe. We also expose all that life in the soil to direct sunlight, which kills it.

Without healthy food and water, we are nothing. We can't purchase our way to a healthy life without them. Our mortality is not our greatest vulnerability, mental limitations are.

An unhealthy soil grows unhealthy plants. We eat the unhealthy and chemically laced plants, which become a part of us and in the process lower our energy levels. Rather than filling our bodies with all the elements that once existed in healthy topsoil, we are devoid of so many minerals and vitamins we can't function on all cylinders mentally, physically, or spiritually. We're disconnected. Our source of reconnection is the energy within the Earth—topsoil. The awakening needed within our bodies must come from our soul or spirit or higher consciousness. Yet we're so out of whack, out of touch, we can't seem to grasp this concept nearly as easily as we should. We're too busy concerning our minds with the next best iPhone, Gucci purse, Ford pickup, or *American Idol* winner. We delude ourselves that our ticket to bliss is now purchased via consumerism and entertainment. Nourishment of body and soul has taken a backseat to this great zeal focused on pacifying our minds.

I can sum up much of our problem with purchasing and eating healthy food in this country with a story. It was to be my "great West Texas organic onion quest". The year was 2006 and early summer, which translates to jungle hot. I'd been working hard to "organize" our garden—doing away with herbicides, pesticides, and commercial fertilizers. Our cotton crop was off to a horrible start due to drought, but our garden was thriving.

The day began like so many before. I woke up with a general sense of optimism that I'd make the world a better place as I contemplated America's continuing downfall over a cup of coffee. Yes, today would be the day I'd make everything better. I saddled up my War Pony (which happened to be a Dodge Diesel pickup), called upon my trusty sidekick Angler (Siberian Husky), and we headed north out of town toward the vast brown of barren fields. That time of the year the cotton should've been boot-high, but it was up to pinkie-toe high at best. That windy morning, pondering the immense disappearing act of the American farmer, I headed to our garden to harvest our sweet onions—pulling, cutting, carrying, stacking. Six farmers getting back to the fundamentals of agriculture. Sweet onions. Yes, nourishment for the body, pollution for the breath.

Dad drove up, got out of his pickup, and stared at the piles of onions.

"Do you want an onion? We're almost out," I laughed, glaring across some 2,000 pounds of breath fresheners.

"What are you going to do with all of them?" Dad asked.

Hell, we hadn't really thought that far ahead.

"Sell 'em."

"To whom?"

Hmm, he had a point. I made a few calls. Okay, I made one call. A friend's mother ran a café in Big Spring. Surely she'd buy some. My logic was simple. We would depend on our fellow residents in the area to purchase our chemical-free goods. It was a brilliant plan.

I mean, everyone loves onions, right? I thought so, too. My first three stops were all a success, selling close to 30 pounds. But the café was my first real sales pitch. "Locally grown—no chemicals, only organic fertilizer."

The café owner was hesitant. "How much do you want for them?"

"A dollar twenty-five a pound."

"Well," she wrinkled her nose. "I'll take some, but I can get a 50-pound bag at Wal-Mart for 15 dollars."

Damn Wal-Mart and their low, low prices. "Yes, but do you know where they come from?"

"No."

"South America. And do you know what they do to those onions?"

"No."

"Exactly. They don't have the same rules for chemicals there. We use no chemicals—nothing. Only organic fertilizers, and it's grown right here down the road."

She reluctantly agreed. "Okay, I'll take that box right there."

I collected the money and left. Five minutes later, I called her back. "Okay, 75 cents a pound, and the overwhelming sense of peace that you're not supporting terrorists when you purchase onions." I had to appeal to her deep-down American values.

'Okay," she laughed. "I'll call you next week."

And just like that, my first regular customer was born. Alas, I was not so fortunate at the rest of the restaurants in town.

"We're not on that health-kick here," one owner snubbed.

"No, we get ours from Cysco Foods."

"That just doesn't make any sense to pay that much for onions."

"No, we're not interested."

"We can't afford that."

"The prices are better at Wal-Mart."

Damn you, Sam Walton!

A couple of owners even sent their teenage children out to deal with me. The word "no" only made me stronger. I ate one onion for courage and one for spite.

Most Americans want the cheapest thing they can get…and that includes food. This is why the American farmer is having such a hard time competing. Are the majority truly aware of agriculture's significant role in feeding their families? Are they interested in the quality of the foods they put into their bodies?

Where their food originates from? Does it matter to them if it is laced with toxic chemicals, human feces, or pixie dust? Does it matter if it came from 4,000 miles away across countless borders? Does it matter if it was grown and harvested using slave labor? We've applied this "the cheaper, the better" logic to our food supply, and we're getting exactly what we're paying for—very little.

Studies show that our bodies are under-nourished because our foods lack the proper nutrients, and this is due to improper farming techniques. We rob the soil of its minerals and put nothing back in their place. It might look like an onion, it might smell and taste like an onion, but what's really going into your body? It is the illusion of an onion. We must begin to question what is inside the onion because that onion and everything else we digest becomes a part of us. That takes a willingness to educate ourselves about food and farming.

I realize Big Spring, Texas, is hardly the fitness or nutrition mecca of the Southwest, but unfortunately it is a microcosmic representation of the overall attitude of the majority in this country. This ideology needs to be corrected. We should educate and enlighten ourselves by propping open our eyes and minds and squeegeeing that third eye. Find the pulse of common sense. Stop, look, and stare through all the smokescreens and mirrors, all the bullshit and misconceptions, every last illusion. Shed the scaly skin around our eyes. Wiggle free from that mindless trance of the majority, the dubious march to the sound of static. Ask questions. Demand answers. Take care of our bodies, minds, and souls. Take care of the American farmer, of the farmer in your respective country. If we don't, nobody else will, and sooner rather than later the farmer will be gone. Will you miss us? Will you notice? Don't wait until all that cheap food disappears from Wal-Mart's low, low-priced shelves.

The decline in American health and fitness reflects our lack of interest in our food supply. From 2000 through 2004, the World Health Organization (WHO) gathered information about obesity in 36 different countries. Among this sample, 29 countries had less of an issue than the United States, including New Zealand, Mexico, Finland, Israel, Canada, Australia, Ireland, Peru, Sweden, Belgium, and Brazil. Today, 28 countries have healthy life expectancies that exceed the United States, including the United Kingdom, Canada, Australia, France, Germany, and Japan. A more recent study, in 2009, by WHO revealed that obesity is becoming more of a problem globally with 10% of adults considered obese according to their body mass index.[1] The U.S. was rated as the third fattest country between 2000 and 2008, behind only the islands of American Samoa and Kiribati. Following the U.S. was Germany, Egypt, Bosnia-Herzegovina, New Zealand, Israel, Croatia, and the United Kingdom.

In the brilliant documentary *King Corn*, Curt Ellis and Ian Cheney show us how much the agriculture and food industries walk hand-in-hand down a destructive road to disease and premature death for many forms of life. The two naturalists have focused their life's work on educating and enlightening others about our food and consequently our health. Since the documentary's release (2007), they've become even more aware of America's demise. According to Ellis:

> The breakdown in the way we eat in America has come hand-in-hand with a breakdown in the way we farm. Both industries—food and agriculture—have been caught in a race to the bottom that has favored bigness and cheapness over sustainability and health. Federal policy has reinforced this through subsidies of big commodities, but culture has reinforced it too. Consumers see a 32-ounce soda and they buy it. Schools see cheap meat and they serve it to their students, without asking (or teaching them to ask) where it

---

1. Laurie Cunningham, "Behold: The World's 10 Fattest Countries", *Global Post*, November 25, 2009.

comes from. Farmers see a herbicide-tolerant crop that's easy to grow, and they plant it. I think some of this is human nature and some of it is American culture and some of it is what's rewarded by our economy, but taken altogether it's turned the thing we most fundamentally need for our survival—food—into something we treat like a plastic toy. So long as it's cheap and it's here to enjoy today, why bother having a long-term care?

The Significance of Gardens

The easiest long-term solution to ensuring a family or individual's healthy food supply is growing one's own in a personal garden. Many people are intimidated by even thinking of starting a garden. It's not as hard as you'd think, and it requires much less real estate than most imagine. Growing your own food is one of the greatest freedoms most never enjoy. In the good ol' days, most people had at least a small garden to tend, but with the emergence of supermarkets, fast-food restaurants, and urban expansion, the gardens slowly disappeared from yards. Gardens are now replaced with patio areas, swimming pools, and expensive landscaping which bears no food. In our area, even most farmers no longer have a private garden of their own, because we no longer consider a garden a priority. Why? Because we're too busy making money instead of quality food. Imagine farming thousands of acres and not being able to feed yourself. It is madness. Growing our own personal food and maintaining a seed supply should now be one of our top priorities both nationally and globally, not some hobby prescribed by a therapist.

Seed can be purchased from a variety of places such as your local farm supply or feed store. Ordering a small supply from organic seed savers can provide you with plenty to get started. Small push planters and tillers can be purchased as well, enabling any and every last one of us to turn a significant portion of our yard into our own food forest. Many gardeners utilize raised bed patterns, which require no machinery, no plowing, and everything is done by hand. It is not necessary to own a tractor or any expensive equipment to have an efficient garden.

Small greenhouses can be constructed out of heavy plastic, PVC pipe, and a little creativity. An old window can be transformed into a handy cold frame or miniature greenhouse, allowing food production year around. I used an "earthship" design for our own personal greenhouse, constructing the back wall out of used tires. These tires were packed with sand and earth, forming a solid northern wall. The rest I framed out of wood, covering much of the roof and southern wall with clear polycarbonate panels. Polycarbonate panels are quite expensive, so using as many old windows as possible cuts down on the construction costs. Metal and old windows cover most of the eastern and western walls. In the winter months, the sun will warm the back wall, releasing heat throughout the night.

I'm far from master gardener status, but each season I gather valuable information about certain plants and planting styles. Constructing an earthen greenhouse on our farm, I've managed to create an efficient environment for growing plants year-around. By saving seeds from heirloom varieties, I keep plenty of seed in stock for three growing seasons (it's always good to save plenty of seed to prepare for droughts and other forms of extreme weather). By planting several types of fruit trees, I've determined which ones do best in our sandy loam soil and which ones I seem to connect with the best. My wife does lots of canning for our family in the fall, preserving tomatoes, beans, peppers, and other goodies for the winter months. We also preserve various fruits and vegetables by freezing and drying. Many old houses are equipped with root cellars underground, providing ideal food storage space. Communicating with older, more experienced gardeners often gives me the guidance I need when experiencing difficulties with a particular crop or plant I'm unfamiliar with. I also search for books that reveal gardening's hidden secrets.

One of the most famous and successful gardeners in the world was Charles H. Wilber of Alabama. In 1987, he boasted world record tomatoes, harvesting 1,368 pounds from four plants. Four plants! Wilber also grew okra plants over 17-feet high and radishes weighing over 18 pounds.

His book, *How to Grow World Record Tomatoes*, is a step-by-step guide to how to yield more fruits and vegetables than one ever dreamed possible. The key to his success was growing his plants in homemade compost (see page 99 above), consisting of cow manure, topsoil, legumes, and ashes (heavy alkaline soil with a pH greater than 7.0 will not need the wood ash). All organic products. No Miracle-Gro, no synthetic fertilizers. By following Wilber's world-record techniques, it becomes clear that an individual can grow plenty of food to feed his or her family.

Current formulas of needing two acres per person to eat for an entire year are based on out-of-date systems of gardening. Instead we can adopt new ideas and approaches. By planting crops closer together, we limit weeds (by creating shade canopy) and also reduce water usage. Whether utilizing raised beds, planter boxes, greenhouses, or hydroponic systems, we can make the most of our space. Companion planting is also an effective technique for maximizing plant production. For example, carrots tend to flourish when planted next to tomatoes. Pole beans, squash, and zucchini can be planted with corn, giving the vine plants a natural lattice above the ground. Hops can be planted beneath large trees, so that their vines have ample room to climb. By doing the proper research and planning, a novice can have a productive garden in his or her first season on a minimal amount of land.

Planting heirloom seeds allows gardeners to harvest optimal seed to plant again the next season. Purchasing fruit and vegetable seed each year is unnecessary when these plants provide plenty of seed themselves. Whether a fruit or vegetable plant or an herb, one or two plants provide a small-scale gardener with enough seeds to plant for two or three more seasons. Some plants, such as onions, require two growing seasons to produce seeds. Patience is often key. Leaving a plant or two in the earth often leads to helpful discoveries. Some plants, such as okra and other perennials, can be left to grow year after year. Some plants do not produce as well if left. Tomatoes and peppers should be uprooted and discarded, as leaving them will encourage destructive insects the next season. Many wonderful gardening books are on the market, as well as those focusing on saving seed (some details are provided at the end of this chapter).

One of the world's most famous gardens is the Findhorn Garden in Scotland. The garden's story and that of its growers was brought to life in the book *The Findhorn Garden*. What started out as a small garden tended by a family transformed into a spiritual journey inspiring an entire community to blossom based on the relationship between man/woman and Nature. By connecting to each plant, to the Earth, to an entire different spiritual world, they successfully turned a sandy piece of land into a gardening oasis. The entire book is filled with incredibly inspiring photos and truths, such as this one:

> This idea of a life and spirit informing nature and directing its activities is not new within human culture; it is the basis for such philosophies as animism and pantheism. The most sacred esoteric teachings throughout the ages have held that in understanding the inner and outer realities of nature, humanity can understand itself, and vice versa. In our time, we are gaining new insights into the nature of identity itself and into processes for self-revelation. Out of this exploration comes an opportunity to reinvestigate and to restate the characteristics of the inner nature behind the outer environment and its forms. We have an opportunity to step beyond the symbols, legends, and mythologies that have tried to express these inner realities, to go beyond the fairy stories of our childhoods, and begin to understand what these images were meant to convey. In so doing, we cannot help but understand ourselves and our processes of unfoldment

more deeply. Such an understanding is the hoped-for foundation for a new relationship between humanity and a world that will be transforming and highly creative, unfolding a planetary Eden for the benefit and growth of all forms of life. Findhorn is a strategy of exploration into the nature of that understanding and relationship.

This story is a true inspiration and is well-known across the organic world. Many scientists, geologists, and botanists have traveled to Findhorn to witness the mystery for themselves. All have concluded there should be no rational explanation for what the people achieved biologically. Whether we believe in devas, Nature Spirits, etc., or not, it is hard to argue there is some life force at work where Love binds humanity and Nature together as one.

It's Elemental, Dear Watson

Approximately 92 elements (that we know of) exist in the Earth. No coincidence—the same as the human body. We focus on *three* in agriculture. While calcium is the building block of life, we concentrate on nitrogen, phosphorous, and potassium. And why just those three? Travel back in time with me, if you will, to the 1860s. Things were a mess here in America, not exactly a "United" States. Overseas a German physicist named Justus von Liebig was experimenting with the elements existing in plants. When a plant was burned, the ashes consisted largely of three elements—nitrogen, phosphorous, and potassium. He assumed plants needed only these three elements to thrive. He was wrong. Within a decade Liebig would realize his mistake and publish his new findings publicly, but commercial agriculture had all the information they needed to run with the proverbial ball. And just like that, a billion-dollar industry was soon born out of an incomplete theory. Yes, plants need those three vital elements. But they desire many more. Furthermore, other minerals can improve the soil itself. For example, calcium, being the important building block that it is, also helps support sugar levels in both soils and plants.

Glenn Rabenberg, owner and founder of GSR (Genesis Soil Rite) Calcium, has studied soil and plant mineralization for more than twenty years. His studies inspired him to begin his company in South Dakota focused on calcium re-mineralization.

"Nature intended calcium and phosphorous to be its two major energy sources, which is the beginning of photosynthesis," said Rabenberg. "The kill-i-cide companies have found it is more profitable to forget about and tie up calcium and phosphorous and use nitrogen and potassium. With a calcium deficiency the plants are more susceptible to diseases, weeds, and insects."

Rabenberg compares calcium to the tour guide and phosphorous to the bus driver of the soil. "Chemical companies are brilliant. They know if they don't talk about calcium and phosphorous, they get to sell you a whole lot of product," Rabenberg said. "It's not about volume, it's about the energy within. If this information doesn't get out, agriculture is dead in 20 years."

The agriculture industry as a whole has gone more than 100 years ignoring crucial elements such as calcium, magnesium, carbon, boron, iron, potassium, and silicon. I hate to stop there because the list undoubtedly goes much farther. By using abusive methods which involve commercial fertilizers (made primarily from natural gas), toxic chemicals (herbicides and pesticides), heavy machinery, and mono-cropping (one-trick pony syndrome), we have created a sick planet by destroying what was once perfectly healthy soil. With excessive plowing, we not only destroy humus and earthworms, we have completely short-circuited the balance of nutrients in the soil, as well as destroying carbon in the soil. Over the past two years, I've read countless articles in *Acres U.S.A.* directly relating the excess of carbon dioxide in the atmosphere to the absence of carbon in the soil.

Commercial fertilizers have also contributed to our topsoil's ruin. Harvey Lisle wrote about the harmful effects of salting the earth in *The Enlivened Rock Powders*. He stated, "When a salt fertilizer is dissolved in water, an ionic solution capable of conducting electricity is formed. This erases all insulation and eliminates any chance of balancing the forces in terms of which we speak."

Commercial fertilizers are ionic salt-based. Basically, we are salting the earth, our own fields, our own home. This same trick was used by the Romans to destroy cropland of their enemies 2,000 years ago. Have we declared ourselves the enemy? Do we not know what we are doing? Or has the need to generate money overtaken our primitive instincts and native senses? The Earth is not just a bunch of dirt. It is our home, our source of Life. Yet, a product derived from natural gas has been cleverly marketed and sold in excess since 1900. How much of this fertilizer does American agriculture mix into the soil? Our friends at agclassroom.org provide us with alarming statistics:

Commercial Fertilizer Use in American Agriculture	
1900-1909	3,738,300 tons
1930-1939	6,599,913 tons
1940-1949	13,590,466 tons
1950-1959	22,340,666 tons
1970-1979	43,643,700 tons

(Statistics attributed to the USDA)

From the 1920s to the 1930s, a decline of about 245,000 tons of commercial fertilizer occurred, thanks mostly to the Dust Bowl era which ravaged the entire Midwest United States. Notice the significant jump following World War II and the industry almost doubling in sales production in the 1970s after Secretary of Agriculture Earl Butz told farmers to "Get big or get out." The progression of television and other media also brought about more easily accessible advertisements from agriculture corporations pushing the "benefits" of commercial fertilizers. I once washed out a water tank with small amounts of NPK commercial fertilizer in the bottom. It killed the grass within days. Five years later, that patch of earth is still completely bare.

Following World War I, an excessive amount of pesticides and commercial fertilizers were dumped upon the agriculture world, as their key ingredients were no longer needed in poisonous gases used in wartime. After World War II, companies like DuPont, Dow, and Monsanto produced fertilizers and other chemicals, as their products were no longer useful for explosives. And the weakening of our soil and crops continued at an astonishing rate, all in the name of corporate good.

The excessive amount of misinformation through corporate brain-staining and an overall refusal to educate ourselves about plant and soil health has left us with an extremely unbalanced soil full of toxins and deficient in life. But as long as we can inject a round of "steroids" (salt-based petroleum fertilizers) into the soil, giving plants that healthy green color, we convince ourselves all is well...and then proceed to downgrade professional baseball players for "cheating" or disgracing our national pastime.

Commercial fertilizers and mono-cropping contribute to soil pH imbalance, which keeps many of the minerals from performing their vital tasks efficiently. Ideal soil pH is around 6.4 or neutral. Much of the soil in West Texas and throughout the Midwest is around 7.8, particularly where irrigation is used. Heavy alkaline water makes the soil pH even higher or more alkaline, as well. Many of the soils near coastlines are much more acidic, registering under a 6.0 soil pH. A soil pH is more or less the blood pressure of the soil. If it is really high or low, it is likely many more health problems exist, preventing a healthy system from functioning properly.

William A. Albrecht emphasized the importance of maintaining mineral-rich soil, including all the needed elements such as calcium and phosphorous, which both the body and mind need to maintain healthy living. His biological studies showed conclusive evidence of soil destruction relating directly to plant, animal, and human health destruction as early as the 1940s. He wrote in *The Albrecht Papers*:

> Little attention is given to the possible long-time deficiencies recognizable only when they approach disaster. Modern farmers farm for economic reasons, for profits, for dollar values, and not for nutritional values. Modern agriculture views itself through the eyes of the industrialist who converts and transforms materials. These he presumes to be available. While agriculture may convert its products, it is not mainly a technology and that alone. It is first biology and technology second. It deals not in lifeless materials. It is concerned with living matters. It promotes the processes of creation, all originating in the soil. Soil depletion, by taking the soil for granted as if agriculture were only a mining industry, has brought us face to face with present shortages of the proteins...Let us hope that knowledge of our soil will arrive before human nutrition goes so low through neglect of soil fertility as to reduce thinking capacities to the point where we cannot save ourselves by saving soils.

There's Dust in Them There Plains!

Late spring and early summer weather in West Texas makes or breaks a farmer each year, as can be the case elsewhere in the country and world. But perhaps West Texas provides one of the greatest tests of grit and guts. This is "next year" country with harsh elements often leaving farmers literally high and dry. If it's not lack of rain, it is sandstorms. If it's not sandstorms, it is hailstorms. If it's not hail, it is bollworms. If it's not bollworms, it is weeds. If it's not weeds, it is your neighbor drifting herbicide onto your crops. You get the picture.

Driving through familiar parts of West Texas upon my return

home, I began to realize how much some areas had changed. The soil had shifted. Old fence lines I once stepped over to cross as a teenager were now completely buried beneath a mound of sand. Sandy soil appeared sandier than I ever remembered. It was as if White Sands, New Mexico, was shedding its skin to share with West Texas. Each day when winds persisted above 20 miles per hour, clear blue skies transformed into a brown haze. Unmerciful are the winds of West Texas. What's to stop them? No trees. No mountains. No hills. And very little grass. Only wrinkles of earth rolling, dipping, and rising gently across the plains.

Our grandparents and great-grandparents witnessed the worst case of soil erosion in what is known as the Dust Bowl of the 1930s. Drought was the primary cause of this catastrophic event. What was the source of the drought? Many scientists blame man's destruction of millions of acres of grassland. The boom of the 1920s gave birth to commercial agriculture in America as farmers plowed under millions of acres of native grass to put in place grazing for cattle and row crops. From 1929 to 1931, wheat production rose 300% in this country. What had taken thousands, hundreds of thousands, or millions of years to become beautiful prairies was destroyed in less than one decade by the farmer and plow in the name of Manifest Destiny.

Farmers tied ropes from their houses to barns, so they might find their way to and from the structures. Wives wet blankets to hang over windows, hoping to keep out the sand. Dinner plates were turned upside down until the last second, minimizing gritty bites of earth. Travel was impossible on windy days. Livestock became disoriented and even starved. Static electricity filled the air. With no trees and no grass remaining for miles, there was nowhere to hide.

The most destructive sandstorm documented in American history occurred on April 14, 1935, which quickly became known as "Black Sunday". Reports state that the sandstorm reached as high as 20,000 feet and spread out over a thousand miles wide. An estimated 800 million tons of topsoil was removed in America's heartland. That much topsoil would fill up the newly built Cowboys Stadium (home of the Dallas Cowboys) ten times to the top of its retractable roof. Three years of constant wind and soil erosion turned 100,000 square miles into a desert.

Hugh Bennett, the father of soil conservation, saw the destructive methods caused by poor agriculture techniques, mainly in the Midwest prairie land. While he was urging Congress to address the environmental disaster two days after Black Sunday, as if on cue, the sandstorms of the Dust Bowl blew some 1,500 miles to the nation's capital. Seeing this stormy wall of sand with their own eyes, politicians knew they had to act fast. President Franklin D. Roosevelt quickly established the Soil Erosion Service. Operation Dust Bowl quickly began, as Bennett helped educate farmers on how to take better care of the soil.

In the next seven years, some 220 million trees were planted in the Midwest from Canada to Mexico, providing windbreak patterns. The building of ponds and reservoirs was included in this project as well. Farmers were paid to plow ridges against the wind. They also were educated on the importance of terracing and utilizing contour row patterns. The lister plow was used on more than 8 million acres, building larger beds to plant crops in the furrows. The Soil Conservation Service replaced the Soil Erosion Service in 1935, and is known today as the National Resources Conservation Service. This agency helps aid farmers to this day with terrace construction, as well as building water reservoirs to prevent excessive soil erosion.

Aw yes, we've experienced the "Dirty '30s", the "Filthy '50s", and the "Nasty '90s" in the past century and we've still yet to attempt to minimize the true travesty of soil erosion as a whole. At least we haven't here in West Texas. I'm most likely farming anywhere between 6-10 inches below what my great-grandfather once broke as virgin farmland. This figure could be higher, since wind and soil erosion is a far greater issue in West Texas than the average agricultural region. At one point, our ancestors rotated their crops. They had to. There was no choice before commercial fertilizer. Those days are gone. Now, we are one-trick ponies per-forming the same tireless act year-in and year-out, exhausting our resources and our audience.

The Dust Bowl of the 1930s single-handedly destroyed the once pristine topsoil of mid-America's heartland. What took centu-ries, even millenniums to build through volcanic ash, glacier melting, organic deposits, and cosmic dust, took commercial farming less than one decade to destroy. West Texas has never recovered. Most likely it never will, because here we are some 70-odd years later, and we continue to pillage the soil, wringing out cotton crop after cotton crop. Driving through West Texas cotton fields, anyone can see the soil is wasting away in many areas. In farming communities between Big Spring and Lub-bock, from Odessa to Abilene, sandy grains sift around like camp-fire ash with winds of 20 mph or greater. Imagine living here on days when winds whip 40 mph and higher. It is Mother Nature exchanging the same unmerciful, unyielding, and unforgiving attitude we've shown her with over a hundred years of commer-cial farming.

We haven't farmed healthy topsoil since the Dirty '30s. It is slowly but surely blowing away. Why else would we be able to find arrowheads in our fields or other primitive tools and weap-ons constructed and used hundreds, even thousands of years ago? Most of the magnetic structure has been destroyed through improper farming techniques, overgrazing, and deforestation.

Refusing to restore our soil is our greatest crime against Na-ture and humanity. Charles Walters, the founder and former editor of *Acres U.S.A*, said in a July 1995 interview for the publi-cation's 25th anniversary, "I view the farmer who wants to leave the land in better shape when he leaves it to the next generation as the role model for civilization."

Those words of wisdom are even more powerfully true today. Although Walters passed away in February of 2009, his son con-tinues to ensure *Acres U.S.A.* provides a strong voice in the world of organic agriculture. The magazine does an excellent job ensuring that the messages of men like Philip Callahan, Albrecht, and other organic agriculture pioneers are not forgotten.

In September of 2009, our friends "down under" experienced soil erosion at its most extreme, as an orange sandstorm blanketed Australia's outback, spreading into cities like Sydney. Sandstorms freak out city folk. I'll never forget a sandstorm brewing outside of Abilene during my freshman year in college. We were lifting weights in the field house, and several of my (football) teammates from tree-friendly parts of East Texas were frightened by the brown sky.

"What is that?" they asked.

I laughed, "That? Oh, that's just a little ol' sandstorm."

"Little? I'd hate to see a big one," one responded.

On a daily basis from January to May, every orifice of my body is clogged with sand. It's not from lying on a tropical beach either. Some farmers leave their fields barren for months on end, creating a recipe for disaster once strong gusts of wind begin to stir. Soil from fields left unattended begins to be blown away, and ends up being blown across well-groomed fields, creating erosion problems for the next farmer. Sandy fields grow larger sandbars along old barbed-wire fence lines, decimating productive acres. Old barbed-wire fence lines are buried in sand as high as rooftops. If the current trend continues another century, this area of West Texas will end up like a scene from the Middle East. What was the birthplace of domestic farming (more than 2,000 years ago) and once the most fertile farmland in the world is now the deserts of Iran, Iraq, and Saudi Arabia. Desertification can and will happen right here in West Texas and other parts of the country if our current farming methods continue.

In West Texas, we have no forests—no real trees other than the fickle mesquite tree. We've destroyed most of the grass that once rolled across Oklahoma, Kansas, Nebraska, and the Dakotas up into Canada. Even with generation after generation living here, vivid memories and stories of the Dust Bowl, the decades of soil erosion and sandstorms, many farmers have leaned toward less labor and fuel, causing more soil degradation. The age of Roundup has given many farmers the perfect excuse to do nothing, leaving barren fields vulnerable to high winds. As farmers and neighbors, we must hold each other accountable. In a sandstorm, a neighboring field left unattended can wipe out a farmer doing everything right.

Callahan, one of the most renowned paramagnetic energy researchers in the world reminds us in *Powers of the Round Towers* that, "Composting, organisms of the soil, and the Paramagnetic force (COP) might well prevent a worldwide famine from destroying mankind. Insecticides and weed killers are the modern curse of environmental health. We never did need them. The simple fact is that they both destroy viable soil."

Soil Destruction Spreading Worldwide

Unfortunately, agriculture continues to be a larger part of the problem rather than the solution. The facts and stats of the undeniable deterioration of our soil reveal a shameful crime. By 2006, in a 10-year time period China had lost over 1 million acres to urbanization. In a 12-year time period the country had lost 16 million acres to desertification. This country needs up to 350 million tons of grain each year. As this desert continues to spread, China's dependence on grain imports will increase and significantly impact grain supply and demand across the world. Although China is the second largest corn-producing nation in the world (behind the United States), it cannot produce enough grain to feed its pigs, much less 1.3 billion people.[2]

What is even more alarming is that the desert shows no signs of slowing its spread despite recent attempts at reforestation by the government, and they abandoned this reforestation project in

2. Joel K. Bourne Jr., "The Global Food Crisis: The End of Plenty", *National Geographic*, June 2009.

2009 after the global "economic crisis". You don't dig for water after you're thirsty, and you sure don't wait to rebuild your soil after desert has spread across fertile land like some Renaissance plague. How has this desert spread so fast? Through years of overgrazing, deforestation, and improper farming techniques, which have robbed the earth of its minerals and caused soil erosion.

The perfect example of this desertification process is the Middle East: once the cradle of civilization and home of the most fertile soil in the world and now predominantly desert. Where rivers such as the Tigris and Euphrates once flowed strong and free, now lie derelict lake bottoms and parched earth sizzling like a forgotten pizza on a summer dorm room balcony.

In a 1990 study conducted by the International Soil Reference and Information Centre, disturbing results revealed the entire world's atrocious practices in soil mismanagement. The causes are predominantly related to agriculture. The three-headed monster of deforestation, overgrazing, and damaging agriculture activities were spread evenly across the world. According to the organization's website:

> On the global basis, the soil degradation is caused primarily by overgrazing (35%), agricultural activities (28%), deforestation (30%), and overexploitation of land to produce fuelwood (7%). The patterns are different in the various regions. In North America, agriculture has been responsible for 66% (primarily the United States) of the soil loss, while in Africa, overgrazing is responsible for about half of the soil degradation.

The leading cause varies from one continent or country to another. Overgrazing is also the leading cause in Oceania (80%), which includes countries such as Australia, New Zealand, New Guinea, and Polynesia. Deforestation is the main cause in South America (41%), Europe (38%), and Asia (40%) and still continues at an alarming rate.

Our forests are destroyed for different reasons, none of them

Soil Degradation Statistics 1990

North America
- 66% - Agriculture activities
- 30% - Overgrazing
- 4% - Deforestation

South America
- 41% - Deforestation
- 28% - Overgrazing
- 26% - Agriculture activities

Central America
- 45% - Agriculture activities
- 22% - Deforestation
- 18% - Overgrazing
- 15% - Overexploitation for firewood

Oceania
- 80% - Overgrazing
- 12% - Deforestation
- 8% - Agriculture activities

Europe
- 38% - Deforestation
- 29% - Agriculture activities
- 23% - Overgrazing

Asia
- 40% - Deforestation
- 26% - Overgrazing
- 27% - Agriculture activities

Africa
- 49% - Overgrazing
- 24% - Agriculture activities
- 14% - Deforestation
- 13% - Firewood

justified in the long run. In Central and South America, rainforests are being destroyed so that ranchers and farmers might graze cattle or grow more soybeans. We're wiping out our most precious and vital forest and turning it into a feedlot. We are ripping out our lungs in order to feed our wallets. We're murdering Peter so that Paul might get rich for a few years. Then what?

A study conducted by Cornell University in 2006 revealed horrific realities about soil erosion.[3] The study pooled together statistics from "more than 125 sources", and it concluded that:

---

3. Susan S. Lang, "'Slow, Insidious' Soil Erosion Threatens Human Health and Welfare as well as the Environment, Cornell Study Asserts", Cornell Chronicle Online, http://www.news.cornell.edu/stories/march06/soil. erosion.threat.ssl.html, March 20, 2006.

- The United States is losing soil 10 times faster—and China and India are losing soil 30 to 40 times faster—than the natural replenishment rate.

- The economic impact of soil erosion in the United States costs the nation about $37.6 billion each year in productivity losses. Damage from soil erosion worldwide is estimated to be $400 billion per year.

- As a result of erosion over the past 40 years, 30% of the world's arable land has become unproductive.

- About 60% of soil that is washed away ends up in rivers, streams and lakes, making waterways more prone to flooding and to contamination from soil's fertilizers and pesticides.

- Soil erosion also reduces the ability of soil to store water and support plant growth, thereby reducing its ability to support biodiversity.

- Erosion promotes critical losses of water, nutrients, soil organic matter and soil biota, harming forests, rangeland and natural ecosystems.

- Erosion increases the amount of dust carried by wind, which not only acts as an abrasive and air pollutant, but also carries about 20 human infectious disease organisms, including anthrax and tuberculosis.

- 831 square miles of forest has been lost in the United States from 2000-2005. The Forest Service actually subsidizes timber companies to the extent of $500 million per year in taxpayers' money.

The evidence in all this researched data unveils one shocking truth. Agriculture is creating more long-term damage than short-term good as an industry. Sure, we expect this from the perverse operations from the timber and oil industry, but agriculture? What went so wrong so fast in an industry that is supposed to represent the very innate beauty of Life? We are part of the problem. This must change. And the only way that change will take place is if the farmer takes the proverbial bull by the horns.

Our precious topsoil is being lost 16 to 300 times faster than it can be replaced.[4] It takes centuries for topsoil to form in its natural state, while man can destroy it in less than one decade. Meanwhile, we've been practicing poor farming techniques for over a century. It's estimated we are losing more than 25 million acres of cropland each year to soil degradation and urbanization.[5]

Soil degradation also means loss of nutrients in the soil, which without tons and tons of organic matter and natural fertilizers will never be regained in our lifetimes. Once soil is dead, it takes ceaseless work to bring it back. Gradually, Nature will heal herself, but how long after our grandchildren are gone? At our current rate of soil erosion, we will lose more than 30% of the global soil by 2050.[6]

With a global population increasing at roughly 1.7% annually, it is not bold to predict billions of people will starve to death over the next 10-20 years. It is estimated that somewhere between 7 and 8 billion acres (3-3.5 billion hectares) are in cultivated production today. What we haven't already destroyed or ruined is already in production. Considering it takes up to 1.2 acres to feed each person annually (using our current agriculture system),

---

4. C. J. Barrow, *Land Degradation* (Cambridge University Press, 1991).

5. D. Pimentel, U. Stachow, D. A. Takacs, H. W. Brubaker, A. R. Dumas, J. J. Meaney, J. O'Neil, D. E. Onsi and D. B. Corzilius, "Conserving Biological Diversity in Agricultural/Forestry Systems", *Bioscience*, Vol. 42, No. 5 (1992), pp. 354-362.

6. Henry W. Kendall and David Pimentel, "Constraints on the Expansion of the Global Food Supply", *Ambio*, Vol. 23, No. 3, The Royal Swedish Academy of Sciences (May 1994).

this doesn't bode well for the 7 billion people inhabiting the Earth. Since America is the number one exporter of grain foods, that means our friends in Asia and Africa will be in even more trouble in less than a decade than they are right now, particularly Asia with its population well over 4 billion people. With the destruction of our soil comes the destruction of our food supply. Even the blindest eye can see where that path leads. Will the country with the biggest gun prevail? What shape will diplomacy take when that point of realization comes? If we'll wage war over oil, what will we do to secure the last remnants of healthy soil?

Economically powerful countries such as China, Japan, and India are beginning to purchase extremely fertile farmland in Africa. If a country is not going to restore and manage farmland properly in their own country, why would they expect themselves to begin doing so on an entirely different continent? That is the equivalent mindset of us trying to build a rocket ship to another planet with plentiful resources because we've messed up this one. Changing planets or continents without first learning from our mistakes would be pitiful.

Gotta Be the Grass

How will we ever clean up the soil erosion mess we've caused? Simple. We use the same philosophy our parents used on us to clean up our mess in our rooms—"Put everything back just the way you found it!" And by us applying ourselves totally to it. Many grass farmers will tell you plowing the earth is the same as ripping the flesh off our muscles, exposing bare muscles to the elements. This doesn't paint a pretty picture of tillage, to say the least.

Renowned organic farmer Joel Salatin of Polyface Farms is a huge advocate of grass. In his book *You Can Farm*, Salatin is adamant in stressing that using grass is the key to restoring our malnourished soil. Salatin says, "Nothing builds soil like perennials. Nothing destroys the soil like tillage. On any farm, we should maximize soil-building principles and reduce soil-destroying principles. That means grass and trees need to be encouraged. Even grain farms should focus on this principle."

While replacing a certain percentage of cultivated acres with grass will help with soil erosion, it does little to alleviate the food supply shortage. Roughly 40% of all grain crops feed livestock, primarily cattle. It takes almost one billion acres of grain and soybean production to feed the world's 850 million pigs. At any given time, there are 1.3 billion cattle and 65 million horses that need to be fed on this planet. As the population continues to grow, our carnivorous appetites will require even more of these animals, which will require more acres to produce their food supply. If an estimated 3.2 million acres are needed to feed livestock alone, and seven billion acres are needed to feed humans, food shortages are going to be more and more common.

Perhaps if we ourselves were to become more herbivorous than carnivorous, we could help balance out the supply and demand of food. By implementing fruit and nut trees in grassland, we would grow our crops vertically rather than horizontally. This would expand our horizons in a totally different direction, allowing us to be less dependent on cereal crops such as wheat and corn. In the future, nuts and berries may very well take the place of corn and wheat as our staple foods. If we reduced our dependence on meat and cereal crops for protein by substituting nuts and berries, we would need less acreage dedicated to feeding livestock.

We started raising chickens on our farm. Chickens are great multi-taskers. They are quite comfortable eating grass and weed seeds, as well as insects and mice. Not only do they produce meat and eggs, they help spread manure of other livestock as well, fertilizing the soil with ample amounts of organic nitrogen. These birds require very little grain feed to supplement their natural diet.

More importantly, if we continued to restore the soil we currently have with natural fertilizers and more environmentally friendly methods, we would also restore more nutrients. This in turn would provide our food supply with more nutrients, cutting down on the amounts necessary to satisfy one's hunger. Animals are no different than us. I've noticed this in feeding hay to livestock. When I feed them hay from our fields where crops have been rotated, the hay lasts much longer than from a field where only one particular crop has been raised. It's obvious that cotton after cotton after cotton crop isn't the answer, but neither is wheat after wheat after wheat crop.

In the immediate future, I am fully convinced hydroponics could have an extremely positive impact on our food supply. As long as healthy water is used wisely, that is. It will be absolutely necessary in urban areas where population levels are becoming overwhelming. Hydroponics allows much more food to be grown in a smaller space and is environmentally controlled. My only problem with hydroponics is you are eliminating a very spiritual and vital element in growing your food—the soil. To me, growing food without earth is like trying to play jazz without any brass instruments. It just doesn't feel right. However, I see no other alternative that will allow us to feed our ever-increasing masses of people in this country and across the globe in urban areas where much of the acreage is suffocated with concrete and steel.

As my experience in the hydroponics field is almost none at all, I will provide resources at the end of this chapter for those interested in more information.

Rotation, Rotation, Rotation

The biggest selling pitch in real estate has always been "location, location, location". A similar phrase is our key to successful farming—rotation, rotation, rotation. Mono-cropping is detrimental to the soil. Depending on the area, most farmers plant the same crop year after year and mask their soil nutrient depletion with commercial fertilizers, which act as nothing more than steroids causing more long-term damage. Rotating legumes for nitrogen, oats for phosphate, and other crops suitable for your respective growing region will help replenish the soil rather than starve it to death. Feed crops improve organic matter and humus, creating more healthy soil life, minimizing soil erosion and allowing rainwater to soak into the earth where it is held in the root zone for a longer period of time.

Donald Allred (my grandfather) was born in 1923 and remembered growing up in the Dust Bowl years. He said that time period provided a huge wakeup call for all farmers:

> What changed was the farmer finally woke up and realized we had to put something back into the soil to build it up. The soil has got to be loosened up with tillage. Terracing has helped the rolling plains as much as anything on wind and water erosion. Today, a lot of farmers think they can get by with just fertilizing, and you can if everything goes just right. But no matter what, crop rotation is the best way to take care of your land and take care of soil erosion. If you're putting nothing into the soil, pretty soon you're going to get nothing in return.

In dry regions such as West Texas, Southern Arizona, and New Mexico, it is more difficult to make any crop at all most years. Minimal rainfall has discouraged a high percentage of farmers from diversifying their operation. Crop insurance is sometimes our only way of survival, and insurance on rarely used crops doesn't pay the bills. But, we can still take over a small percentage of our acres with planting spring or winter legume crops and plowing them under so we are growing our own nitrogen. Once the benefits are noticeable, a larger share of acres can be dedicated to this type of rotation program. By supplementing with an oat crop, a farmer would see a vast improvement in his or her next cash crop. Over a 5-10 year period, it is more profitable financially to use this approach. We know it is definitely more beneficial to the soil and environment.

As part of the Baby Boom Generation, Dad has, like most

farmers, seen enough decades of farming to realize the benefits of crop rotation. But it often comes down to what a farmer can afford to do to stay in business through droughts and financial hardships. He said:

> Everything became about the dollar. Farmers stuck to the one crop that would enable them the highest profit. In our area, that was cotton. Our infrastructure wasn't set up for grain or other crops, because we didn't have the combines and trucks. It was financial survival. If you tried to plant grain all those years here, you'd be working at the bank or Wal-Mart.

Strained Relations Between Farmers and the Legume Industry

All farmers understand the importance of legumes in a farming operation. Legumes replenish the soil with organic nitrogen that can't be substituted with vulgar amounts of commercial fertilizers. Crops that follow legumes receive ample benefits, allowing them to flourish in a nitrogen-rich earth. Legumes are not only beneficial as a green manure crop, they are a food crop which will help feed our country's people instead of them depending on the heinous ideas of NAFTA (North American Free Trade Agreement) and CAFTA (Central American Free Trade Agreement).

Unfortunately, the legume industry appears to be run primarily by dishonest businessmen who are more concerned with making more money than ensuring that agriculture thrives. Any farmer who has planted black-eyed peas, mung beans, guar, or other legumes will shake his head telling horror stories of not getting paid by the business he had a set contract with. The doom reports of low grades seem to dominate any hopes of making a profit from legume crops. It is common for neighbors to deliberately deal with two different legume dealers to compare. They plant on the same date and harvest at the same time, yet one will get low grades while the other will receive Grade 1 across the board. Peanuts remain a valuable crop, but require large amounts of irrigation to produce efficiently.

Whether it is black-eyed peas, mung beans, or guar, farmers in many parts of the country can't seem to do well consistently in the legume business. I'm not sure what goes on behind the scene with these dealers. Are they getting pressed on by the big boys and passing this on to their customers? Nobody is willing to say. Legume dealers have more or less gained a monopoly in most areas of this country. If one dealer has a very large area, he can afford to "cheat" a few farmers here and there and not have to worry about losing a little business as he moves on to the next area. But that adds up over time, and what we've ended up with is a hell of a lot of farmers scared to death of planting legumes, because they fear they won't ever receive a dime. It truly is a black-eye on the agriculture industry. If we could ever de-corrupt this side of the business, it would do wonders for farmers, the economy, agriculture, and Nature. Everybody would win.

Significance of Weeds

With eyes wide open upon my return to the farm, I noticed weeds were more widespread than ever before. Not just careless weeds and tumbleweeds, but several species I'd never noticed before reared their heads as summer crops progressed. This was attributed to various reasons, including less intensive cultivation, hay trucks spreading weed seed, and land placed in CRP (Conservation Resource Program) grass spreading more weeds. No doubt these didn't help, but weeds seemed to pop up where no other fields or major roads bordered. Books were my main means of discovering why weeds thrived.

Ehrenfried E. Pfeifer wrote in *Weeds and What They Tell* that:

Weeds are specialists. Having learned something in the battle for survival they will survive under circumstances where our cultivated plants, softened through centuries of protection and breeding, cannot stand up against nature's caprices. Weeds resist conditions which cultivated plants cannot resist, such as drought, acidity of soil, lack of humus, mineral deficiencies, as well as one-sidedness of minerals. They are witness of man's failure to master the soil, and they grow abundantly whenever man has missed the train—they only indicate our errors and nature's corrections.

This made sense to me. There exist about 1,800 different plants labeled as "weeds" here in America. We use the term weed as if it is an absolutely useless and pointless part of Nature. Nonsense. There is no such thing. Everything in Nature happens for a reason. Everything in Nature has a purpose just as we as humans do. The beauty is to not only recognize their existence but determine what their presence means. Let us not look at them as weeds, but as herbs and teachers. Any farmer knows weeds spread from the plants going to seed via the wind, birds, or other grazing creatures. Weeds also spread due to soil compaction and mineral deficiency. What we fail to realize is that perhaps weeds are trying to tell us something. It's the land's way of giving us a good hint about what the soil is lacking. Weeds should be viewed as innate monuments showing the key elements that the soil lacks. They are the Earth's manifesting message of what it is needed.

Charles Walters wrote in his book *Weeds: Control Without Poisons* that:

> When weeds grow, there is always a good reason. When they travel and propagate themselves, there is always method to their madness. They are born teachers, if we have the wit to learn. They have character, sometimes more character than the production crops we cherish.
>
> There are many factors that have a bearing on weed pat-

terns and crop performance. They're all interrelated. The ideal is to have pH control, good loamy soil texture, enough decaying organic matter to set the things in motion for better crop and changing weed patterns. The bottom line is simply that good soil structure, good soil drainage and good aeration can control biological activity in the soil. In turn, the farmer can increase the nutrient supply and grow a high-yield crop even if a few weeds are supported underneath. But a sick soil with inadequate nutrient release and conversion will have a depressing effect on the yield potential. This allows the weeds to have a more negative effect simply because there are not enough nutrients to feed both the desired crop and the weeds. It also allows weeds to impose water limitations.

If everything is energy, it is easy to apply an electrical viewpoint to all living things, including the soil and weeds. In his book *Science in Agriculture*, Dr. Arden B. Anderson translates an analogy that truly drives the thought home of how important soil fertility is. He states that much like a stereo system, the system (soil structure) is only as good as its weakest component. For example, if you have a high-priced receiver and poor-quality speakers, the entire system fails to produce what you want. We want sweet music from our soil and crops, not the sound of static. Few have put it into words exactly like Anderson:

> To summarize the analogy between the soil/plant system and a stereo system, one could say that the soil-mineral component relates to the stereo antenna and receiving mechanism whereas the biological component relates to the multiple-component tuner and speaker mechanism. The stereo system as a unit emits music at some degree of quality, at some level of yield or power (watts). By analogy, our natural system produces a crop at some degree of quality, at some level of yield or volume. Both stereo and soil/plant systems are energy con-

verters. One converts radio waves to sound, and the other converts solar energy to matter. The design or blueprint for the biological system is held by the DNA, which is the master "information chip" for designing the system. It then acts as the feedback mechanism to keep the system on track.

Always view the soil/plant/atmosphere system as an electrical apparatus. If you apply something to the soil that interrupts the mineral balance, organic stability, or microorganism activity, you de-tune the circuit reducing its efficiency. At first, nature attempts to re-tune the circuit with additional antennas and conductors in the form of weeds.

Weeds are simply another form of Nature's many messages or messengers explaining what we should or should not do. When I closely examine these unwanted plants, I truly ask them why they are here. I'm aware that talking to weeds might seem silly, but they respond as well as house plants or tomato plants in the garden. Many weeds are physical manifestations of specific elements. In our area of West Texas, it is usually calcium and iron. Sometimes, weeds are scabs. Since we've ripped off the earth's flesh (native grass), the soil knows it must cover itself. As farmers, bare earth is natural to us. Not to Nature. What was covered for thousands, if not millions, of years, we stripped clean in less than a century. If our own flesh is injured, if its epidermis is scraped off, will it not scab over in an attempt to heal itself? The Earth is no different.

When our government first tested the atomic bomb in the deserts of New Mexico in the 1940s, guess what was the first vegetation to grow back? Russian thistle—otherwise known as the tumbleweed. Here in West Texas, the tumbleweed might as well be the state tree or flower. It thrives here. Many German farmers brought wheat seed to the States from Europe in the 1800s, which was littered with tumbleweed seed. If tumbleweeds thrive in radiation-polluted environments, are we also creating a toxic environment through decades of chemicals allowing the tumbleweed to thrive? It certainly appears that way.

We've used certain herbicides on our fields, and I've watched weeds intensify, mutating. They grow larger, tripling the amount of stems and consequently produce more seeds. I've seen careless weeds (amaranth or pigweed) transform into giant gothic candlesticks with roots the size of a grown man's forearm. Tumbleweeds can expand as large as a Volkswagen Beetle (this occurred in extremely dry conditions when the herbicide did not take). Sometimes, the herbicide just seems to annoy the respective weed, making it even more determined to stand its ground.

As I watched these changes occur, I couldn't help but wonder how much shock the soil must be going through, attempting to digest all that poison. Perhaps it was expressing its message of contempt by producing a mutant weed. I knew this was not the way I wanted to farm. I couldn't. These weeds were telling me so. Plants appreciate our presence, our love, and our care. Our focus and footprints are the best fertilizers. If we sit in our fields and gardens among the plants and ask for their guidance, Nature will tell us exactly what we need to do.

Resources

BOOKS
Bread from Stones by Julius Hensel
Carrots Love Tomatoes by Louise Riotte
Diet for a Dead Planet by Christopher Cook
Enlivened Rock Powders by Harvey Lisle
Fast Food Nation by Eric Schlosser
Four-Season Harvest by Eliot Coleman
Gardening Indoors with Soil and Hydroponics by George Van Patten
How to Grow World Record Tomatoes by Charles H. Wilber
In Defense of Food by Michael Pollan
Science in Agriculture by Arden Anderson
Secrets of the Soil by Peter Tomkins and Christopher Bird
Seed to Seed by Suzanne Ashworth

The Albrecht Papers by William Albrecht
The Findhorn Garden by the Findhorn Community
The New Self-Sufficient Gardener by John Seymour
The Non-Toxic Farming Handbook by Philip A. Wheeler
The Omnivore's Dilemma by Michael Pollan
The Secret Life of Plants by Peter Tomkins and Christopher Bird
The Secret Teachings of Plants by Stephen Harrod Buhner
Weeds: Control Without Poisons by Charles Walters

WEBSITES
findhorn.org
fukuokafarmingol.info
gardeningrevolution.com
gsrcalcium.com
hydroponicgardening.com
hydroponics.net
kingcorn.net
michaelpollan.com
motherearthnews.com
naturalfarming.org
organicfoodconsumers.org
organicgardening.com
permaculture.com
postcarbon.org/report/41306-the-food-and-farming-transition-toward
verticalfarm.com
wholeearth.com

VIDEOS
Black Blizzard
Dirt! The Movie
Fast Food Nation
Food Inc.
Fresh, The Movie
King Corn

Chapter 4

KNOWLEDGE OF NATURE AND SELF
Forming One into Another

Everything in nature that has actual form
can be treated as an antenna,
that is, as a resonant shape for collecting
some type of energy.
PHILIP CALLAHAN

We are only beginning to comprehend
the language of nature, its soul, its reason.
The "inner world" of plants is hidden
from our gaze behind seventy-seven seals.
I. ZABELIN

Student and Teacher

Growing up on a desolate farm, I took much of Life for granted. Even as the son of a farmer, I failed to witness the natural beauties around me. Resentful, I focused on the barren emptiness of West Texas. Mesquite trees and prickly pear cactus were merely an eye-sore. The flat horizon was nothing more than a prison confining my hopes and dreams from the rest of the world. As a young man, I fled to the Rocky Mountains of Colorado. Magnificence surrounded me each waking day, but still the wondrous offerings of mountains and rivers took a backseat to a lifestyle of decadence. As my years progressed, so too did my appreciation for everything. Spending an entire summer in Alaska, working on fishing boats I witnessed Nature unmolested, basking in its brilliant mysticism. Clouds danced overhead. Trees swayed in the breeze. Undisturbed Earth possessed a youthful bounce felt each time my foot touched the ground. Grassy mountains propelled each step forward with newfound energy. The ocean blurred into sky. My eyes could not discern where one began and the other ended in the blissful beauty.

Further travels confirmed this feeling. Each place offered its own individuality, its own brilliance, its own poetry of expression. Even my beloved West Texas—the very place I had grown to loathe— expressed more splendor in its desolate ruggedness. In my mind the rugged beauty and empty fields resembled an oasis of sorts. I embraced the cumbersome thorns of the prickly pear as much as their flowering blooms. The open prairie became my church, and the desert wind the voice of my prayers.

Within Nature rests an answer to each question and a solution to every problem. She provides for us all things possible. It is a relationship we must cultivate. We simply cannot take much more than we give. Any relationship with a spouse, child, parent, neighbor, or friend cannot succeed for long based on that formula. There must be balance. The circle must be complete. There must be mutual respect, love, and admiration. It comes from within. Nature constantly speaks to us, whispering words of wisdom and comfort. We only have to be still and listen.

Our failure to observe accurately and learn from Nature has brought us to where we are today—stumbling around in a dark room, taking directions from complete strangers hoping to profit from our lack of knowledge. It's like us wandering around in a downtown metropolitan alleyway on a Saturday night and asking gangsters for directions to the nearest ATM. Someone's going to profit from our disorientation, and it is not going to be us.

Disorientation from Nature is laughable, considering the history of our species. From the dawn of man through Neolithic times, and even into the early 1900s, we were very much in tune with our environment, but our obsession with money, the industrial age, technology, and our ever-pressing expansion into urban living has damaged our relationship with the Earth. Rather than including Nature in all our constructional "progress", it's as if we are attempting to exclude her. As we bulldoze forests to put up another restaurant chain or shopping mall, a token tree or shrub is conveniently placed here or there for decorative purposes. Seldom is Nature welcomed into our homes and neighborhoods. This is something we must recognize and correct. Parking lots are a poor substitute for prairies.

Dedicating a small portion of time each day to Nature works wonders. Simply sitting underneath a favorite tree, gardening, or walking down a nature trail breathes healthy energy into our spirit. It connects us with Life.

These days are here for us to feel all things. These days are here for us to understand the language of mutuality within everything. We must enlighten ourselves by clearing our minds of social clutter, setting free the origins of our intent. Forget entertainment. Forget laws. Forget registered realms of normality. Let us allow all the purity we've denied for too long. Let us become part of all we've met so that a sense of familiarity comforts our greatest fears. Nature is our greatest teacher if we sit still long enough to hear her speak.

One man who persisted in educating himself in Nature was Philip Callahan. Feeding off the curiosity he developed as a child, questions persisted in his adult years. This desire to seek answers led him to become not only one of the world's most renowned entomologists, but one of the most heralded naturalists in American history. He has written several books dedicated to insects and their behavior patterns. His studies on various energies, particularly infrared and ultraviolet light, reveal fascinating information about the insect kingdom—not to mention his studies on electromagnetic and paramagnetic energies, as well. Early theories in his studies of insects revolved around the role of various light spectra. While infrared and ultraviolet energy is invisible to the human eye, his experiments concluded that insects were able to visualize these light spectrums, as well. This allows insects to determine the difference between plants with strong or weak energy, an ability that influences flight patterns of moths, for example. Callahan also considered the significant relationship between paramagnetic (male) and diamagnetic (female) forces as the yin and yang energy in Nature, influencing magnetic properties in our soil, plants, and trees.

He clearly states the futility of pesticides in *Tuning into Nature*. "Early in my career, I studied pesticides, as did all entomologists. But the findings I release in this book taught me that attempting to poison insects was at cross purposes to nature and would, in the end, prove futile," said Callahan.

The former WWII radio operator puts the insect issue in plain terms for all of us to understand:

> A sick plant actually sends forth a beacon, carried in the infrared, attracting insects. It is then the insect's role to dispose of this plant deemed unfit for life by nature. By learning how to "tune in to nature", may you learn to better understand God's beautiful design and come to work with nature by enhancing her energies rather than attempting to overpower and rule over her.

Most American farmers could have saved hundreds of thousands, if not millions of dollars by eliminating the use of pesticides (as well as GMO crops) over their individual careers. In the 20th century alone, trillions of dollars were wasted on this man-made scam. It is humiliating for us to even consider Callahan's words to be the truth. Pride often blinds rationality. Crazy, the lies we've been told and still believe because we thought there was no natural alternative. Is it too humiliating to believe the answer is as easy as changing our brainwave pattern? Can we not send our thoughts in a new direction by altering our frequency or changing the station or at least adjusting the antenna just a hair?

Callahan was once an entomology professor at Louisiana State University. His teachings did not go over well with the Agriculture Department. He was informed in an official letter from the

Dean of Agriculture that he was "teaching his students too much". Teaching too much? *Too much* meant too much truth. Callahan later resigned, leaving the university, and continued to explore more truths in Nature.

th About Insects

The folks in Enterprise, Alabama, learned the importance of rotating crops back in 1919. They even built a monument in celebration of what they learned from the boll weevil insect which destroyed their cotton crops. They introduced peanuts to their rotation and eliminated the relentless insect. And here we are 90 years later, wondering why insects destroy our crops.

Let's break it down to as basic a concept as it really is—un-healthy soil equals unhealthy plants. Unhealthy plants equal destructive insect issues. Yet we treat the issue of destructive insects the typical American way—cosmetically. We think as long as we wipe out the insect *right now*, we are solving the problem. Sadly, by impatiently eliminating one problem with chemicals, not only are we creating many more problems, we're allowing the problem to escalate to chronic status. It's the equivalent of curing an illness with toxic pills that weaken the immune system.

Many farmers will tell you the reason they haven't rotated their crops is because they "can't afford to". If it is money we are trying to save, think about how many millions and billions of dollars we've flushed down the toilet with insecticides and genetically engineered crops. How much land could be purchased by using the money an individual farmer has wasted away on these toxic chemicals? How much seed, organic fertilizer, or better equipment could be bought? How much more money could we save to invest in diversification? How much easier could we pay off our debts? What is the price tag we place on a healthy environment? And how does destroying an entire ecosystem of truthful insects justify our refusal to learn how Nature truly works and why?

We've been brain-stained. Many farmers now believe we can't farm without pesticides or GMO crops. Many have no idea how insects function in the Nature kingdom. Most farmers have believed lies for so long we really have no idea what the truth smells like, much less sounds like anymore. We rely on people who call themselves entomologists or crop consultants who wear shirts and hats with Monsanto or Bayer Crop Science blazed in visible sight. We rely on individuals who are part of a perverse system created to keep us uninformed and underachieving.

County extension agents and entomologists will usually side with the chemical companies in offering their expertise on insects. They have to. Most of them went to Texas A&M University or some other agriculture-based institute of higher learning that convinces its students that chemical agriculture is the greatest thing since indoor plumbing because chemical companies help fund its programs. Texas A&M insists on teaching students the brilliance of chemicals rather than the insect's significant role. How many entomologists are taught how insects function? Why do they flock to a particular field and devour the leaves or fruit of the particular plant? Unfortunately Callahan's methods are still not accepted as universal truths.

"Hey, Johnny Appleseed!" you scream. "That's just what they do. Bugs eat plants! They get hungry so they eat!"

But why these particular plants? Why not dandelions or roses? Why not marigolds or tumbleweeds? Ask your entomologist next time. Ask the chemical company selling you expensive pesticides. Ask a Monsanto dealer trying to sell you that high-dollar insect-proof seed. Test their knowledge of the insect kingdom. My question to my fellow farmer is, "Why do you believe complete strangers who are selling you the stuff?" It is equivalent to walking into a barber shop and asking the barber if you need a haircut.

In 2005, I was determined to find the answers to my questions about why certain insects destroy certain crops. I enrolled in a weekend seminar designed for training "bug scouts" at the Texas A&M Research Center in San Angelo, Texas. There I sat for several hours in a room full of high school and college students who wanted to make some summer money scouting farmers' fields for insects which damage cotton crops. The respective entomologists were benevolent in their attempts to educate us. They showed us slide after slide of insects, explaining in detail how to identify thrips from aphids and bollworms from loopworms or beat armyworms. We learned the characteristic differences between the good guys and the bad guys and which eggs belonged to whom. In that aspect, I honestly did learn quite a bit. They confessed there existed thousands and thousands of types of insects and that they had no idea what many of them were.

After the two-day course and a trip to a cotton field outside of Austin, I left more confused than educated. Their information only inspired me to ask more questions. Many of the questions I asked, they could not answer with confidence. As a result, I knew there existed a great deal of significance in the insect world that we didn't know about in agriculture.

One of my questions was "Why can't we grow corn in our garden?" That was one of those things that was keeping the butter in my mind churning. Our farmhands were stumped by the fact they hadn't been able to grow corn for years, because the corn earworms wiped the plants out every year. I had told them I'd figure it out sooner or later.

One of them had told me, "If you can figure out how to grow corn here again, you're really onto something."

As I began to ask around, people just shook their heads in disbelief. "It's gotten to where you just can't grow corn around here anymore." Most had turned to the Bt corn, which is genetically modified. Determined to find a healthy alternative, I refused to go that route.

The only answer the entomologists gave me was to try GM corn or applying *Bacillus theringetus* to each individual plant. Neither was the solution I was expecting to hear from "experts". However, I did try applying *Bacillus theringetus*, as well as vegetable oil, the following spring to several 100-yard long rows of corn. My attempts were futile at best, and we managed to harvest only a meager 30% of the corn. The rest had been devoured by corn earworms. But as we slowly built up our soil, increasing the organic matter by rotating wheat and increasing organic nitrogen with legumes, we reaped the rewards with an excellent garden corn crop in 2007.

Our cotton crops were a true blessing in 2005. Timely summer rains fell perfectly. Each day I walked the fields studying leaves, bolls, stems and blooms, noting changes each week while looking for signs of destructive insects. But inside I knew bollworms would overwhelm us. Slowly but surely moths arrived, laying endless amounts of eggs. Quickly I learned to look for insects much like one hunts an animal. Often, I found their excrement before I found the worm. Bollworms leave trails of brown digestions as they make their way to the next meal. Instead of a scout, I became a hunter. This made the job more exciting. I got some pointers from more experienced bug scouts and entomologists.

One leathery-skinned veteran told me, "You'll get to the point where you can smell them."

My first reaction to this was "This guy is nuts." But he was right. After a while, the smell of their excrement lingers in the muggy heat, clinging to your nostrils. The smell of their greasy, slick flesh will haunt your nasal cavity at night as you hear them munching away through your beloved crops.

Despite my disdain for pesticides and my gut feeling that insects do what they do for a reason, I followed the pattern laid down by 75 years of commercial farming. "The insects must be destroyed" mentality prevailed. By the end of August, bollworms spread like a plague throughout our fields. Following the model set before me I estimated insect population per plant and acre. I informed Dad it was time for us to spray for bollworms. Planes swarmed our fields over the next few days, blasting the cotton crop with poisonous liquid. My stomach gripped to my ribs. "What the hell am I doing?", I asked myself.

Only two days later all of our neighbors were spraying their fields, as well. It was like a perverse chain reaction creating a war zone around us. All day, the constant buzz of planes could be heard overhead as they dipped down, drenching the earth with toxins. In my dreams I could hear the screams of insects. Perhaps it was the plants, as well, begging for my help.

A few days later, I was back scouting our fields. Sure enough, the insecticides had worked like a charm. No signs of bollworms anywhere. But now there was a bigger problem—no lady bugs or lacewings either. Another negative issue with insecticides is that they kill *all* insects—the good guys, too. There is no moral disclaimer involved with insecticides. Like an atomic bomb, it kills one and all. With no beneficial insects remaining to protect the plants, it was just a matter of days before aphids returned and began to thrive.

The crazy thing about aphids is that all they do is eat and produce babies. I'm not even sure they sleep. They reproduce asexually and can have as many as 20 babies a day. So, it doesn't take long for these tiny little creatures to wreak havoc on a field of plants. They leave behind a sticky film, creating a waxy shine as they suck the life out of the plant's leaves. And the solution? Well, more pesticides naturally. And with another egg-lay by bollworms and beat armyworms, we had to spray one more time before the plants were passed the point of suffering significant insect damage. All the time something inside was telling me we were causing even more damage with our destructive, poisonous solutions.

Some startling trivia about insects is learned when a little research is performed. For instance, certain moths detect a female's presence from up to five miles away. That's far more impressive than across a crowded bar. With such a highly tuned internal communication system, how easy would it be for a host of moths to detect 640 acres of sick plants?

Our cotton crops harvested record yields in 2005. We averaged about 750 pounds of lint per acre. Which may not sound like a lot, but 1.5 bales per acre of dryland cotton in West Texas is a crowning achievement. It was truly a blessing to be welcomed back with such an amazing crop that first year. While I felt extremely fortunate to experience a record crop, I couldn't help but think it could be better. What if we could achieve even higher yields without using pesticides? Studying our costs for the year, the thing that really got me was the fact we had spent anywhere between $30-40 per acre on insecticides, which was more than double what we had spent on fertilizers. That year, we had used only commercial fertilizers, which I despised. In the back of my mind I knew there was a better, healthier way to farm. Despite what all the farmers around me kept saying—"That's just the way it is. You have to use these chemicals."— I refused to accept that.

After the harvest season, I talked Dad into joining me for lunch with Jim Burnett, owner of Texas Earth, an organic fertilizer business in Brownfield, Texas. I was determined to use healthy products, sure they would in turn create a healthy environment for our plants and soil. The meeting did not go well. Jim presented a high-price plan in order for us to balance our soil and replenish it with various minerals. It would've cost more than $40 per acre. While farmers will spend that much on insecticides some years, it is only to save a guaranteed highly productive crop. Planning to spend that much per acre before the seed is even in the ground is not so appealing.

Dad left the meeting saying, "If I can make a bale and a half per acre without this stuff, then what's the point in spending all this money?"

Jim simply blushed and nodded, "Well, I understand where you're coming from."

In retrospect, the proposal was way over budget and unrealistic for us. I knew it would take a lot more to convince Dad, but I was determined to try a more economically friendly version. Jim understood the financial constraints involved. In dryland farming, it is easy to get into financial trouble by overspending before knowing what kind of crop will be harvested.

Inspired to be around someone from West Texas in the organic world, I kept in touch with Jim and we soon became good friends. I would call him with a question as a wide range of thoughts entered my mind, and we would chat about various products and theories. Looking back, I think I inspired Jim as much as he inspired me. His insight into the biological world helped propel me down a path of enlightenment. For that, I will always be thankful. Over the next few years, Dad was able to see the benefits (when it rained) of organic fertilizers on our crops. By our 2009 crop, he allowed me to dedicate our entire acreage to organic fertilizers, eliminating commercial fertilizers. (Unfortunately, we did not receive late summer rainfall. Our crops suffered in severe drought conditions.) That was a huge step for my old man. This I know. And for that, I am extremely grateful. Dad, however, is much more open-minded than many farmers. Hopefully, more "old school" farmers will follow his lead.

From his experience of selling organic fertilizers for more than 15 years, Jim said that many challenges exist in convincing most farmers that something from Nature will benefit them more than the commercial fertilizers that have been widely used for half a century:

> It's hard to change a farmer from thinking chemically to thinking dynamically. When you're dealing with chemicals, one plus two equals three. When you talk about dynamics, now you're talking about biology and physics being thrown into the equation, and nothing is the same. It is affected by everything from the weather to soil tension to a number of things. When you start trying to educate people, they have a lot of excuses not to listen. I try to focus on the ones looking for an answer. Getting people to accept something when they're not ready, it's just not going to happen.

Biggest Pest of All—the Pesticide Industry

Perhaps the biggest scam of all was the creation of the pesticide industry, which began to take off soon after World War I.

Most non-organic fruits and vegetables we buy at the grocery store today contain high traces of pesticides—particularly the ones with thin skins, which more easily absorb chemicals. Several websites and books list the fruit and vegetable products with the highest levels of pesticides, as well as the lowest. The Organic Consumers Association's (OCA) website (organicconsumers. org/organic/pesticide-residues.cfm) has a detailed list of foods with the highest traces of pesticide residues. According to the OCA, the top ten are the following: strawberries, bell peppers, spinach, cherries (U.S.), peaches, cantaloupes (Mexico), celery, apples, apricots, and green beans.

Pesticides are pure "cancer" to our bodies. Poison is poison no matter how much it appears to help our food crops flourish. Again, we are treating the problem cosmetically. What we see is a healthy fruit, but what we are putting into our bodies is a toxin-ridden substance doing more long-term damage than providing short-term fulfillment. How many trips to the doctor's office? How many different prescriptions are filled because of the sickness we create? How many surgeries are needed because of the cancer-causing toxins with which we flood our bodies? Can anyone tell me how this broken system we've followed for decades has served anyone well? Do we feel compelled to follow it, no matter the price?

Thick-skinned fruits such as asparagus, avocados, bananas, broccoli, cauliflower, corn (but most is genetically modified), kiwi, mangoes, onions, papaya, pineapples, and sweet peas have the lowest levels of pesticides. The downside to that is nearly half of those are imported from thousands of miles away. Only broccoli, cauliflower, corn, onions, and sweet peas can be grown predominantly across the United States.

From the Mouths of Tiny Creatures

They say, "When the student is ready, the teacher will appear." Well, I was ready, and my teacher arrived in the form of a textbook courtesy of Jim.

We met for lunch one day in the summer of 2006. Smiling a warm smile, he shook my hand with enthusiasm. He cradled a book next to his chest as we walked into Pal's Corner Café in Ackerly. We'd been chatting for several weeks over the phone about insects, various fertilizer programs, and agriculture in general. Jim knew I was determined to find answers to my questions. That day, he had an answer for me.

"Lookie here," he said. "Read these first two pages and tell me if that doesn't make complete sense or what."

The book was *Exploring the Spectrum* by Philip Callahan. On the cover was an illustration of an ear of corn being eaten by a worm. I thumbed the pages to the book's introduction and read with much anticipation. The words began... "The corn earworm larvae are one of the most efficient scavengers of sick (chemical farming) corn in the moth world. It is a feeder on the fruiting parts of the plant and is known by the crop it attacks, e.g. *tomato fruit* worm, *cotton boll* worm, *strawberry* worm, etc."

Wait a second. Scavenger. Sick plants. It was already making sense to me. The book continued...

No other insect can be considered a better representative of the electromagnetic spectrum than the corn earworm, even its generic name Helio (sun) signifies light.

The earworm eye can see in both visible and UV portions of the spectrum. It lays its eggs at night primarily between 2:00 to 4:00 a.m. when the ultraviolet flash floods the night sky. The night sky UV light puts energy into (pumps) the airborne molecules from corn or sex (mating) scent in the atmosphere. It is like the condenser spark that ignites (lights up) the mercury vapor in the fluorescent light tube. Laser like, narrow band emissions stimulated by blue and UV night light, emit in the infrared portion of the spectrum. The spines (sensilla) on the moth antenna are dielectric waveguide antennae that are tuned by their shape and length to the molecular infrared emissions.

As the moth vibrates its wings before and during flight, its body is stimulated to emit both sound and radio waves plus IR light. The male can home in not only on the infrared from the female scent molecules, but also the broad band infrared heat light generated from the body. The sound and radio waves, from the body, modulate (put energy into), along with the night sky blue and UV, the flowing atmospheric plume so that the antenna sensilla can resonate to them. We may understand then that this important agricultural moth utilizes four important parts of the electromagnetic spectrum: UV, visible, infrared and radio.

The author has published over 50 papers on the life history, morphology, reproduction, communication, flight and feeding habits of this one species. These are the papers that led directly to the present work on paramagnetic soil, ancient stone structures, cancer, AIDS and atmospheric group frequencies, thus proving, as John Muir stated, everything is connected to everything else.

As I read that last line, it was as if the clouds parted and angels sang in harmonic chorus. Yes! I knew it. I knew there was a reason. I hadn't been that excited in a very long time. Everything was connected. We were all as One. These moths and worms were teaching us a valuable lesson by simply performing a needed task—taking out the *garbage*.

The bollworms are Nature's garbage collectors. Whether it be a tomato hornworm, bollworm, or corn earworm, this particular family of worms attack their respective crop of weak plants so that the strong plants might thrive. Much like how a cheetah, tiger, or lion seeks out the slowest gazelle, deer, or other four-legged prey. It was one of Nature's greatest laws exhibited in a very blatant and rigorous way—only the strong survive. Our problem in commercial agriculture is that all our plants are sick and weak. So, once the Air Force (moths) makes the drop (eggs) in the battle zone, the Marines (worms) commence taking out the enemy (sick plants) one by one. It is a miniaturized war zone we only want to avoid, ignoring the *cause* of the problem. Our modern way of thinking tells us that if a problem exists, we must destroy what is causing the problem by whatever means necessary. In the political world, war is the remedy. In the agriculture world, poison is the cure.

As farmers, we tend to think if a plant is lush, green and receives plenty of water, it is a healthy plant. We only notice if the plants' leaves turn yellowish or the ends of their leaves begin to curl due to stress from drought or disease. Our eyes are limited to visible energy, while the insect kingdom functions visually and electronically on the ultraviolet and infrared energy scale. As moths and other insects fly through the air, their wings are vibrating at a constant rate. For example: the corn earworm moth vibrates its wings at an average of 2,500 beats per minute (about 40 beats per second), while the honeybee wing vibrates much faster, at 250 beats per second.[1] Simultaneously their antennae are also vibrating at approximately the same rate, sending and receiving signals. Tiny sensory hairs or sensilla along the antennae also help translate messages to their nervous system or more specifically their nervous receptors (Johnston's organ) at the base of the antennae. They are more or less living and breathing radars or radios. Where do we think man got the idea for infrared and ultraviolet tracking used by our armed forces such as the Air Force?

Nematodes are becoming more of a problem in our area, causing damage to cotton crops in certain spots of various fields.

---

1. Philip Callahan, *Insects and How They Function* (Holiday House, New York, 1971), p. 82.

These worms are some of the most diverse creatures and the most multi-cellular animals on the Earth. One of their main purposes is to process organic material in the soil. Because our crop soil lacks life and organic matter, they feed on the only existing forms of life, which happen to be cotton plants. By rotating in a forage crop and creating stubble, which digests into humus, the nematode goes back to eating what it wants to eat and therefore not having to survive solely on our cash crops.

Soil Technology

It's crazy how we'll accept anything in technological terms as long as metal gadgets with complex wiring and buttons are visible; yet mention this same hardware pattern in the context of Nature, and we become skeptical. Such is the way our brains have been stained. We perceive modern man-made technology as superior to that of Nature's. Think of cell phones, for instance. Everybody has a cell phone these days. How do these things work? A receiver is in communication with a tower or very large antenna. Audible, literary, and visual information is passed via electromagnetic waves from one transmitter device (phone) to the tower and on to another device (phone), and voilà! We have instantaneous communication that has changed the way our human world now functions in business, entertainment, and everyday social behavior. No wires connecting them. Just the miracle of modern technology. This same principle operates in Nature. Where do you think man gets these electrical ideas and theories from anyhow? Yet, when we talk about this principle in agriculture, most farmers think this is crazy nonsense. Put a little piece of molded petroleum with buttons and a screen in our hands, though—then you have a bona fide believer.

Silica is supposed to compose up to 27% of our topsoil structure—healthy soil, that is. Most farmland is devoid of this vital element. With the depletion of silica, gone are the magnetic properties so important to the Earth's surface. Herein lies one of the major consequences of the Dust Bowl affecting my beloved West Texas landscape today. We've lost silica. We've annihilated traces of basalt from volcanic eruptions in the Rocky Mountains and decades of fertilizing courtesy of the buffalo and other animals which traveled in herds across these areas.

Without silica and crystals there would be no computers, no televisions, no cell phones and none of the clever electronic devices we use to entertain, educate, or stimulate our brain cells on a day-to-day basis. Take away those two gifts from Nature, and our modern world would be radically different than it is today.

Let's revisit Dr. Arden Anderson's model of the soil system as an electrical system. The role of the insect becomes even clearer as an indicator of deficiencies in the soil:

> If the circuit is de-tuned badly enough, nature calls in the garbage collectors, the insects, to clean it up. Disease organisms are simply an indication that the circuit is way out of tune and is building up debris as a result. Have you ever noticed how an overloaded electrical circuit will start to erode or break down, or how an engine that is out of tune will build up debris?

The use of petroleum-based fertilizers encourages higher populations of destructive insects in our crops. These fertilizers are high in ammonium. Moths are attracted to ammonium. Another misconception about insects is that they are unable to survive cold winters. For years, I heard old farmers say, "What we need is a good hard winter." The thinking is that this will kill all harmful insects. This isn't true of many insects, particularly the insects which destroy crops. Pay attention the next time you have a week or two of hard winter—insects will be flying around again afterwards after just one or two warm days.

Insects such as bollworms and corn earworms go through diapause, which is a hibernation phase that allows these insects a prolonged resting stage. They are protected from the seasonal elements. The amount of sunlight and the temperature tell them when it is the optimal time to emerge. So insects, much like a grizzly bear or a snake, hibernate through cold spells during winter. This dormancy period, much like that which plants go through, allows these insects to survive harsh elements such as freezing temperatures. An exception to this rule may occur when there is a late freeze or snow like we experienced here in West Texas during the 2007 Easter weekend. After several weeks of sunshine and warmth in mid-spring, a high percentage of these insects had most likely been told by the sun it was okay to come out and play. But the sudden change in weather and freezing temperatures got some off-guard. I'm sure they sense changes in Nature much better than we do, but as weather patterns are becoming crazy and unpredictable, I'm sure even insects are thrown off from time to time.

Raising Energy Levels of Plants

Raising the energy level of crops to the point where each plant transmits a healthy signal will tell the moths to keep cruising along until they find a field of sick, unhealthy plants down the road or perhaps just across the fence. How do we achieve this? By using organic products that will only enhance, not harm, the plant and soil. Think of the plants we raise as our own children. If you don't have children, think of them as an extension of yourself. Treat them in the same manner by which we maintain our own health or ensure that our children grow up physically healthy. The plants we grow have the same requirements—moderate amounts of water (rain), exercise (sunshine), healthy food (natural fertilizers), and an abundance of love.

Here's where it gets interesting. What if we could utilize a basic, harmless, all natural product on our crops to send a healthy signal to moths flying overhead in the wee hours of the night? In fact, what if we could use a variety of healthy products to also promote plant growth and higher fruiting rates, all while maintaining healthy production? It is absolutely possible.

Foliar feed sprays are one of our greatest remedies for improving plant health and production with immediate results. Today there are numerous products on the market with recipes consisting of bat guano, fish emulsions, seaweed, various other liquid manures, trace minerals, and even molasses.

"Hold on there," you interrupt. "Did you just say *molasses*?"

Sure did. You can top off some pancakes from your nozzles while on a little break out in the field. Beats trying to wash off a blend of 32-0-0. Using molasses in a foliar feed, I've also seen it kill bollworms dead on the plant within 24 hours of the application. Molasses, or sugar water, is toxic to worms, proving fatal. These types of insects do not have a pancreas and cannot digest sugars, which will then ferment into alcohol in their digestive system, killing the insect. Many feed lots carry large volumes of molasses. Ask as many questions as possible about the source of the molasses to ensure it hasn't been treated with something that might damage your plants.

We know from our trusty high school science books that photosynthesis is the process of a plant transforming solar energy into sugar, which enables the creature to mature and fruit. Therefore, by applying sugars in the form of liquid molasses, we are speeding up the process of photosynthesis, and the plant is able to conserve its own natural energy for whatever it needs the most. So feeding the leaves also enables the plants to endure other hardships, such as drought and soil mineral deficiency.

The downside to foliar feed sprays is that they must be used in a timely manner preferably in temperatures under 85° Fahrenheit so that the leaves may have time to absorb the product before evaporation takes place. A plant's leaf cells are more open in cooler temperatures. Once the sun's heat reaches a certain point, the molecular structure tightens up to prevent heat damage from occurring. The heat also evaporates the liquid, preventing the plant from receiving the maximum benefit. So early mornings and late evenings are really the only time you can apply these products...unless you happen to catch some cloudy cool days late in the summer.

One thing we have to watch with sugars is that we can apply too much sugar and shut down the plant's growth entirely, forcing it into fruiting early. Sugars are best in moderation. An application every two to three weeks late in the growing season is recommended. One way to ensure you're not overdoing it is to make one pass and wait about two hours. Use a refractometer and it will easily tell you whether it is helping or hurting the crop.

The brix level is a measurement of the dissolved sugar-to-water mass ratio of a liquid. In a nutshell, it is the easiest way to measure whether the plant's energy level is healthy or not. A farmer can spray a few plants or acres, wait about 30 minutes and take a brix reading to make sure the energy levels of the plants are raised and not lowered. This is simply precautionary to keep you from giving the plants too much or not enough fertilizer per acre. A refractometer (or brix meter) can be purchased for under $200 and will enable you to measure the plant's brix level before and as you begin applying the foliar feed. Best to make certain you are not overdoing it.

A combination of healthy organic matter and a good foliar feed program will also speed up the crop's maturity rate, allowing for an earlier harvest each season. This is a huge advantage as winter nears, bringing with it snow and rainstorms that can delay harvesting for weeks on end. Imagine gathering your crop two or three weeks earlier! Neighbors will wonder how you've done this. And your answer will be so simple, it will puzzle them even more. Perhaps your actions will inspire them to try these natural and healthy alternatives. Envision spreading such a trend that empowers the farmer with larger profits, higher yields, and independence while enhancing the environment by creating healthier soils and plants.

Making use of locally produced livestock manure as fertilizer is also key in producing a bountiful garden or crop. Converting these manures into compost and foliar feed recipes will supply farmers and gardeners with efficient fertilizers healthy to the soil and plants. A panty hose and a five-gallon bucket are all one needs to convert manures into a foliar spray. Again, a refractometer helps in monitoring energy levels before spraying an entire crop or garden. Producing and utilizing organic fertilizers will save lots of time and money in the long run, particularly as fuel prices and mining costs escalate. Remember that in the near future as energy prices rise, commercial fertilizers will not be economical to purchase.

Ladybugs, Earthworms, Bees, Bats—Oh My!

As soil and crop management skills are slowly yet surely honed into an organic and all-natural mindset and practice, one will notice a significant shift in what types of insects will dominate your garden or fields. More beneficial insects such as ladybugs, lacewings, wasps, bees, and other hard-working creatures will buzz, zoom, and zing over your plants instead of crop dusters.

By restoring the soil, we are creating an entirely healthy ecosystem that will benefit all forms of life. Just as plagues and diseases are contagious, so too is healthy energy. With an increase in organic matter and minimizing the use of the steel plow, earthworms will return. Once these magnificent creatures appear, it is such a joy to know you are breathing back life into once-depleted soil.

Charles Darwin championed the earthworm's cause. Years of studying their behavior inspired his conclusion that earthworms digested the earth, creating not only more soil but extremely fertile and healthy soil. With the publication of his book *The Formation of Vegetable Mould Through the Action of Worms, With Observations on Their Habits* in 1881, the world of agriculture soon learned of the earthworms' importance to soil and crop health. Darwin theorized that a healthy earthworm population could create one inch of topsoil every four to five years. Astonishing when you consider it takes hundreds of years to achieve the same results without their assistance.

Compost piles stored in a cool, dark area are an efficient place in which to "grow" your own earthworms. Fishermen love them as well as gardeners. Nightcrawlers are sold worldwide as fish bait. Many gardeners have an earthworm hatch in their greenhouses, covered with plywood or other pieces of lumber, allowing easy access to feed kitchen scraps. Earthworm castings are also sold as a rich fertilizer.

Bat guano also acts as an excellent fertilizer. Rich in organic nitrogen and phosphorous (10-3-1 NPK [Nitrogen-Phosphorous-Potassium] ratio on average), bat guano helps stimulate plant growth. Caves are not needed for a colony of bats. A simple wooden construction about two feet high and two feet wide is sufficient. Allow four inches between the sheets of wood, creating a mini-cave den for bats, and hang the structure about eight feet or higher from the ground. Simple plans for building a bat house are available at batmanagement.com.

Bee colonies act as highly skilled pollinators for crops, trees, and other native vegetation. Bees help pollinate at least one-third of our crops. Many serious gardeners also have a beehive/house on their property to enhance pollination. Bee Colony Collapse Disorder (CCD) worldwide has appeared in headlines for a few years now. A few beekeepers I know are vehemently insisting on an organic diet for their bees. Rather than electromagnetic pollution via cell phones and other electronic devices, some think the reason for CCD is poor food management by beekeepers feeding their bees food products based on substitute (fake) sugar, or their failing to keep a sterile environment for their colonies. Others believe that man is the cause through other means. For example, commercial pesticide use and GMO crops are also proving fatal worldwide to bee colonies.[2]

---

2. U.S. Environmental Protection Agency, "Pesticide Issues in the Works, Colony Collapse Disorder", EPA, http://www.epa.gov/opp00001/about/intheworks/honeybee.htm, October 2008.

Over the past century, pollinated crops have risen dramatically, while managed beehives have declined. The National Research Council released a report in 2006 revealing a loss in habitat suitable for bees due to increasing urbanization and intensive corporate agriculture that requires widespread use of pesticides and herbicides, as well as disease, parasites, and climate change. CCD in Europe resulted in 30% annual losses in honeybees in 2008 and 2009.[3] The 2008 Farm Bill includes the Pollinator Habitat Protection Act of 2007, encouraging the preservation and conservation of pollinating insects.

Honeybees are creatures we should all embrace. Honey has wonderful healing qualities, particularly raw honey. It has been used for thousands of years to heal burns, scrapes, and other flesh wounds. Bees eat pollen from flowers. In turn, their honey supplies our bodies with much needed iron, copper, manganese, silica, chlorine, calcium, potassium, sodium, phosphorus, aluminum, and magnesium. Why purchase man-made vitamins when a spoonful of honey can do the job even better? Honey is also a healthy substitute for sugar. I literally wake up in the land of milk and honey every morning, adding a little honey and milk to my coffee to cut down on its acidic qualities.

Imagine a farm with honeybees, bats, and earthworms supplying much of what is needed for healthy plants and soil to thrive. These creatures would also contribute to the health of the individuals overseeing this well-balanced piece of land. By implementing more beneficial creatures in the landscape, the quality and production of all crops and wildlife gets a severe boost, allowing Nature to thrive as well as the steward.

Another key Earth-friendly product to have around the farm is diatomaceous earth. Known as a key ingredient for dynamite, this powder has multiple benefits. Not only is it an excellent mixture in pump filters for swimming pools and hot tubs, it prevents

---

3. Lynn Betts, "An Impending Pollinator Crisis?", *The National Farmer-Stockman* (February 2010).

damage from certain insects. Diatomaceous earth is essentially ancient crustacean fossils. Under a microscope, their spiked forms are visible. They are deadly to certain insects such as weevils and ants. It is an excellent substance in which to preserve stored seeds in large amounts. It can also be sprinkled around ant beds. The powder gets into the joints of their bodies, irritating the tiny creatures. Annoyed, they begin to lick those body spots, swallowing the powder. Their intestines are shredded by the spikes of the diatomaceous earth, resulting in death. Harsh, I know, but very effective. Weevils can destroy an entire season's worth of wheat or any other stored seed, so this product comes in very handy. It is better than using other forms of poison. Incidentally, it also works on termites.

Perhaps one of our greatest faults as a species is that, as we've been at the top of the food chain and animal kingdom for so long, our arrogance exceeds our intelligence. We refuse to admit that pesky little creatures such as insects perform such a vital role in our existence. Through the eons of time we've adopted a "god-concept" for our own existence, somehow convincing ourselves we don't need anybody or anything to "rule the world". This concept continues to unravel our proverbial yarn, daring to expose the vulnerable marrow of our spool. Without certain insects, we will perish. Many crops require the services of bees, flies, etc., to pollinate efficiently. We are all one here. Being at the top of the pyramid shouldn't give us the impression that we are the entire pyramid.

Lightning in a Bottle

When lightning storms occur in the Earth's atmosphere, it is the massive explosion of energy we *ooh* and *aw* at in wonderment as spidery veins charge across the night sky. Each lightning bolt is like a rock thrown into a pond—it creates a ripple echoing in all directions until it reaches the shoreline. Likewise, if a lightning bolt occurs anywhere on the globe, it begins a wave pattern, known as the Schumann wave, oscillating at approximately 12.5 feet above and below the Earth's surface. Apparently there are about 1,000 lightning storms each second. Imagine if we were able to harness a fraction of that energy and use it in an absolutely benevolent manner in Nature.

The world-renowned inventor Nikola Tesla understood the importance of harnessing Nature's energy. Although he invented the first radio, Tesla was never officially given credit for the patent. That honor went to Guglielmo Marconi. The scientist Tesla was decades ahead of his time, spending most of his life dedicated to perfecting his understanding of the principles of free energy. Of course, the day after his death, the FBI and other governing agencies ransacked his home and laboratory, confiscating all of his notes, equipment, and any other clues to his ingenious discoveries. Rest assured, many cool inventions have come about in the past half century due to Tesla's genius.

Experimenting with literally millions of watts of electricity, Tesla wore three-inch thick cork soles on his shoes. During one experiment in 1899, he shut down the city of Colorado Springs' entire power system, as his dome-antenna caught a huge bolt of lightning. This was exactly what he designed it to do. Harnessing the energy from that lightning bolt was his goal. Tesla was attempting to send a radio signal to Paris, France.

The modern wizard knew "the earth was alive with electrical vibrations" from lightning strikes pulsating across the globe—Schumann waves. A single lightning bolt carries on average one million kilowatts of electricity. One lightning storm gives enough energy to supply the entire United States for about 20 minutes.

How can we ever have an energy shortage with this type of power snapping, crackling, and popping overhead? Imagine the possibility of harnessing Nature's power to supply us all the energy we could ever dream of needing. Solar energy, wind energy, and other expensive forms of alternative energy would quickly diminish in costs. Perhaps the FBI could publish Tesla's journals so humanity might benefit from his free-energy concepts. No? Well, a man can dream, can't he?

It has been proven that the human brain (when in a meditative state) and a bolt of lightning operate on the exact same frequency—about 7.8 Hertz or cycles per second. There are coincidences and then there are relative facts we must acknowledge as divine reason. So, if in a meditative state, our minds are already on the same radio station as lightning bolts, why then could we not transmit a message to bring a little rain our way? If we are all a part of one another and consequently an extension of the universe, why is it so hard for us to establish or re-establish our cosmic communication with the elements, with the Heavens, with the weather? If we are the rain, how can we deny ourselves access to all parts of our whole?

Take a moment. Let that marinate for a spell.

In various native cultures, there exists a strong connection between certain individuals and the weather elements. Many native tribes across the globe have certain members—whether they be shamans, medicine men, or witch doctors—who have the gift of connecting to the Spirit of Nature and helping influence the weather one way or another. I believe it to be true that certain blessed individuals possess this gift and can at anytime bring rains, winds, or snow to bless the Earth.

Even in recent American history, we have documentation of successful rainmakers. In the early 20th century in America, Charles Hatfield made quite a name for himself in California as a rainmaker. The song *Hatfield* by Widespread Panic is one of my all-time favorite tunes. Hollywood provided us with *The Rainmaker* (starring Burt Lancaster as a Charles Hatfield-like character), and the book *Wizard of Sun City* details the triumph and tragedy of Hatfield's accomplishments in ending Southern California droughts in Los Angeles and San Diego. His most documented rainmaking services were known to cause the catastrophic flood in San Diego in 1916. He was to be paid the sum of $10,000 for filling Lake Morena. He succeeded and then some, as more than 40 inches of rain fell in less than a week. In a long, drawn-out dispute, the city of San Diego refused to pay Hatfield, as the floods caused hundreds of thousands of dollars in damages. Dozens of people drowned, as well.

Stories of shamans, medicine men, and other Native leaders "bringing the rain" have been told for centuries—people with strong connections to Nature, with "power" to make it rain. The Hopi, Navajo, and Sioux tribes all tell stories of rainmaking, whether from rain dances or other sacred ceremonies. Native tribes in Central and South America also speak of these abilities. Aboriginal tribes also have been known to influence weather patterns, particularly rain. Does this power, this ability lie within all of us? We will never know unless we continue to explore the depths within.

Other technologies are in existence regarding energy frequencies and wavelength manipulation. The High Frequency Active Auroral Research Program (HAARP), located near Gakona, Alaska, is the most controversial technological "weather manipulator" currently known. Protected by both our U.S. Air Force and Navy, this system (covering some 40 acres) possesses the capabilities to alter frequencies in Nature, disturbing natural wave patterns oscillating across the globe into the ionosphere. While said to be strictly a communications experiment, some scientists claim HAARP has the ability to influence weather. This subject could form a book in itself, but is one the reader is encouraged to further explore. Scientists, such as Dr. Nick Begich, worry that HAARP is creating a serious strain on Nature as well as the ionosphere. His book, *Angels Don't Play This HAARP*, explains in great length how our government has advanced Tesla's ideas but is using these highly advanced techniques in destructive ways.

It may be difficult for many to accept such things are possible. Simply because we do not think it is achievable, doesn't mean it cannot happen. If our minds were more open to all possibilities, it would help us in the mental transition necessary to lead us to a new way of doing things.

Resources

BOOKS

Ancient Architecture, Modern Visions by Philip Callahan
Angels Don't Play This HAARP by Dr. Nick Begich
Bees by Rudolf Steiner
Crazy Like Us by Ethan Watters
Exploring the Spectrum by Philip Callahan
Insects and How They Function by Philip Callahan
Pyramid Power by Dr. G. Pat Flanagan
Resource Wars by Michael T. Klare
Tesla: Man out of Time by Margaret Cheney
*The Formation of Vegetable Mould Through the Action of Worms,
With Observations on Their Habits* by Charles Darwin
The Intelligent Farmer by A. F. Beddoe, DDS

WEBSITES

acresusa.com
cropservicesintl.com
batmanagement.com
beecare.com
honeybee.com
opticsinfobase.org
radionics.org
texasearth.com
wormfarm.com

VIDEOS

A Farm for the Future
Polyface Farm

Chapter 5

EVOLUTION OF MIND, MONEY AND ENERGY
Revolution of the Soul

> *Every generation needs a new revolution.*
>
> THOMAS JEFFERSON

> *Who knows that the universe is but one*
> *vast sea of compassion, actually.*
> *The veritable holy honey beneath*
> *all this show of personality and cruelty.*
> *In fact, who knows but that it isn't the solitude*
> *of the oneness of the essence of everything.*
>
> JACK KEROUAC

Is This Thing On?

A worldwide revolution is slowly spreading. Widespread rebellion is already happening in countries like Iceland and Greece, but we won't hear about it from our mainstream media. Global banks are being bombed, and average Joes are already flying planes into IRS buildings. Our own government knows a revolution is looming. They are taking every precaution, I'm sure. As banks crumble, oil prices boom, and unemployment soars, this world will experience more radical shifts and changes than many people are willing to accept. How ugly this revolution could get depends on so many undetermined factors.

For 99% of the 20th century, the price of oil was so low that the destructive excesses of our lifestyles were not limited by the cost of fuel. Needless to say, energy prices can crush our greatest sense of freedom. In the 21st century that restriction of freedom is leaking more and more into the general population with volatile oil prices. Our vantage point is so clouded, so distorted, because we cling to our dream, our life-long misconception of what this world is supposed to be. Whether it is through futile childhood bedtime stories, traditional expectations, Las Vegas delusions or Hollywood's happy endings, we're expected to be hypnotized into this false premise where everything is fine. Perhaps we're so distracted by our immediate surroundings that the rest of the world seems far too complicated to ever interpret, let alone change. This whole concept of perpetual growth can only go so far and encourages perpetual war. Just like every good rubber band, each expansion has its breaking point.

We are destroying a perfectly good planet. Why? Because we're making money in the process. More than 60 years worth of greed and gluttony has caught up to us in a very unforgiving way. The continual depletion of non-renewable resources simply to afford us a certain lifestyle of wasteful decadence is psychotic by nature and irrational by design. Allowing oil, coal, and timber companies to ransack our planet claiming these to be our only logical energy sources is perhaps the biggest fraud the Powers That Be have sold or will ever sell the people. It has proven to be the ultimate scam (along with fiat money). And now, our leaders are touting nuclear energy as our energy savior. Really? Perhaps we should ask the people of Chernobyl, Ukraine, how that story ends.

To rebel against the destructive aspects of the current system in this country, each and every individual should remove his or her money from Wall Street and all national/international banks. To kill the snake, we must cut off its head. If we can't cut off its head, starving it is just as effective. By removing our money, we send a very powerful message to the bankers and other well-dressed, slick-haired executives who irresponsibly play with our money. Let them play with their own money. We should place ours in locally owned banks we can trust. Forget the big boys "too big to fail". Let them see just how significant the cash from "the little man" really is. To have a truly effective revolution in today's world, everything starts with taking our money out of the system.

Now—more than ever—it is vital we come together, not only farmers but all people, and learn from the mistakes of our past. We must realize the importance of all things. We have the blessed opportunity of creating a better world rather than destroying what remains. If we are to see this world improve we must become fully fledged scouts and pathfinders for a new way of doing things. Let us turn away from corporations like Monsanto, DuPont, Bayer Crop Science, and Dow Chemical; insurance companies like AIG; and national banks/wannabe banks like Chase, Goldman Sachs, Bank of America, and CitiBank, as they are all obviously the ones running this country, empowered by the elite families.

As farmers, if we are to survive this next phase of life, we must unite. Why do we allow seed companies and global markets to set commodity pricing? Why do we not buy or begin our own seed companies, producing and storing our own seed? We are not helpless. We are the ones with all the land, all the machinery; and we are the ones who provide all the labor, all the risk, and spend all the money from seed to harvest. We are creators, not producers. We are guardians, not sodbusters. We are living, breathing souls, not consumers.

How did we ever allow ourselves to lose our seat at the agriculture bargaining table? It is our failure to have a long-term plan other than making money off a one-trick pony show. It is our failure to diversify. It is our failure to create multi-faceted infrastructure. It is our failure to organize together. It is our lack of proper planning. It is our refusal to unite and agree as One. We've allowed greed and pride and short-sightedness to blind our true vision, muzzle our voice, and paralyze our ability to act as the single most important vocation in the world. Each day we wake and put on our boots is our Little Bighorn. Will we remain disbanded and vulnerable or come together to strengthen our purpose and justify our existence as true stewards of the soil, as flesh and bone guardian angels of the Earth? Will we stand to fight or sulk back into an eternal state of surrender?

We must create core groups while maintaining a concern for

all. We must do what is best for farming and present and future generations, not what is simply best for a few individuals this year. If corporations, lawmakers and politicians will not allow us into their boardrooms, let us not allow them into our fields. We are the Gatekeepers. How many people walk into a restaurant and begin dictating what they will pay or not pay for the food on the menu? One does not walk into a gardener's field and begin dictating the price of home-grown food. Yet, this is what we've allowed in agriculture. We have all the power, yet we've allowed these groups to convince us that we can do nothing. This is absurd. We have *all* the power. We are the food chain. We are the Earth and water. We are drought and rain. We are the most vital gatherers this planet will ever know. Banks can fail. Agriculture cannot. We do not eat or drink money. Food and water have always preceded paper in survival significance and always will.

For now, we are being beaten over the head with globalization's perverse pipe dream. With Peak Oil very much a reality, it is ridiculous to think we will continue to import the majority of our food across our borders. We must think local. We must unite locally. We must put the *unity* back in community. Yet, how can we unify without rebelling against the current standards and expectations which we deem as laws? Laws often exist solely to test the limits of our intention, purpose, or ability. We adhere to so many laws of scientific and social origin that we forget the spiritual possibilities of exceeding their very existence. How is it that maintaining a healthy water and food supply is voided simply because we adhere to the influences and controls of corporations? Often, too distracted by dollars and cents, legalities and illegalities, we are unable to make sense of our purpose, the true miracle of bringing more Life to Earth.

We must reprogram the wiring of our minds in order to survive. It is a different world we live in now than just a few short years ago. The continual submission to corporate agriculture is nothing short of a sluggish suicide for the American farmer. In fact, our mindless approach with a stockyard-like mentality is a lethal injection to Life itself. Finding a new way that avoids the restrictions of commercial agriculture will in time be seen as an act of heroism.

The development of a network of local food supply feeding each community, city, or region in this country is imminent. The same goes for every other country. Pursuing the exhausted method of transcontinental shipping of our groceries is short-lived and insane. Farms should be evolving into the nucleus of communities around the world. How much longer do we really expect to receive an ample supply of exotic fruit that has to be shipped from thousands of miles away? How much more energy will be required to make that coveted meal to impress your family and friends? One does not need to be a genius to figure out the impractical nature of our current eating and consumption habits.

The United States makes up about 4.5% (roughly 305 million people) of the world's population, yet we consume 25-30% of all goods (oil included) and produce 25% of the pollution on this planet. We are the epitome of excessive consumption. Whether it be food, cars, houses, furniture or clothes, we are hoping to consume or purchase our way to bliss. Statistics say that this isn't working out too well for us. Americans have slipped to 42nd among nations in life expectancy (down from 11th just two decades ago), being leap-frogged by developing countries such as Jordan and many others.[1]

Many of you may be scratching your heads by now, saying, "But, how are we going to feed the entire world and maintain a local food system for communities across the country?" We can't. The rest of the world, rather than relying on the importation of our cheap, highly subsidized food crops, must go back to producing their own staple crops. This would greatly benefit themselves and their own farmers.

---

1. Associated Press, "U.S. Ranks Just 42nd in Life Expectancy", August 11, 2007.

Less Oil + More People = Very Expensive Fuel

The above equation sums up our near future. Accept it. When the cheap oil is gone, there will be a collapse of catastrophic proportions, and it will dwarf the 2008 economic meltdown. Let's factor in that the United States is running out of oil reserves, so too is England, Europe, South America, Russia, and Mexico. England is most likely in worse shape than anyone. China and India can no longer keep up with their demands. That leaves the Middle East, Africa, Canada, and whatever other scraps remain for the big boys to fight over for the next 20 or 30 years.

Through basing an entire economy on a non-renewable resource, time has now become of the essence as we've collectively chosen to ignore many warning signs of energy price-spikes over the past 30 years. In 1949, world-renowned oil geologist and physicist M. King Hubbert informed us of our rapidly declining discoveries and production in the oil world. His prediction in 1956 that U.S. production would begin to decline after 1970 was frightfully accurate. His theory on global Peak Oil production became known as Hubbert's Peak. His continual warnings of world production peaking in the 1990s were scoffed at and mostly ignored by the rest of the industry. Hubbert's report *The Nature of Growth* was submitted as testimony to the hearing on the National Energy Conservation Policy Act of 1974, which were hearings before the Subcommittee on the Environment of the Committee on Interior and Insular Affairs of the House of Representatives. He detailed specific graphs of oil discovery declines and how demand for oil would increase with population growth.

He said, "On such a time scale, it is seen that the epoch of the fossil fuel can be but an ephemeral and transitory event—an event, nonetheless, that has exercised the most drastic influence so far experienced by the human species during its entire biological existence." Apparently his words fell upon deaf ears, as the world continued down a path of excess.

In the 1960s we were using 60 million barrels of oil per day on a global scale. Fast forward some 40 years and that figure has jumped up to 85 million barrels per day. Peak Oil is really not an argument about us completely running out of oil. It is about us running out of affordable oil. Mike Ruppert has proven to be one of the leaders in modern-day Peak Oil education. His latest book, *Confronting Collapse* (originally entitled *A Presidential Energy Policy*), points out many hard-to-swallow scenarios regarding our lack of preparation with alternative energies and the continuing digressions of oil discoveries. It boils down to how much energy (money) it takes to get a barrel of oil.

Ruppert writes:

> The world will never run out of oil. Once it takes more than the sale price to extract one barrel, or it takes more energy to extract a barrel than one gets from burning it, there is no point in using it. The term "nonconventional oil" is important. Because it is through understanding that term that we begin to look at how much energy we expend for how much energy we get in return. Unconventional oil sources like Canadian tar sands or oil-from-coal—which has not been proven to be commercially viable and is very destructive to the environment—put us face to face with the fact that nothing will ever provide an energy return for energy invested like the oil we began pumping at the beginning of the 20th century. Nature made that oil over millions of years. There is no free lunch. The Laws of Thermodynamics are as fixed as the law of gravity.

A documentary centered around Ruppert's research came out in 2009, entitled *Collapse*. Highly recommended viewing for everyone.

Colin Campbell, a world-renowned petroleum geologist, is one of the modern leaders educating the general public about Peak Oil. He founded the Association for the Study of Peak Oil and Gas. Campbell predicted global oil production would peak by 2007, and his prediction appears to have been accurate. In

1998, Campbell (along with Jean H. Laherrère) estimated there were 1,000 billion barrels of oil left to produce.[2] At our current consumption of 85 million barrels per day, that would leave us with less than 36 years of oil. Since this is already 2010, that would mean less than 24 years of oil remain to be produced. But as oil consumption rises every year with the momentous economic expansion of countries like China and India, that figure can rapidly decrease over time. Bottom line—*we're very near the end of the Oil Age.*

The wildcard in all of the future supply predictions is China. Their economy and dependence on fossil fuels is growing 8% annually. That means their demand for oil will double in 10 years. Those escalating demands from the most populous nation in the world would drain remaining sources much sooner than anticipated. We could be looking at serious oil shortages between 2012 and 2015.

With the tar sands of Canada and Venezuela, we are using much heavier, even more polluting fossil fuels than ever. These take more time and more money to achieve usable fuel status. This means more money at the pumps. Here we are in agriculture operating multi-thousand acre farms with 200 horsepower tractors guzzling on average one gallon per two acres each trip across the field. No matter how many corners are cut, a minimum of four or five trips (from pre-planting to harvest) is necessary for most crops each season. Even Roundup farmers will find it difficult to farm as much land once fuel prices climb. The fact that oil companies are already tapping heavily into tar sands for oil production should be a very big clue that we are well past Peak Oil production not only in America, but worldwide! Particularly when mining tar sands for oil means more deforestation, soil destruction, and pollution simply to attain the oil crumbs in the Earth. Some tar sands oil production has produced as little

---

2. Colin Campbell and Jean H. Laherrère, "The End of Cheap Oil", *Scientific American* (March 1998).

as 1.5 to 3 barrels of oil to 1 barrel of oil used in this horrific mining process.

Over-exaggerated oil reserve estimates from OPEC countries help calm the general public's fears of us ever running out of cheap oil. We put all our future's fate in the hands of countries we cannot afford to trust. Their oil reserve estimations are linked directly to the amount of oil they can produce and sell each year. The higher their reserve estimation, the more money they make. The war on terror has been a convenient means for our U.S. military to protect the largest productive oil patch on the planet. War is inevitable as other giants jockey for position to secure this type of energy. Considering it takes more than 23,000 hours of human labor to equal the energy produced by one barrel of oil, it is simple to see how much more is accomplished with the convenience of oil. Perhaps the Amish knew something long ago that we failed to accept—keep life steady and simple. Instead, we've fed the beast far too long.

The impact of expensive fuel on agriculture will spread into the rest of this country in the form of rising food prices due to input and transportation costs. Everything from ball bearings to tires to plastics to transportation of any and all goods comes into the equation. Prices will continue to escalate. When will we get to the point in time where what we currently do for work, for pleasure is no longer economically affordable? We must become less dependent on heavy gas-guzzling machines and long-distance transportation to perform our daily routine. Our transition to a lifestyle less dependent on former habits will make the realities of the near future much more bearable.

Unless there is a significant decrease in global population through war or fatal disease, it is inevitable our fuel supply will not afford us the many luxuries we're accustomed to for more than one decade—in the best case scenario. The math just doesn't add up. How many more years will the average person be able to afford air travel? Eight years? Five? Two? The world economy continues to spiral downward with false props trying to keep it at its standard pace, but when the eventual collapse occurs it will be very harsh, and unfortunately the aftermath will linger for decades on end.

Even with discoveries of shale natural gas, truth-speaking experts warn these fields will dry up within five years. Oil analyst Arthur Berman discovered that the Barnett wells in Texas declined by 50% and the Haynesville Shale wells in East Texas and Louisiana by 95% after their first year of production.[3] Much of the hoopla and hope around ethanol production via corn went belly-up with the crash of oil prices in 2008. Ethanol is not our savior. The idea of using more energy to attain a gallon of fuel than you are producing by burning it is pointless. Ethanol wastes away corn and maize—key components of our food supply. Biodiesel makes much more sense as it can be derived from any vegetable-oil seed such as cotton and sunflower. But still, biofuels are simply a drop in the ocean when it comes to replacing our fossil fuels as energy, and mass world-wide production of food crops for fuel would compromise our food supplies.

America will be hit harder and faster by Peak Oil than any other nation on the planet. Why? Look at our city infrastructure. Suburban America is built on the premise of commuting 30-50 miles back and forth from work to home each day. Brilliant concept when there is plenty of cheap oil bubbling. But when that cheap oil translates into $6, $8, $10, or even $14 per gallon there will be much less congestion to the rush-hour traffic. When a family is faced with the choice of long commutes to and from home versus putting food on the table, cooling/heating the house, and keeping the lights on at night, reality becomes ruthless. We are accustomed to driving long distances and think nothing of it, but that soon will change along with our lifestyles. Most current civilizations predate America, and will not experience as much difficulty dealing with their commutes. European cities and most other nations' urban areas were built long before oil, but most of our larger cities depend on having easy access

---

3. Chris Nelder, *The Next Oil Crisis is Just Ahead,* Energy and Capital, http://www.energyandcapital.com/articles/oil-gas-outlook/975, October 16, 2009.

to plenty of cheap oil. If we don't act soon, suburban families will be nomadic pilgrims in search of a more suitable place to survive. Crime will surge. There will be much more need to focus on basic survival than driving long distances to make money, which will by then be virtually useless anyway.

Relocating now to an area where much is available within a short distance, preferably walking distance, will benefit families and individuals tremendously in the near future. We must shorten the space between our homes and our necessities. Long-distance commutes from home to work just won't make much sense anymore. We must seriously plan for this transition. Spending the majority of a paycheck on fuel is not practical economics for anyone. We cannot relive the old Wild West mentality of riding our horse to the point of exhaustion, stealing another when it can no longer move. When you're riding alone in the desert, you better treat that horse better than yourself. Because nothing we have thus far found can equal the amount of energy produced from fossil fuels. As that black gold production slows from a gush to a trickle, so too will much of our current lifestyle.

Agriculture will change as much, if not more, than any other industry. Transforming our farms into smaller, more efficient and diverse operations will prevent economic stalemates in the future. Imagine running 400 horsepower fuel-guzzling machines across 5,000+ acres. Imagine a season where the fuel bill costs more than the crop itself. Will fuel become more valuable than food? Most of the technological products derived from petroleum will not be there to help us either once the price of fuel begins its unforgiving climb. Everything we do and how we do it will change simply because the era of cheap oil will soon vanish.

Planes, Trains, E-Cars, Horses and More

Transportation is in need of a major overhaul in America. Why we're spending billions and billions on more new highways and interstates in this country is beyond me. Can anyone explain why we've nearly abandoned our precious railroad system as a primary means of private transportation? It is the very reason we were able to "tame" this country, with railroads expanding from New York City to San Francisco, much faster than anyone had anticipated. Europe has its electric train system reaching from one country to another and is far superior to our rusty tracks and system powered by diesel engines. While we've been busy waging wars for profit the past 60 years, other countries have focused on infrastructure. While American corporate giants have bought up patent after patent of goods that would prove beneficial to people and the environment, they have secured their status as profit-generating machines. This is at the expense of everything else.

I know a mechanic who patented an invention that would allow engines to run on vapors from gas or diesel. This invention (patented in the early 1980s) would've transformed cars and pickups into highly efficient means of transportation, averaging between 60 and 80 miles per gallon. His life was threatened by government officers, and he gave up manufacturing and installing his patented device. And if that is one mechanic in my area, imagine how many dozens of other innovative minds have created something wonderful we never saw.

Let's think about our American automobile industry for a moment and why there is a very good reason General Motors and Chrysler went bankrupt. In 1923, the Model T could get 25 miles per gallon. Some 87 years later, that is still better than most cars today. The Model A (manufactured from 1927-1931) got between 25-30 miles per gallon, while weighing over 2,200 pounds. A 2009 Ford Focus, with a weight of 2,300 pounds, gets 38 miles per gallon. That is only a 21% increase on one of Ford's most fuel efficient automobiles. A 6-cylinder Ford Ranger (4WD) gets less than 18 miles per gallon. We can put men on the moon less than half a century after the first Model T, yet we can't produce fuel-efficient automobiles after nine decades of production! And who killed the electric car in the mid-1990s? Yes—the oil industry. It is beyond ridiculous.

Due to the greedy actions of corporations and lack of proper leadership and foresight by the past four Presidents (Ronald Reagan, George Bush Sr., Bill Clinton, and George Bush Jr.), we are where we are in regards to energy. We should be laying down electrified track directly beside our current railways. This would allow efficient long-distance travel between cities and communities. It would also cause no direct pollution and use much less fossil fuels. Electricity is still, of course, largely generated from gas-powered and coal-powered electric plants.

Who needs cash for clunkers? Let's do "clunkers for Clydesdale horses". It'll provide huge savings. I mean those big creatures are strong, and they always bring beer! Can you imagine cruising into a dealership in the future in your 2005 Chevy Tahoe and pulling away in a horse-drawn buggy built for a family of four? Forgive me—my sarcasm knows no bounds. But even horses require fuel in the form of grass or hay. If you haven't at least one to two acres, how will you fuel your horse, mule, or donkey? In 2001, I was traveling in Morocco, and the people had an interesting saying that went, "My grandfather rode a horse, my father drove a car, I fly an airplane, my son will ride a horse." Full circle. I thought it was poetically funny then. Now, it is quite sobering.

Food for Fuel, Fuel for Thought

Following the 2007-2008 crops, headlines were circulating about lack of enough grain production to supply both the food and biofuels industry. China cannot produce enough grain alone to feed their own hogs, much less their entire human population. Russia witnessed economic hardship and its harsh effect on food supply firsthand in the collapse of the Soviet Union in the early 1990s. Dmitri Orlov, a Russian-born journalist, warns us of such downfalls.

Orlov spoke to an audience at Cowell Theatre in Fort Mason Center in San Francisco on February 13, 2009. He said:

> In the United States, the agricultural system is heavily industrialized, and relies on inputs such as diesel, chemical fertilizers and pesticides, and, perhaps most importantly, financing. In the current financial climate, the farmers' access to financing is not at all assured. This agricultural system is efficient, but only if you regard fossil fuel energy as free. In fact, it is a way to transform fossil fuel energy into food with a bit of help from sunlight, to the tune of 10 calories of fossil fuel energy being embodied in each calorie that is consumed as food.
>
> Their food inputs, such as high-fructose corn syrup, genetically modified potatoes, various soy-based fillers, factory-farmed beef, pork and chicken, and so forth, are derived from oil, two-thirds of which is imported, as well as fertilizer made from natural gas. They may be able to stay in business longer, supplying food-that-isn't-really-food, but eventually they will run out of inputs along with the rest of the supply chain. Before they do, they may for a time sell burgers that aren't really burgers, like the bread that wasn't really bread that the Soviet government distributed in Leningrad during the Nazi blockade. It was mostly sawdust, with a bit of rye flour added for flavor.

According to the Piedmont Environmental Council, the average distance food travels from the field to the dinner table is an appalling 1,500 miles. With practically every region within America capable of growing bountiful crops, there is no logical reason why we should continue to import food from such long distances. Such reliance only increases our chances of suffering a severe food crisis.

Utilizing Other Forms of Renewable Energy

In a food crisis the only way you might be able to feed yourself is to destroy a vital part of your whole and if this is done eventually the rest of you soon follows. I have to wonder if subconsciously that is what we are choosing to do right now. Are we so far in we cannot simply reverse or are we simply convinced we haven't the strength or knowledge to regroup and retreat?

It's easy to say or think that sustainable or renewable energy is our lasting savior to lead us out of this mess. But we don't appear to be heading that way fast enough. After steady and substantial growth in the industry from 2004 to 2007, renewable energy only experienced a 5% growth in new investments in 2008 at $155 billion. Undoubtedly, the financial crisis of the global economy didn't help spur significant business toward clean energy. Then oil prices dropped back down under $50 per barrel, and all of a sudden we forgot about the importance of renewable energy when our pocketbooks were only getting nibbles instead of huge chunks chewed out of them monthly.

According to BP (British Petroleum), renewable energy accounted for a paltry 1.5% of the world's energy supply in 2009. Denmark leads the way as 20% of its energy derives from wind and 11% in Spain. America did become the largest wind energy producing country in 2008, surpassing Germany as the world's leader. While Germany has more wind turbines, our stronger winds helped push us into the lead. Texas alone accounts for 25% of the wind energy in this country. But wind accounted for only 1.2% of America's total energy production. So, there is still a long, long way to go.

The main problem with wind and solar energies is that all of their main components (wind turbines, solar panels, batteries, inverters, etc.) are made using the same basic ingredient—oil. As long as manufacturers do not seek renewable alternatives to make these vital components of renewable energy systems, it is impossible for the prices to ever become affordable for most people in this country. There is huge potential in magnetic energy, as Nikola Tesla showed. He was able to generate light from a light bulb simply by creating a magnetic field, using no connecting wires or switches. Again, I'm no scientist, but surely other minds are pursuing the possibilities of getting energy from high-powered magnets.

As oil prices continue to climb, so too will the prices of these products. It is doubtful solar and wind are feasible alternatives for the average middle class family. That is unless one educates himself or herself on how to construct and install these energy systems. Educational courses, workshops, or seminars could be offered by local community colleges, universities, and other benevolent institutes. These would benefit individuals and families because they would be learning something essential to their survival, as well as the schools making a little income in exchange to help with teacher salaries, books, and other costs. Solar and wind still offer our best chance of supplying our homes and businesses with clean energy. When the President mentions "clean coal" I have to laugh as I think about my kid having a "clean" dirty diaper at the end of a day.

With the recent economic crumbling of our current fiat system, perhaps now is the best time to alter our viewpoint on money. This will in turn make us realize what is truly valuable and important at this moment, and for posterity's sake. Even if you have neither children nor grandchildren, surely you've realized you can't take your money with you once you're gone. Because no matter how much you have in the bank, none of us is getting out of this world alive. Perhaps the Cree Indian tribe had a better perspective on economics in an old proverb that states, "Only when the last tree has been cut, the last river destroyed, and the last fish caught will we realize we can't eat money."

My question to all parents is simple: "Would you rather your children and grandchildren live in larger houses, drive more luxurious cars, and eat heavily poisoned foods instead of having healthy air to breathe, adequate shelter, and toxic-free food and water?" Call me crazy, but I'll take what's behind door number two every day of the week.

Currently, commercial farming is no better than the timber industry, the coal mining industry, or the oil industry. We are every bit as much a part of the problem. Yet, because we are continuing a wholesome vocation, we do not think of ourselves as selfish or greedy. But we are if we continue to ignore our poisoning of the soil, water, and air. We are just as guilty as North American Coal, Halliburton, and DuPont if we continue to pretend our actions have no consequences. We are just as shortsighted as Monsanto if we continue to destroy the future rather than enhance it.

We must change, and that change must occur now. The move to us each farming less land will be in our very near future. The reasons we are operating 3,000+ acre farms is because of government subsidies, chemicals, and affordable fuel. We've fallen for the corporate scheme. We've become the rural version of Wal-Mart—more of an inferior product at a low cost. Somewhere along the line we stopped being farmers and started calling ourselves *producers*. How many true farmers are left among us? We must shed the factory mentality rooted in a love for money and replace it with a family mentality based on a love for our work and a love for Mother Nature.

As energy prices continue to rise at an unprecedented rate, we'll finally wake up from our corporate approach to agriculture. Smaller farming operations will mean more freedom, higher yields, less soil degradation, and less financial risk for us. Soon, very soon, I hope we completely remove the factory mentality from the farm. When we begin to look at ourselves as true stewards of the land instead of mere producers perhaps our path, our purpose will materialize to the point of undeniable recognition. If we immediately begin the transition of farming 6,000 acres rather than 10,000 or 2,500 acres instead of 5,000 or 500 acres instead of 2,000, then there will be no frantic rush to run across the fields with a 120-foot wide spray boom pumping toxic fumes and liquids into the environment. We will lose everything if we continue at our current pace. Yet if we change, we have everything to gain—a healthy life for all creatures and a brighter future for our children and their children.

The main challenge lies with the Baby Boomer farmers and the 45-55 age group of farmers. Their general mentality is, "I've done it this way all my life, so why change now?" Perhaps some can limp to the retirement line. Perhaps change is too difficult for them. I am not sure, but I have witnessed some change in their methods, my father included, as they slowly but surely acknowledge many of the problems caused by decades of commercial/chemical farming and the decadent lifestyle of the American dream.

Legalize Hemp? Shiver Me Timber

Let's begin with one of my favorite plants. We could start this evolution/revolution by legalizing hemp. It is one of the most diverse and useful plants known on this planet. Hemp still grows wild over much of the Midwest. Yet, since 1937 it has been drilled into our thick skulls how evil it is. Hemp and marijuana are sister plants. You can get high or stoned on marijuana. You can't on hemp. It would be like getting drunk on O'Douls (non-alcoholic) beer. Hemp has been used by ancient civilizations dating back to 8000 B.C. in Europe and Asia to make clothing, ropes, and other helpful products.

The illegalization of these two plants has nothing to do with hemp or marijuana being bad for you. It has everything to do with hemp being good for the farmer, the economy, and humanity as a whole and marijuana aiding one's mind in peering through the doors of perception. While I'm an advocate of legalizing all natural plants that offer us a peek into what truly lies beyond our current "normal" perception of reality, I realize and respect many are not comfortable with this. I could go on and on about pharmaceutical companies or our privatized prison system profiting from the illegalization of marijuana and hemp or the "War on Drugs" hoax wasting tax payers' money, or the success of other countries decriminalizing psychedelic plants and how they encourage mind expansion, but I will simply focus on the helpful benefits of the hemp plant in agriculture. The topic of the decriminalization of many plants such as marijuana, peyote, magic mushrooms, etc., can be explored in a number of other books, websites, and further sources.

What most people fail to realize is that hemp is practically the only plant you could use to build a house, build a car, fuel your car, make a little food, paper, plastics, and clothing from, and you'd never have to leave the continental United States for any of the production process. Yes, this is the big, bad plant our government continues to persuade us to think of as the evil of mankind.

Thankfully, someone in politics had the gall to try and do something about the ridiculous prohibition of hemp in this country. U.S. Representative Ron Paul from Texas proposed the Industrial Hemp Farming Act of 2005 to help get this wonderful herb back in agriculture production in America. And it went over like a fart during a church prayer.

Let's look at this logically. Whenever there is a ridiculous law in existence, we must examine who benefits financially from it. Follow the money. Which corporations would suffer greatly from the legalization or even the decriminalization of hemp?

Perhaps the timber industry. The very industry ridding this country of its oldest and most fantastic trees. How could these billion-dollar companies profit off a plant grown annually nationwide across millions of acres owned by individuals and not corporations or the government? They couldn't. Hemp plants can grow 20 feet high if given the proper space and time, providing excellent materials for building construction. So why do we continue to rape our national forests by cutting down trees that have stood for thousands of years (and help us breathe) to build homes and buildings when we could just as easily do the same thing with hemp? Hmm, let's think about this. Well, the timber industry contributed $3.4 million dollars to the Republicans in the 2000 elections, over $1 million of that going to George W. Bush and Dick Cheney. The timber industry has maintained a strong connection to the political scene to ensure its survival, buying off politicians, election after election, and destroying one of our most precious resources in the process.

Then there is the DuPont family. Fact is, DuPont along with the paper mill and timber industry did a hell of a number getting hemp to vanish from the scene. Yes sir. The year after the ridiculous Marijuana and Hemp Tax Act of 1937, DuPont patented nylon, a clever little fiber that does everything hemp once did. How blatantly obvious was the DuPont family's role in ridding this country of hemp? President Richard Nixon appointed Richard DuPont his drug czar in 1973. Richard DuPont was also the Vice President of DuPont and the great-grandson of Charles DuPont, founder of the company. DuPont simply created a billion-dollar industry by roasting the hemp and marijuana plant. How convenient that our "drug czar" enabled his family to build a hugely wealthy company by outlawing a precious resource. All the little plastic trinkets they contrive to make in unison with oil companies could be made with plastic hemp, which is a stronger and more viable material than petroleum plastics. DuPont's 1938 patent on the invention of nylon is more than coincidental—it occurred one year following the Marijuana and Hemp Tax Act. In 2008, DuPont's total revenue exceeded $30 billion and their profits totaled more than $2 billion. They are currently ranked 75th in the Fortune 500. Not bad for a company that got started making gunpowder. Most of their clever inventions between 1938 and 1970 (Nomex, Lycra, Orlon, Mylar, etc.) exist because nylon became the opportune man-made substitute for hemp.

Hemp would also help reduce the need for metals and other goods used to construct automobiles, tractors, airplanes, boats, and any other vessel of transportation. In 1941, Henry Ford produced his "Plastic Car", which was derived from the fibers of hemp and wheat straw combined with asbestos. We could substitute fiberglass for asbestos now. The body was lighter than steel and 10 times stronger. Videos can be seen on YouTube and other websites on the internet of Ford beating the fender with an axe and no dent is visible. The car also ran on hemp fuel. So why then did production of this car not take off in America? There was a little distraction called World War II, then it appears the idea vanished forever as hemp growing was deemed illegal.

By growing hemp, we could make so many useful products such as soaps, shampoos, and other cleaning products. By keeping large containers of hemp, lavender, or peppermint liquid soaps, we could mix in other essentials such as borax, washing soda, and baking soda to make any of the household cleaning products we need. Hemp and most of our other bi-products from our crops could be used in packaging, replacing plastic bags, bottles and other wasteful shipping products harmful to the environment.

The really ironic thing about the whole hemp issue is that it was against the law for farmers not to grow hemp in the 17th and 18th centuries. They were jailed in the colonies. Yet, with modern progress in the 20th and 21st centuries, it has now become a felony to let the plant grow. We even legalized hemp temporarily in 1942 to help produce sails and ropes for our Navy during WWII. From 1942-1946, farmers from Kentucky to Wisconsin raised 42,000 tons per year. Hemp farming is an answer to our economic problems. It is not a problem. We've been lied to for more than 50 years. It is high time the truth got out, and that we begin making changes immediately.

With Our Minds On Our Money

From the outside looking in, farming may appear to many to be like a luxury cruise. They see the big fancy tractors with auto steering and GPS, big fancy pickup trucks motoring up and down country roads, and large houses and barns. Yeah, it looks like a walk in the park. What they don't see is what goes on to make the payments on those tractors and high-priced equipment. Consider that in 1950, my grandfathers and great-grandfathers paid less than $5,000 for a tractor and pickup (combined), while receiving around 40 cents per pound for their cotton. Fuel was 27 cents per gallon and the minimum wage was 75 cents an hour. Fast forward to 2009 when I received a little over 60 cents per pound for my cotton, while paying more than $100,000 for a good *used* tractor and $40,000 for a new pickup. Fuel averaged $2.50 per gallon, and minimum wage was $7.25 an hour. If we both yielded a mere half a bale per acre, it is easy to figure my great-grandfather was much better off (factoring in the devaluation of the dollar and the consumer price index) with his 160 acres and $16,000 gross profit than I would be with 1,600 acres and a $240,000 gross profit. The input prices are out of control in agriculture. It doesn't matter how many bells and whistles John Deere puts on our air-conditioned machines when commodity prices have refused to climb at a comparable rate with the consumer price index over a 70-year time period.

Dad moved back to the farm in 1972, when farm diesel cost 14 cents per gallon, compared to $2.28 in 2009. He is now selling his cotton for roughly the same price 38 years later.

When I asked him about the lack of price progression over the years, he said this:

> We're more in a world market today. China has become more of a major player today. The cost of labor and production in America today can't compete with their production prices. Domestic sales have gone down drastically over the past 10 to 20 years. Once the product leaves our hands, the corporations mark it up. Everything we buy is priced by corporate America to make a profit. We don't have that luxury of dictating prices, because farmers won't stick together. You can't get farmers to agree on the same row pattern, much less agree to hold your products off the market. Cor-

porations like John Deere just mark their products up to reflect labor costs. We can't do that. We're at the mercy of the federal government to send us a subsidy payment to make up for our lack of parity.

Consider that in 2008-2009 a farmer received about $350 for a bale of cotton, which weighs just under 500 pounds. On average, one bale of cotton makes 215 pairs of blue jeans from a company like Levi Strauss. The average pair of Levis at Wal-Mart costs about $20 a pair, resulting in $4,300 income. I don't know anyone who can invest $350 in stocks, bonds, real estate, and turn a 1,200% increase overnight. Consider many blue jeans cost between $40-60, and that percentage doubles or triples.

The same concept goes for wheat. Consider a farmer received $5.50 for a bushel (60 pounds) of wheat in 2009. Mrs. Baird's Bread can produce 100 loaves of bread from one bushel of wheat. H-E-B, Albertson's, or Stop & Shop charge customers around $1.50 per loaf. Somewhere between the farmer's field and that grocery aisle, some $145 is pocketed on a bushel of wheat the farmer never sees, resulting in a 2,700% increase in the commodity value to the finished product. The same can be said about any and every fruit, vegetable, or other commodity crop. Even a head of lettuce is marked up about 1,000% from the farmer's cost. This huge price gap has left the farmer scrambling to farm more land in order to generate more product. Dad's generation of farmers have witnessed this as much as any other generation.

"We have to farm more acres to spread our costs out to be able to stay in business. You've got to have a minimal amount of acres just to cover your costs. You've got fixed costs, variable costs, equipment costs, and costs of living, so you have to have so many acres in order to survive," said Dad. "The average consumer's attitude has changed. We're another generation removed from the farm. They don't care where anything comes from. If it is cheaper, they'll buy it to give them more money to spend on cars, houses, or whatever they want."

Unfortunately, his evaluation is accurate. When I returned to the family farm, Dad was coming off a very good dryland cotton crop here in West Texas. My first task was to help him get caught up on bills. But as the stacks of astronomical debts towered over my immobile body, the cold truths and outright horrors were quick to permeate my unsuspecting mind. The horrors. My god, the horrors. I received a crash-course lesson in Finance 101, Psychology 202, Ag Economics 303, and What-The-Hell-Did-I-Get-Myself-Into? 404.

One check after another I signed, wondering if I'd ever see the light of day…or at least a net gain. Carpal tunnel soon started in my right hand. My throat tightened. Vision blurred. Sweat trickled from armpits to toes. Back muscles clung to the spine. Needless to say, it was an awfully humbling experience. At that moment it was abundantly clear to me that when the Federal Reserve was snuck in as law in 1913, the labor and freedoms of Americans and American farmers were sold down the river so that perpetual debt could float in as the true waterway of America's economy.

The main source of our financial struggles in American agriculture is the exact same source as it is for all American economic enterprises—the manipulative control of money by large corporations along with the Federal Reserve. The main idea behind modern survival is money. You must make more money than you spend in order to operate a business. And with today's expenses in comparison with today's commodity prices, that clear-cut task has become near heroic.

Where is our money going? Labor, fuel, pesticides, herbicides, tractor payments, implement payments, operating loans plus interest, and don't forget our precious taxes. We can't eliminate all of these, but we can minimize the costs of each. We get double-dipped with self-employment taxes: on top of our federal income tax rates, we also pay self-employment tax. In many years, this simply doubles the amount of tax money we pay the U.S. Treasury.

As I walk out across these dusty plains of West Texas, I am

constantly asking questions, seeking solutions to our economic problems. While there may still be more questions than answers and more problems than solutions in my mental quests, I am certain there are at least ten things we must do as farmers:

1. Boycott Monsanto and GMO crops!
2. Save our seed.
3. Rotate our crops.
4. Remove all funds from Wall Street and large banks.
5. Refuse to do business with any monopolistic businesses.
6. Strive for self-sufficiency in everything.
7. Get smaller.
8. Get in tune with Mother Nature.
9. Stop looking to chemicals as the solution to all our problems.
10. Help one another.

Sooner rather than later we'll realize paper money is more useless than toilet paper, because it certainly won't keep us clean. Nor will it keep us warm, nor prevent us from starving. One of the most brilliant essays I've read on fiat money is by Johnny Silver Bear. The article is on his website (silverbearcafe.com/private/06.09/natureofmoney.html) and explains much of the history of paper money, gold, and silver in America.

Our attitude to money must change if we are going to change anything. One of my fellow young farmers and neighbors informed me he had Texas A&M University conduct a 10-year study for his farm, and they concluded he would "make more money" by planting cotton every year rather than any other crop. My first reaction was, "Please don't tell me you paid them for this information." My second reaction was, "Did they happen to recommend Monsanto's most expensive seed?" If making the most money over a decade is our top priority as young farmers then we are in big trouble. Maximizing profits will do us no good when our soil is depleted of all life, our food devoid of any nourishment, our bodies exhausted, and our minds spent. Perhaps we can use all that cash money we made as tissues to wipe away our tears.

Bartering and Alternative Currencies

Confusion sets in. Emotions swing wildly like drunken young men desperately disguising insecurity. All because Love has left the party. Life without Love is meaningless. Yet, as fast as Love left the party, Money rushed in to take its place. Freedom is forgotten and forgery takes its place—forgery of power and control, which gives birth to manipulation, lies, and persuasion.

Just look at the New World Order (or Trilateral Commission or whatever the Elite of Wealthy and Greedy are calling themselves these days) and all the immoral attitudes of those who connived its meaning and purpose. While the Bilderberg Group and the Council on Foreign Relations plot and scheme for world dominance, the rest of us can choose to live in reality. What we need are small communities based on sustainable living with an economy focused on locally produced goods, with particular attention paid to food and seed supplies. Each region would differ in what those goods and foods would be, but we must get back some of our manufacturing in this country if we are going to function with any efficiency. That is one of our greatest challenges at a time when, for example, almost all our textile mills have been relocated to Mexico or Asia.

Here is an eye-opener. From 1776 to 1912 (136 years) the value of the American dollar increased by 11% in relation to the consumer price index. After the creation of the Federal Reserve in 1913 to the present (97 years), the American dollar has decreased in value by 97%.[4] Let that marinate for a spell. It takes 95% more money now than it did in the early 1900s to buy food,

---

4. "Why the U.S. Dollar Constantly Loses Value", theTrumpet.com, http://www.thetrumpet.com/index.php?q=3037.1530.0.0, November 24, 2006.

fuel, clothing, and other raw materials. So, can anyone tell me how the Federal Reserve has helped America? As this book is being written, U.S. Representative Ron Paul and others are attempting to audit the Federal Reserve. Thus far, those efforts have failed.

Instead of everything revolving around the American dollar, the euro or an ounce of gold, why not base a barter system on what is of real value—food. Whether it be a bushel of wheat or corn or apples or whatever staple crop is of great significance to your area, all things can stem from that. Wheat is a crop that can be grown practically anywhere in America, so initially this might work well for most areas. Common-grown fruits, nuts, or vegetables might provide a more long-term fix, as no plow, planter, or large tractor is needed to plant them. We can certainly minimize fiat money's overwhelming power and persuasion in our daily lives.

Silver would be a more acceptable measuring stick than gold. If gold is to boom toward $5,000 an ounce like some are predicting, only a small minority of people will be able to own any gold, unless they started purchasing it before 2008. Sure, hindsight is nice, since gold was around the $275 an ounce area as recently as 2003, but let's not kick ourselves, shall we? But it's really not necessary to even involve the precious metals if you reside in a community or area where all you really need is food, water, and shelter.

Another option we have regarding money is an alternative currency adaptive to each specific region. Don't scoff. It's already working in southern Massachusetts with their "BerkShares" paper money. Five local banks have printed more than 2 million paper notes with roughly around 200,000 in circulation. In Ithaca, New York, they've adopted a currency dubbed Ithaca Hours, which is accepted by city transportation. A local currency is a perfect way to encourage local commerce within the community rather than people traveling outside of the community or importing goods from another country. It also promotes wealth amongst the people rather than sending it to someone you'll never meet or know. If we don't support one another in as many ways and means as possible, slowly but surely we'll see more people around us suffer during a Greater Depression in the years to come.

Each community or city could determine its own type of currency and its value. Perhaps a unit could equate to one hour of minimum-wage labor, a sack of flour, a loaf of bread, a bottle of beer or whatever (okay, probably not a good idea to base a currency on alcohol!). This type of action would require effective leadership and the creation of a sincere bond within the community suggesting strength and unity. Rather than buying all our goods online or over the phone, we could have actual face-to-face encounters with our fellow people.

All this talk about the absence of real money may sound incredibly off the charts, but talk to anyone who lived through the Great Depression in the 1930s. Nobody had any money in rural areas. They had chickens, hogs, cows, horses, and gardens. Their currency was manual labor. And guess what? They made it work. How? Because there was no other choice.

Instead of towns and cities dominated by Wal-Marts, retail malls, (corporate chain) Chili's Restaurants and their colossal parking lots, we would have small shops and homes selling homemade soaps, candles, leather, tools, and locally grown fuel, food, and clothing that never had to travel more than 100 miles. Tradesmen/women such as welders, blacksmiths, carpenters, seamstresses, healers, and mechanics could barter their services for other goods and services with other local citizens. Once a month there could be a trade-day with neighboring communities that may specialize in other crops or goods. Currencies, silver, or gold would only be necessary for goods and services needed from outside the community. It is really up to us what is or isn't developed. Everything may not run smoothly at first, but if we continue to work together we will find the best system for our particular situation related to geography, local vegetation, and resources. As long as we are focused on sustainability, independence, and preserving our resources, not only will our communities prosper, but posterity will thrive due to our inspired hard work and innovative diligence. We could combine the romantic heritage of "the old West" pioneer towns with a keen sense of community at the heart of the spiritual-awakening version of Manifest Destiny.

Some of you are wondering, "Wait a minute. How is anyone going to get rich?" Maybe none of us will. But we will be rich in resources, rich in health, rich in strength, and rich in a love for all things of true significance. We would eliminate the previous standard of an upper, middle, and lower class system. We would become a species unified in purpose, a real community instead of a place littered with individuals. Even if one doesn't agree completely with Darwin's theory of evolution, you still must agree with his statement that, "It is not the strongest of the species that survives, nor the most intelligent that survives. It is the one that is the most adaptable to change." This applies more to our species than any other at this point in history. If we continue to live as we always have, then very little hope of peace exists. Yet, if we labor together like a colony of bees or ants or other successful, hard-working species, we will succeed in overcoming these immediate hardships and translate them into a prosperous means of Living.

Getting and Staying Out of Debt

Native Americans noticed that the white man's obsession with gold made him crazy, causing him to commit crimes he would not otherwise have done. And we haven't stopped yet. Norm Franz wrote in *Money and Wealth* that "Gold is the money of kings; silver is the money of gentlemen; barter is the money of peasants; but debt is the money of slaves." Staying out of debt in the future will be a necessity. Not exactly a lifestyle to which farmers are accustomed, but as this economic crisis furthers, our banks will not lend as much as is needed to pay off current debts. We will all have to adapt to a new philosophy of living off what we make rather than what we can borrow on credit. Debt enslaves us.

Getting and staying out of debt will be a must for us to survive and live freely in the immediate future. Most farmers, who do not have oil wells or wind turbines to support their farming habit, will find things difficult if they don't change their approach. Those who have relied on oil well production for most of their lives will be lost once the pump jacks stop pumping. It will be impossible to continue by following the current trend. Imagine running a 5,000 acre farm as oil rockets over $250 per barrel. Imagine purchasing tractors that cost over $200,000 and harvesting equipment over $300,000 per machine. How does one finance those payments? A second and third mortgage? Why risk your home and land to continue a lifestyle dying like the dinosaurs? Farming less land with less equipment is the only solution. Some farmers remember paying 21% interest rates in the late 1970s and early 1980s. If that happens again, we are toast, unless we begin necessary changes now. Bankers know this to be true, as do most experienced farmers. And this could happen in the very near future with our economy still in Code Egg Shell.

Debt is a prison. Despite the absence of barbed wire fences and caged cells, it is nothing more than financial enslavement preventing us from living life to the fullest. How will banks pay for the drastic increase in FDIC memberships and insurance? Higher interest rates or more fees for things which were once free. I highly support banking with a locally owned bank rather than a national chain. The local bankers need our support. Why give more money to the big boys run by the elite and Wall Street? Your local banker will usually keep you from making huge financial mistakes as opposed to "banksters" linked to a large corporation. Trillions of dollars were needed to keep the big banks from failing when they were the very ones who failed us by corrupting the entire system and robbing hard-working people of their life savings.

In 2008, the average American owned five credit cards. This is the greatest economic trap of all—living on debt. We must realize that hard work is our only true currency. Not paper money. A real "economist" could show you hundreds and hundreds of pages of literature informing you of the perverse history of money in this country, the lies, the manipulations of currency, and the fraud of paper money. I only know enough to say that we've been getting used and manipulated for a very long time. The research is up to you. (Please check the Resources at the end of this chapter.)

In the near future, bartering will be the greatest friend for most of us, as we are the peasants of this world. The kings and queens will continue to own gold, while silver will be our greatest purchasing ally. If I have any advice at all as far as investing goes, I would tell anyone to get out of the stock market or anything controlled by Wall Street. While gold and silver are shamelessly manipulated along with all other commodities, no matter how much pressure is applied, all corks will eventually resurface. Gold and silver are the only true currencies in this country. Someday, we will all know this to be true.

The Changing Role of Government

One fact overwhelming us election after election in these United States is that our government no longer exists to protect the freedoms and liberties of "We the people". On the contrary, each year, little by little, more freedoms and liberties are stripped away from us, leaving us more vulnerable and less free. Each such law is preceded by some ridiculous crime or mistake committed by one individual or group, so lawmakers rush a bill to committee, punishing the entire nation like an elementary principal does an entire school for one student's disruption.

With each election come more empty promises. The best liars win. What's even crazier, we still believe the two parties represent two entirely different sets of principles. Republicans are the conservatives. Democrats are the liberals. It's ridiculous for this country to remain divided by two political parties who have nothing but their own personal agendas to pursue rather than the

American people's liberty. Grandstanding on certain issues makes great sound bites on the local news, but it is what happens behind closed doors that counts. Why waste our loyalty on either party, when they continue to spearhead political Ponzi schemes? We've got to wake from this zombie-like trance.

Incorrigibly, we are lead to believe that new bills and laws are passed for our own safety and our own freedom while our freedoms are actually stripped away. We continue to exchange liberty for security. As our current system of sociality melts, so too will the power of our federal government. Municipalities, counties, and even states (Michigan, Arizona, and California leading the way) will go broke. If President Obama and his administration "transfer" money from hard-working middle and lower class people to international banking cartels, the American economy will collapse sooner rather than later.

The Wall Street crash in September 2008 was nothing more than a highway robbery of America's retirement prospects. As Baby Boomers neared the age of a much-deserved break from the working world, the banking industry pulled the proverbial rug from underneath them. All little parties must end, and the lights were shut off with a room full of partygoers looking desperately for their car keys and coats only to discover that those too had been stolen.

The battle between the "banksters" and the rest of us has been ongoing since the 1830s and perhaps even goes back to when this country was gaining its independence. There were always the fat cats sitting patiently in the shadows, waiting for the right moment to take over as much of the world's wealth as possible. It has always been about money in this country. Always.

Andrew Jackson summed up the central banking system (which is now our Federal Reserve) best when he said:

> Gentlemen, I have had men watching you for a long time
> and I am convinced that you have used the funds of the
> bank to speculate in the breadstuffs of the country. When

you won, you divided the profits amongst you, and when you lost, you charged it to the bank. You tell me that if I take the deposits from the bank and annul its charter, I shall ruin ten thousand families. That may be true, gentlemen, but that is your sin! Should I let you go on, you will ruin fifty thousand families, and that would be my sin! You are a den of vipers and thieves.[5]

"Vipers and thieves" is putting it politely. If all our presidents had the courage of Andrew Jackson, our country would've never been stolen from us and handed over to the "banksters". As long as our government continues to employ people like Hank Paulson and Tim Geithner (from Goldman Sachs) as the head honchos of our Treasury Department, we haven't a prayer. We must stop supporting the fat cats of banking. Yes, the Rockefellers, Rothschilds, Morgans, their puppets, and whoever else are sitting in the shadows these days. We must restructure our banking and money system immediately to prevent further mayhem and destruction passing to the rest of humanity.

Unfortunately, our government continues to reward incompetence and corruption with trillion-dollar bailouts. All the while, they expect us to batten down the hatches and be good little Americans, not ask questions, and continue to bend over with a smile, saying, "Thank you sir, may I have another?" The current system has been compromised time and again, proving it is broken beyond repair. This system has been too perverse for too long. The foundation upon which our Constitution was drawn is a threat to the elite. We've been taught socialism, fascism, and communism to be perverse forms of government, but let's not forget the warning from our forefathers regarding the

---

5. Stan V. Hinkles, *Andrew Jackson and the Bank of the United States: An Interesting Bit of History Concerning "Old Hickory"*, 1928 (As obtained from original minutes of the Philadelphia committee of citizens sent to meet with President Jackson, February 1834, by Stan V. Hinkiles Sr.).

potential evils of democracy: Thomas Jefferson once said, "Democracy is nothing more than mob rule, where 51% of the people may take away the rights of the other 49." Benjamin Franklin gave us a fitting metaphor of democracy when he said, "Democracy is two wolves and a lamb voting on what to have for lunch. Liberty is a well-armed lamb contesting the vote." What form of government do we have today? Where has the Republic fled?

A return to a Republic makes more sense for future purposes. Each state should retain and exercise its sovereign powers. This will empower us to exercise our Constitutional freedoms. The abolition of slavery in this country was celebrated worldwide more than 140 years ago, yet we've come full circle without even realizing or accepting it. Let us proclaim emancipation once more.

A few members of our government are taking active roles in disbanding our current money system. In February of 2010, South Carolina Rep. Mike Pitts introduced legislation that would mandate gold and silver to replace the federal currency as legal tender. One month later, Idaho's House State Affairs Committee voted in favor of HB 633. That bill would allow citizens of Idaho to pay their taxes with an official state silver medallion. Both cases cite fears of devaluation of the American dollar due to the government's reckless spending.

The Federal Reserve should be disbanded and tossed aside with yesterday's garbage. Since its inception in 1913 this privately owned bank has done nothing but rob from the poor and middle classes and give more to the rich. It is the robber holding the gun, only it cowards behind the power of our own government. It is not government. It is not even federal. It is a privately owned bank run by the richest of the rich. So long as the Federal Reserve remains the head of our financial system, we have no hope of owning a real or trusted currency in this country.

Why President Woodrow Wilson signed the Federal Reserve Act in 1913 is beyond me. Just a few short years later, in 1916, President Wilson obviously regretted it himself, writing:

A great industrial nation is controlled by its system of credit. Our system of credit is concentrated. The growth of the nation, therefore, and all our activities are in the hands of a few men. We have come to be one of the worst ruled, one of the most completely controlled and dominated governments in the civilized world. No longer a government by free opinion, no longer a government by conviction and the vote of the majority, but a government by the opinion and duress of a small group of dominant men.[6]

Yet still to this day, some 94 years later, not one U.S. President or Congress has had enough courage to rid this country of its greatest money-leach sucking Americans dry of all monetary fluids until they wither like a stack of wrinkled corpses.

As we continue blinded down this path of indignity, surely we'll soon stop and ask ourselves, "What is worth saving?" It is obvious our government considers the bankers and money launderers top priority in this country. Perhaps I should say it is the bankers who give themselves and the money launderers top billing, since they are the ones who really run this country anyhow. As these "banksters" flex their iniquitous muscles, squeezing dry the nest eggs of hard-working people and suffocating the American dream, I've realized their persistent theme: we don't matter. Not to them. "Useless eaters" was the term used by Kissinger. "We the people" are now regarded as bottom feeders no longer willing to fuel the excess of consumerism.

As a trillion dollars is used over and over again as the American government's version of the quicker-picker-upper, we will all soon remember just how frail and useless a wet paper towel becomes once a spill dries and hardens—it will remain and thicken like morning-after dumplings on a forgotten stove. And who will then be called upon with mops, sponges, and hellfire elbow grease? The

---

6. Woodrow Wilson, *The New Freedom: A Call for the Emancipation of the Generous Energies of a People* (New York and Garden City, Doubleday, Page & Company, 1913).

bottom feeders, that's who. Instead it is time for us to formulate our own plans, build a new system, and derail our minds from the track leading to inevitable and continuous collision of a broken system run by suited executives.

We spend most of our adult lives making money to pay for things we don't really need. Often, we simply get in over our financial heads and are forced to become slaves to debt, mortgages, car payments, college loans, farm loans, or other pieces of paper telling us we must slug away our energies for the rest of our days as mortal creatures. Yet all of this is really a scam. Paper money is an illusion made with woven pieces of plant flesh boasting Masonic symbols and dead white presidents of the land.

Nothing Left to Lose

As several of my friends and I were about to graduate from college over a decade ago, we nervously shuffled to the edge of the cliff, wondering if we could make the leap into the next stage of our lives. Would we too fall for the oldest trick in the book? A lifetime of labor under the scorching sun for financial gain?

One late night I posed the question: "Why don't we all just learn to do different things and have our own town? We need houses, right? Well, one of us goes into construction. We need cars? One of us becomes a mechanic. We need food. I'm the farmer. We'll need a doctor, too." And so on, and so forth.

It was the perfect plan. Everyone agreed, opened another beer, laughed, and...I guess forgot all about it. I never did forget that epiphany. Today I feel as if the times are demanding very much that model of communal living. The one we long ago accepted has worn itself thin. It is time to try something else.

If any group of young people was preparing to embark upon the perpetual voyage of adulthood, I would encourage them to explore such methods. My advice would be to surround yourself with love, family, friends, music, laughter, hard work, goals, intelligence, enlightenment, and a keen sense of survival. Do not take the current trend of modern living as the norm or accept it as the only way to experience day and night on this glorious planet.

Credit cards, mortgages, college courses, corporate employment, slave wages—those things are not meant for all of us. Six billion people are not wired exactly the same. Why pretend like they are? Why should we settle for some out-of-date, feedlot cattle-like form of life? Let us roam the prairie. Break free from such prisons. Create our own world. Live our own lives.

Even governments have no fool-proof guarantee against their own bankruptcy or financial ruin with large debt. California and Arizona are perfect examples of states that have mismanaged tax dollars. In September of 2009, Arizona Governor Jan Brewer signed a bill to approve the sale of the state capitol building (along with 32 other state properties) to help pay a historic $3 billion deficit. Four months later (January 2010), the State of Arizona officially sold its capitol and 13 other state facilities for a grand total of $735.4 million, which allowed the state enough money to operate until the end of the fiscal year.[7] The economic ruin and unemployment rate (over 40%) of Detroit could be the tragic example of what many American cities could undergo if finances are continually mismanaged by our elected officials. In January of 2010, Colorado Springs, Colorado, city officials were forced to make drastic cutbacks in spending, as citizens refused to vote for large tax increases. Colorado Springs cut off one-third of its street lights, laid off many firefighters, policeman and employees, and severely cut back on watering and maintenance of public parks.[8] Will life become less comfortable if we force our local governments to cut back on spending? Yes. Will it be necessary for things to stay afloat

---

7. Mary Jo Pitzl, "State gets $735 Million in Sale-leaseback Deal", *The Arizona Republic* (January 14, 2010).

8. Michael Booth, "Colorado Springs Cuts into Services Considered Basic by Many", *The Denver Post*, http://www.denverpost.com/news/ci_14303473 January 31, 2010.

if we reach this point? Yes. The painful reality is that digging our-selves out of colossal debt requires massive sacrifices.

Cities, schools, and counties propose multi-million dollar bond elections to construct or renovate over-the-top projects. Voters go to the polls, checking box after box, without realizing the consequences of drastic property tax increases needed to pay for such projects. The vast majority of Americans do not own their own homes, let alone land. Millions of Americans have no idea what property taxes even mean, much less cost. Farmers own large areas of land, and in turn we pay large amounts of property taxes. One of my fellow farmer friends suggested to me that the old laws of a republic should still be in effect where only property owners have the right to vote on such issues. That strip-ping-way of a basic freedom for many is drastic, but we must be conscious of what we are voting on and how if affects property taxes paid by small businesses and individuals on a fixed income.

The emergence of the Tea Party, an anti-tax group organizing pro-tests across the U.S., was initially encouraging, but the group appears to have been hijacked by the Republican Party and Fox News. The Tea Party has focused its energies on attacks on the Democratic Party alone, rather than the entire political system. We need an organized movement with intelligent policies and brave leaders not easily per-suaded or tainted by the current two parties. Excessive taxation will become more of an issue, but to remain effective in challenging this, the Tea Party must remain focused, ensuring their candidates are not merely hitching their wagon to please the crowds.

Jobs are hard to come by in this economic meltdown, as well. In November 2009, 125 metropolitan areas reported jobless rates higher than 10%.[9] As the farm and farmer continue to vanish, governments fail, and metropolitan unemployment rises, where will we turn for productive labor? What will the solution be once we pass the point of no return?

---

9. United States Department of Labor, Bureau of Labor Statistics, http://www.bls.gov/news.release/metro.nr0.htm.

Looking back over the past 20 years or so, the concept of freedom has been marketed and sold like the latest and best laundry detergent. While the concept of freedom is pushed our way, the reality is that more of our freedoms are being taken away. Slowly but surely, we're marching silently behind barbed-wire fences too high to climb. Before long, we'll find ourselves locked inside a room with nothing but the glow of a conveniently placed television and the sound of static to comfort us at night.

We the people must be very careful what we accept and tolerate from our government. We've been fooled into thinking the masses have no voice, no persuasion in the making of laws that affect our daily lives. The truth is that we are much more powerful than that. And if our elected officials want to come after our silver or our gold, then it will be time to serve them their walking papers. Let us not forget President Franklin D. Roosevelt executing Presidential Executive Order 6102, which demanded the confiscation of Americans' gold. This became known as the Gold Confiscation Act of April 5, 1933. How many wealthy bankers or high-rollers do you think turned in their gold? And this confiscation was executed so calmly and coolly, with most people still fooled with ideas of patriotism. You were doing it "for your country".

The truth is, it was done to make the rich richer. And they are doing it again. This time, they'll take everything, and fulfill the prophecy of President Thomas Jefferson, who said:

> I believe that banking institutions are more dangerous to our liberties than standing armies. If the American people ever allow private banks to control the issue of their currency, first by inflation, then by deflation, the banks and corporations that will grow up around [the banks] will deprive the people of all property until their children wake-up homeless on the continent their fathers conquered. The issuing power should be taken from the banks and restored to the people, to whom it properly belongs.

Bothered by the stripping away of our rights and the chiseling away of our Constitution, the core issue of freedom pushed itself to the front chamber of my skull. What is freedom? How would I explain it to a child? Wrestling with the literal meaning, I allowed myself to free my mind to explain it to the rest of me. Freedom is the ability to fall into the abyss that is your true self. In that fall you find every last admirable and pathetic quality of your fiber. At one point, you frantically search for the bottom. Full of fear you desperately try to grab hold of the sides, clawing and scratching. Overcoming that fear, you realize there is no bottom, no sides, no top—only the fall. Once that idea is embraced, the fall transforms into a beautiful and graceful flight. That flight is freedom.

Without the flight there is no progression. Without the flight, we're all just prisoners held captive by our own fears—never becoming who we're supposed to be, never accomplishing what we should to evolve. If you are utterly confused or frustrated at this point, that is good. Confusion is the step just before enlightenment. Life is often not a matter of understanding the reason for some things, but rather realizing the importance of all things.

Resources

BOOKS
Blackout by Richard Heinberg
Confessions of an Economic Hit Man by John Perkins
Confronting Collapse by Michael Ruppert
Crossing the Rubicon by Michael Ruppert
Desert Solitaire by Edward Abbey
Peak Everything by Richard Heinberg
The Coming Battle by M.W. Walbert
The Emperor Wears No Clothes by Jack Herer
The Informant: A True Story by Kurt Eichenwald
The Fed and the Farmer by Edward Kennedy

The Outlaw Handbook by Claire Wolfe
Twilight in the Desert by Matthew Simmons
Unforgiven by Charles Walters
Walden and "Civil Disobedience" by Henry David Thoreau
Web of Debt by Ellen Hodges Brown

WEBSITES
derrybrownfield.com
dieoff.org
fromthewilderness.com
hubbertpeak.com
lemetropolecafe.com
mikeruppert.blogspot.com
oathkeepers.org
oilcrisis.com
oilrelease.com
peakoil.net
postcarbon.org
richardheinberg.com
silverbearcafe.com
theoildrum.com
votehemp.com

VIDEOS
A Crude Awakening
America: From Freedom to Fascism
Capitalism: A Love Story
Collapse
Crude
The Informant!
Life and Debt

Chapter 6

YIN AND YANG, TIT FOR TAT, EGGS OVER EASY
Enlightenment

> *It is not hard to find the truth.*
> *What is hard is to not run away from it*
> *once you've found it.*
> **ALEXANDER JABLOKOV**

> *Knowing others is wisdom;*
> *knowing the self is enlightenment.*
> *Mastering others requires force;*
> *mastering the self needs strength.*
> **LAO TZU**

New Laws Threaten Farmers

Whether it is our health industry or agriculture, interference from government agencies and dominant corporations forces us into one way of thinking or doing. One of our main problems is an excessive amount of unnecessary laws benefitting the big boys. Each year Congress allows corporations and lobbyists to write new laws or amend old laws, all of which seem to restrict our freedoms as individual citizens while empowering monopoly-like control by large corporations. With the exception of the original Constitution and amendments securing the freedoms to "we the people" and criminalizing those who invoke harm against us, most laws are merely to test the limits of our intention, purpose, or ability.

We adhere to so many laws of scientific, criminal, and social origin not knowing why. Because we have to? Are we mere infants? Because we think there's no alternative? Because some group or individual motivated by selfish desires has the power to press in our skulls the message that no other means may be deemed possible? I don't get it.

How may we progress if we allow ourselves to be controlled by such set standards and limitations? It seems to me the true leaders and innovators in the hidden pages of history are those who broke established barriers, laws, and previously accepted attitudes. These people are the true and righteous pioneers and history makers/changers of our world. Where the heart, mind, and soul are involved, how dare any book or any other man dictate what we can or cannot accomplish?

As our minds evolve, so too shall the laws. What was once thought unwavering can and will be waived with the passing of a thought willing itself into action. Let us not completely accept limitations of the first three dimensions until we have looked under every last stone of the fourth. Even if the rest of humanity will not accept these mental revolutions, let us write them in our own hearts, minds, and souls. This is where the real story is told.

On July 30, 2009, the House passed HR 2749, or the Food Safety Enhancement Act of 2009. The purpose of this bill is to improve the safety of food, drugs, devices, and cosmetics in the global market, and for other purposes.[1] While this bill includes needed legislation such as the "country of origin labeling" (COOL), it also places small farms and local facilities producing for local markets under the same regulations and facing the same potential fines as Tyson Foods, Del Monte, Frito Lay, and other multi-million dollar food factory corporations. HR 2749 is now awaiting approval by the U.S. Senate.

While I am writing this book, Bill S. 510 (formerly known as HR 875) is officially in committee in Congress. Bill S. 510, or the FDA Food Safety Modernization Act, was introduced to protect the public health by preventing food-borne illness, ensuring the safety of food, improving research on contaminants leading to

---

1. http://www.govtrack.us/congress/billtext.xpd?bill=h111-759.

food-borne illness, and improving security of food from intentional contamination, and for other purposes.[2] Sounds harmless enough, but the bill offers the possibility of million dollar fines to small farms too. They use terms like "food establishment" which not only includes factory farms and slaughterhouses but private and individual gardens, as well. This bill uses one giant brush to paint all food producers—whether private or corporate—with the same stroke.

The bill allows the administrator (FDA) to "detain and seize any food regulated under this Act that the Administrator has reason to believe is unsafe, is adulterated or misbranded, or otherwise fails to meet the requirements of the food safety law". The seizure of this food may not exceed 30 days, but by that point the produce becomes worthless. In civic court, an individual or company may receive serious fines under this law. Section 405 states, "Any person that commits an act that violates the food safety law (including a regulation promulgated or order issued under the food safety law) may be assessed a civil penalty by the Administrator of not more than $1,000,000 for each such act." Perhaps Tyson Foods Inc., ADM, or Cargill can pay one million dollar fines without blinking an eye, but imagine if you are an organic farmer with a 100-acre farm simply trying to sell a few tomatoes and peppers at a local farmer's market. The perimeters must be more clearly defined so that each fine fits the crime. A farmer selling 100 tomatoes should not be fined the same amount as a corporation packaging millions of pounds of beef each year.

The concept of this law is necessary, but fair punishment must be stipulated so it does not apply the same penalties on a family farm making a few thousand dollars compared to Tyson Foods, a billion-dollar company. A fine should equal that of the farm or corporation's annual income, so farmers are not bankrupted by a single mishap. Will the FDA truly target billion-dollar corporations contributing large sums of money to key political cam-

---

2. http://www.govtrack.us/congress/billtext.xpd?bill=h111-875.

paigns or simply use this law to challenge some defenseless small-scale farmer as an example to make us believe that they are looking after our best interests? These corporations operate factory farms where diseases and other contaminations are more likely to occur. Enforcement of this law on any small family farm ruins that respective business for good. Without proper boundaries in place, this bill could prove ruinous to many food growers. This puts the power of "search and seizure" into the FDA's hands, allowing them to enter any farmer's field or private property at any time for inspections, violating our constitutional rights.

Congress has also considered the necessary funds (around $300 million) to implement the NAIS (National Animal Identification System), which is a system requiring all livestock, including cows, pigs, chickens, goats, sheep, etc., to be implanted with a microchip to track its origin and movement. The NAIS would cost small farmers and ranchers more than seven dollars per animal to tag each creature, while large confined animal feeding operations (CATOs) would average just over two dollars per animal. This system also requires not only factory farms but all farmers and ranchers to pay for the implementation of this program for their animals. Proper documentation and records are required for the monitoring and movement of all animals from birth to slaughter.

A similar system was implemented in Australia in 2004 called the National Livestock Identification System (NLIS). Most reports I've read on this system concluded that it proved costly and ineffective. Tracking diseased animals to their original location is the main objective, but it is simply more government control imposed upon the freedoms of farmers, ranchers, and other independent families. These laws must specify factory farms and large corporations in order to limit the power of government officials and prevent them from raiding anyone's farm at any given time. Again, it is the factory farms or large corporations this law should be intended for since they move thousands of animals on a weekly basis to and from food establishments all across the world. Private farmers and ranchers should not have to be punished for the crimes of these corporations.

Organizations such as the Farm and Ranch Freedom Alliance in Texas have chosen to fight the NAIS, protecting the rights of farmers. The USDA announced earlier in 2010 it was dropping the NAIS, which was a huge victory for farmers and ranchers. However, the USDA also said it was refocusing on a "new flexible framework" involving interstate commerce of animals. We must continue to be vigilant with these issues. The very idea that these types of laws are even being considered is not only a threat to agriculture and farmers, but also a threat to our very basic freedoms as Americans to grow our own food, to dare to be independent from corporate America.

Localized action by communities, regions, and even countries provide hope that we may unite as one and stand up against invasions of our freedoms and health. As early as 2004, areas such as Mendacino County, California, began taking a stand against GMOs. Mendocino County voted and passed Measure H, which bans cultivating, propagating, raising or growing any type of genetically modified organism. The new law was enforced by the County Extension Agent, and if anyone was caught growing GMO crops, the crops were destroyed and they were subject to fines. This was the first legislation passed in the United States banning GMOs altogether. Other California counties followed their lead over the next few years including Santa Cruz, Marin, and Trinity. Delaware and Hawaii also passed legislation banning GMOs. Across the world, about 35 countries have some form of bans on GMO importation and/or planting. These countries include China, Japan, Spain, Italy, Austria, Norway, Germany, Thailand, Algeria, Egypt, and the Philippines.

We must remain vigilant as legislation is largely influenced by lobbyists of multi-billion dollar corporate giants and billion-dollar commodity crop markets. Farmers put their livelihoods in the hands of their own lobbyist groups, who do their best to look after the farmers' interests. Cotton farmers have the National Cotton Council. Wheat farmers have Wheat Government Relations. Soybean farmers have the American Soybean Association.

Corn growers have the National Corn Growers Association. Not to mention countless other crops with their own national, state, and local organizations, boards, and committees working in favor of their respective industry. But who is working for the betterment of agriculture as a whole? Each organization pushes for legislation in the next farm bill or crop insurance plan to benefit their respective crop. Why is there no legislation providing incentives for crop rotation or planting multiple crops on every farm each season?

Currently farmers are essentially penalized if they farm more than one crop at a time per field, as crop insurance and the USDA require more fees per each entity of crop grown on a particular field. For instance, if a farmer wants a healthy crop rotation of three crops on a leased field, an additional $1,200 is needed to insure the other two crops. (Each crop requires each entity, the farmer and landlord, to pay $300 per crop per field in order to have protection against drought, hail, or other destructive acts of Mother Nature.) Crop insurance rates also favor the one staple crop in each particular farming area, discouraging a farmer from diversity. Crop disaster payments in times of extreme drought or flooding also do not compensate farmers with alternative crop production. To encourage healthy crop rotations in commercial agriculture, our Farm Bills must provide favorable legislation for the farmer to do so. Punishing us with more unnecessary fees will certainly not provide such encouragement. If we were to receive a fair and balanced parity price for our crops, all these subsidized forms of government intervention would not be necessary anyway for farmers to make things work financially.

Again, my granddad, at 86 years old, provided honest observations from an old farmer who has seen farming progress from a mule and a plow to 400 horsepower tractors:

> A big problem has been that the people we have in political office do not know what they are talking about. None of them are connected to the farm anymore. The main thing

that will help the farmer is price. The return on our money has gone down, down, down. Why is the farmer the only one who has to give in order to help the consumer? Everything else is higher, except agriculture products. This is what's killing the farmer. Somebody is making a lot of money that way, and it's not hard to figure out who it is. We need to get rid of the middlemen, and we need farmers helping to design legislation and the Farm Bill.

Parity Not Charity

Whatever happened to the "Parity not charity!" battle cry? It's as ancient as the "Make love not war" and "Give peace a chance" slogans filed away in the dusty room of past revolutions cut short. Parity is defined as "the equivalence of a commodity price expressed in one currency to its price in another; equality of purchasing power established by law by different kinds of money at a given ratio". In short, we should be getting a value equivalent to the value of what our crops are worth on the open market once they go into making a shirt, blue jeans, box of cereal, or other goods, when in reality we are getting about 50% of that value or parity.

Farmers received parity from 1909 to 1914 and thrived economically. The Federal Reserve's power soon came into government play, and parity slowly faded away. Part of the New Deal during President Franklin Roosevelt's administration in 1933 included the Agriculture Adjustment Act of 1933, requiring farmers to plow up one-third of their crops, destroy newborn calves, and kill one of ten dairy cows, as well as many of their hogs, to receive any government subsidies. This was the American farmer's introduction to the modernization of government subsidies. By utilizing less of their land and cutting back on livestock, this would keep demand in check with supply. The Steagall Commodity Credit Act, which was signed July 1, 1941, guaranteed farmers would receive no less than 85% of parity price. The Agriculture Act of 1954 guaranteed farmers a minimum of 82.5% parity. Parity slowly faded into a rural legend and more subsidies ushered in a new era of farmer welfare.

Government subsidies are the proverbial carrot on a stick for us to chase. We continue to farm mass amounts of land to collect our welfare and produce enough food and clothing for most of the modern world. Is this really necessary? Truth is, we would be much better off with parity prices instead of government subsidies. Our dependence upon government weakens us. Apparently, that's the way our government wants us—weak and vulnerable. So long as they have us dependent upon them, we are forced to do as they say.

Acres U.S.A. magazine published a chart comparing USDA parity price versus the producer's market price in the August 2009 issue. The parity is more than double in most crops:

Crop	Parity ($)	Producer's market price ($)
Wheat, per bushel	13.60	5.98
Corn, bushel	8.37	4.10
Cotton, lb.	3.14	1.13
Milk, cwt.	44.80	12.10
Beans, cwt.	65.40	30.08
Potatoes, cwt.	19.20	9.79
Soybeans, bushel	20.40	10.81
Apples, lb.	0.77	0.18
Beef cattle, cwt.	239.00	83.65
Hogs, cwt.	131.00	44.54
Eggs, dozen	2.13	0.75

The only exception I take to this chart is that cotton prices were actually more like 60 cents per pound rather than $1.13, which represents the organic cotton market price. But one certainly gains a whole new perspective of what portion the farmer is actually getting for his or her crop.

Following the North American Free Trade Agreement (NAFTA) in 1994 and the General Agreement on Tariffs and Trade (GATT), the World Trade Organization (WTO) was given unlimited power over agriculture commodities. In 1996, the U.S. Congress passed the Freedom to Farm Act with the new Farm Bill. If freedom's just another word for "nothing left to lose", then farmers lost just about all of their bargaining power in that bill. Commodity prices crumbled. Cotton, for example, climbed strong up over 80 cents per pound in the early and mid-1990s. After the new Farm Bill increased subsidies and erased borders, cotton prices dropped to 48 cents in 1997 and crashed to 28 cents in 2000.[3] A heavily subsidized commodity such as cotton encouraged more farmers to grow the crop than ever before. An excess of cotton flooded the market, as subsidy programs and insurance programs influenced farmers to be those "one-trick ponies" to ensure financial survival.

With each election in the past 20 years, agriculture has slowly drifted farther and farther into the background. It's as if it is some nuisance to our politicians. The Farm Bill is paper-clipped on the back pages of this country's welfare program. Washington, D.C., created the very mess we're experiencing in agriculture, causing farmers to be dependent on subsidies. They've weakened a once strong and proud industry. Now, it is merely individuals struggling to survive in a rigged game designed to fail over the long haul.

Many people on the outside of farming can't understand why

---

3. Will Allen, Eddie DeAnda and Kate Duesterberg, *Cotton Subsidies: Who Needs Them, Who Gets Them?*, Organic Consumers, http://www.organic-consumers.org/clothes/willallen011504.cfm, December 9, 2003.

farmers receive such large amounts of subsidies. Often, farmers are the subject of ridicule because of these government "handouts". What people fail to realize is that those very subsidies are what keep food and clothing at such low prices. With the current commodity price structure and without subsidies, farmers could not make sense out of farming large amounts of land to produce the crops needed to feed and clothe this world. Subsidies are the super glue holding this entire system in place.

Our own federal government owns 624 million acres, which is 27% of the country's land. The majority of subsidies once went to the largest landowners, who are usually neither farmers nor ranchers. In the United States alone, just 10 individuals/families own 10.6 million acres.[4] Ted Turner is at the top of that list, owning more than 1.8 million acres in 10 different states. He and other wealthy, powerful landowners are the reason why two-thirds of annual government subsidies went to just 10% of farmland owners, not the average farmer. That was until the 2008 Farm Bill introduced an adjusted gross income cap prohibiting subsidies being paid to entities whose non-farm annual income exceeded $500,000 or whose farm income exceeded $750,000 in a single year.

It is much easier to chastise the farmer for getting "hand outs" from the government. Farmers don't like the way the government program smells any better than the rest of the world. We, more than anyone, realize it is a broken system that must be fixed. And farmers have tried for decades to get this message across.

The American Agriculture Movement of the late 1970s shed light on this topic as farmers joined together, shutting down railroad cars and trucking companies in the food industry on a number of occasions. I remember as a child driving to Big Spring, Texas, and seeing hundreds of tractors in a row with American and Texas flags. Farmers huddled together with signs.

The protests came to a head on March 1, 1978 in McAllen,

---

4. Monty Burke and William P. Barrett, "This Land is My Land", *Forbes*, http://www.forbes.com/forbes/2003/1006/050.html, October 6, 2003.

Texas. Farmers protesting the importation of fruits and vegetables labeled as "Made in the USA" were ambushed on a bridge between McAllen and Hidalgo. A canister of tear gas was fired on the bridge to control the protestors. More than 200 farmers were thrown into jail as goon squads, deputy sheriffs, Texas Highway patrolmen, and other policemen imposed their will against these emphatic American farmers.

The intensity of the standoff magnified over two days as more farmers gathered outside the Hidalgo County Jail to protest the incarceration of their relatives and friends. Emotions were highly charged as dynamite and hand grenades were in the possession of many wanting to storm the prison's perimeter. Negotiations were ongoing between a small group of organizers and the sheriff's department. More protestors arrived, numbering more than 2,000. A Georgia farmer sat atop a tractor revved at full throttle with its nose against the front glass doors of the jail. Snipers aimed machine guns directly at the mob. Negotiations tightened inside the jail. Both sides knew emotions would soon create a bloody battle. The sheriff finally let the farmers walk free (on $28 bail each) and reduced the charges, avoiding a dark day in American history.

In the winter of 1979, more than 6,000 farmers convoyed in tractors to the nation's capital in what was to be known as the infamous Tractorcade demonstration in Washington, D.C. One farmer atop a tractor was blinded for life during the incident by tear gas used by local police to disperse the crowd. Many West Texas farmers were involved in the American Agriculture Movement. One of those was Marion Lea Snell, who was brutally beaten by goon squads in McAllen, and one of the 200-plus farmers arrested. Reflecting on his active participation in such a movement, Snell said:

> The more involved we became, the more we realized how bad we'd been getting screwed. The farmer is the only businessman that pays retail, sells wholesale, and pays the freight

both ways no matter what we buy or sell. The farmer is the first level of business that makes money, but the bankers of the world don't want us to get out of their control. That's what we were trying to do, to get out of the bankers' control with parity pricing. With parity, we wouldn't need to borrow money to farm, but they do not want the farmer to have parity. When you get to bucking the system like we did, it worries them. If we could ever get 80% of the farmers together now, we could control it.

These moments in history are just a few examples of the farmer's stand against the abuses of a corrupt system. Getting farmers to unite once again has been difficult as we've grown more complacent with the system, with borrowing large sums of money to operate, and accepting subsidies in exchange for parity.

As I write these words there has been much in the media of my beloved Texas (as well as Vermont) seceding from the United States and once again becoming its own country. While I doubt it is likely, we are one of very few states with enough resources (oil, natural gas, wind energy, electrical grid, farmland, crops, water, and timber) to pull off such a transition. However, I am not confident that certain political grandstanding is sincere. But make no mistake, many Texans would love for this to occur. Each state in America must regain its sovereignty if we are to truly function with any efficiency. Each state should be accountable to our original Constitution. Federal law should be expelled in favor of each state interpreting what is or is not lawful so that "we the people" can once again restore the true meaning of freedom and liberty. The perverse propaganda of false patriotism should be extinguished with a true vision of how Life should be without corruption in government, greedy corporatism, and a faulty economy run by bankers and billionaires pursuing nothing but more money and more control.

We must unite in the pursuit of our true liberty. The greatest threats to our freedom are not terrorists dressed in robes and turbans. Our greatest threats come from American men and women in dark suits, who call Wall Street, the United States Government, and the Federal Reserve home. They are the wayward souls behind pristine financial entities such as Goldman Sachs, AIG (now AIU), Merrill Lynch, CitiBank, and Chase. Yes, the night is darkest just before dawn, but when you've been locked in a dark room with windows painted black, you must break free to embrace the sun's warmth once again. The freedoms we are given by Nature, not man, give us that right to live. And we should not let anyone take those freedoms from us without a fight.

The Tribe Has Spoken

It's time to circle the wagons. A return to some form of tribal living makes sense, particularly in rural areas. Come to think of it, we never really abandoned this group instinct in our sense of survival, whether it be high school jocks, cheerleaders, street gangs, religious sects, social cliques, or whatever group we've felt safest with throughout the various stages of our lives. We will return to some extent to being hunter-gatherers. Not simply ones who drive around in pickups and shoot animals, but ones who are knowledgeable of their environment, respectful of the surroundings, and take only what is needed rather than more than is necessary. Once the concept of financial profit is no longer an issue, the principle of enough will welcome us back with open arms.

The need for and importance of relying on several others mean that living in the near future will be much easier if we cooperate with others rather than if we all persist in being lone rangers unwilling to let any friend, relative, or neighbor into our world. Strengthening trustworthy relationships will build our confidence rather than heighten our paranoia in future day-to-day affairs. Each tribe should not separate itself off from others outside their group but rather work on ensuring the formation of trusting bonds in reference to trade and in relation to bonding together in times of distress, trouble, or interferences from outside forces. They should become allies rather than competitors. This was the downfall of Native Americans—their stubborn refusal to join forces in times of hardship. There is strength in numbers, particularly when the multitude is unified in a particular effort.

Please relax. I'm not talking about painting our faces, beating our chests, and going out on raiding parties late at night, but rather focusing on creating small core groups consisting of individuals with specific skills and knowledge beneficial to more than just one person or family. Strengthening local ties through commerce, friendship, barter, and the family, social, and entertainment segments of our lives is one of the most important efforts we should be making right now.

Restructuring Communities and School Curriculum

It's much easier to hold the broken pieces once they're all put back together—even if it is in an entirely new arrangement. This is really what we need in rebuilding and restructuring our homes, communities, towns, neighborhoods, and cities. The average age of the American farmer is 62 years old. If more people are going to practice farming methods, the proper guidance and education is needed. Most of us had fathers and grandfathers to teach us the necessary skills, but that isn't now always the case. Imagine half a million young men and women trying to not only survive off the land but also make a profit and feed and clothe the rest of the world, and you are talking about one huge mess. This isn't 1959, much less 1929—we've grown to be severely disenchanted with Nature, and no longer make anything in this country. With our population exceeding 300 million, farmers comprise 0.32% of that—less than the amount of prisoners in this country.

Before people start growing gardens, they need education

about agriculture. I'm talking about families in both rural and urban areas. Education is needed immediately in how to begin and maintain healthy soils, seeds, and plants. We must relearn what grandparents and great-grandparents instilled in many—how to grow and preserve our own food. That is one of our greatest freedoms we took for granted. In the near future Wal-Mart, H-E-B or other national retail supermarkets may not always have their shelves fully stocked to supply the multitudes year-around—particularly if we are hell-bent on depending upon Central and South America for the majority of our fruits and vegetables. Whether it is through the models of transition towns and eco-villages, or whatever other means of transformation, our cities, towns, and communities must blend in with Nature, rather than exclude her.

Each community—whether a small town, rural area, or metropolitan area—should dedicate a set number of acres or city blocks to reforestation so that we will no longer continue to rape our national forests and state parks. And yes, these localized forests should partly consist of the hemp plant. It should be the star of the show for its many uses. These forests should be located right next to a community garden. Each town or community should appoint a chief gardener (who would not literally need to have the pedigree or even a college degree) to oversee these projects. In the future a chief gardener should be just as important as the city mayor, sheriff, or police chief in each and every single community. And the individual should be elected to this position by the local people only—not a county, state, or federal employee. We just need this person to be of high character (not swayed through bribery by the likes of Monsanto) and in tune with Mother Nature. This could be a seasonal position occupied by two or three different individuals and overseen by the community or a smaller committee.

Each school should utilize Nature courses in their curriculum. Reading, writing, and arithmetic should be balanced with agronomy, ecology, and botany. Classrooms should be transformed from bricked asylums with no windows by including hands-on experience in greenhouses, fields, and gardens. We must let Nature regain its level of importance in our lives, and that starts with educating children and young people so that they will share the same knowledge with the next generation. As big a fan of sports as I am, it is safe to say we've really overdone our indulgence in entertaining ourselves with visions of grandeur for our adolescent athletes. On average, about 4% of high school kids ever play college sports, and less than 0.3% go on to play professional. Compare that to 100% of high school kids who drink water and eat food, and it really seems like we've gotten our priorities out of order in our school system. A textbook jump shot or form tackle only takes us so far in life.

Seed banks should be started for heirloom fruits, vegetables, herbs, and grain and fiber crops in each town, community and neighborhood, along with each high school, junior high and elementary school. Greenhouses need to be constructed to ensure that no outside genetically modified seed may contaminate this vital project if such crops are grown in the area. Honeybee colonies should be implemented into each community to ensure we preserve their pollinating role as well as the miracle of honey. A program for locally adaptable bat colonies would be extremely beneficial to each area, as bats help keep mosquitoes and other pesky members of the insect population in check. Contests and challenges between the public schools would be a healthy way to encourage new ideas and innovative methods focused on creating and living in an entirely self-sufficient manner.

Instead of just applying the Nature "band-aid" (this term is attributed to Jim Kuntzler) to our urban areas with the token tree and shrub, vegetation will be the heart of each neighborhood and community. Trees can cool sidewalk strolls and provide shade for other outdoor activities in the heat of summer. A reasonable combination of winter trees could also form a perimeter windbreak in the cold of winter.

There needs to be a more aggressive transition into alternative energy as well in communities. Who says you have to spend an arm and a leg on wind energy? There are various websites and books offering cheaper, handmade wind turbines. We should make sure we practice rainwater harvesting from our houses and buildings to a significant degree to harness every last drop from the sky. Each cotton gin, grain mill, or other agriculture center should also serve as the main source of local fuel, installing a small-scale biodiesel plant with local field crops as the staple ingredient. Shares could be bought based on the individual's participation or contributions to the community in regards to his or her own trade or occupation. Again, the barter system would work well here.

Home Construction

Rather than continuing the insane modernized construction of cookie-cutter houses and pre-fabricated buildings without a soul, why not blend in the Spirit of the Earth with our dwelling creations? Instead of an entire house framed in wood, insulated with synthetics and fiberglass, how about rammed earth, concrete, or straw bale construction? Rammed earth houses, though highly labor-intensive, have been constructed for thousands of years and last longer than modern constructions of wood and even metal.

We could be using our own local resources for construction purposes, requiring little to no travel for materials. For instance, we added on to our house in the spring of 2010 using earthen mega-blocks as the walls. Dirt is compressed in a hydraulic machine, making 18-inch thick blocks up to eight-feet long. By utilizing soil from a pond built on our farm, we saved trailer loads of lumber. We used SIPs (structural-insulated panels) for the ceilings. These panels are over eight-inches thick and a metal roof is attached directly to them. No attic was needed. No wood was used in the construction of any of the outside walls or roof, saving lots of trees. I love the idea of living in a home constructed using the earth from our own farm.

With the thick walls and ceiling, the new part of the house is highly energy efficient, with no need for an air-conditioning and heating system that requires substantial amounts of electricity. No synthetic insulation, no crawling in dusty, dark attics, and no crawling underneath the house. Geothermal methods such as radiant flooring heating underneath the concrete floor will help keep the floor warm in the winter, hopefully eliminating the necessity of a wood-burning stove (we're not sure yet, as we've yet to spend a winter in the addition at the time of publication). The concrete floor is cool in the summer months, and this, along with ceiling fans, provides all the cooling we need. And the construction process is much cheaper than conventional building. There is no need for us to build a tornado shelter as these heavy walls will provide plenty of protection from destructive wind force.

I've attended countless talks and seminars where savvy architects aren't just trying to capitalize on the green building movement. They have figured out many of the inefficiencies that exist in the average American home construction process. Take attics for instance. Why do we waste so much space on an attic? This is where much heating and cooling air leaks out, resulting in larger energy bills. And the vents on the side of the house for an attic are about as handy as racing stripes on a Yugo. One architect told me it was like, "climbing into a microwave oven with a bowl of boiling soup and trying to blow on it to keep it cool". Smaller vents could be used to prevent molding in attics.

Handmade devices such as solar ovens are an inexpensive option for cooking. A medium-sized cardboard box lined with tinfoil with a glass or plexiglass pane can easily cook any meal on sunny days. More elaborate solar ovens are available on the internet, as are many clever hints on constructing your own. It isn't difficult. By putting up a clothesline, a family can save hundreds of dollars on a dryer, not to mention increasing the shelf-life of clothes. Any appliance with a heating element (clothes dryer, coffee pot, etc.) requires between 800-1,200 kilowatts to operate. This is handy information for those wishing to go off the grid with a solar and/or wind energy system.

We must look, think, and live outside the box. Current standards simply aren't good enough. They're neither sustainable nor efficient. No matter how grim or great life gets, it all boils down to the fundamental essentials—food, water, shelter, and love. Everything else, we can do without.

We tend to think in *always* terms. People will say things like "Oh, that's just the way it's always been, and that's the way it's always going to be." Really? Is a century our definition of always? Probably so in America. But this ol' globe has been spinning round a lot longer than Ford Motor Company, Exxon, and General Electric.

We're blinded by pride and ego, numbed by meaningless mirages, and misled by marketing schemes and propaganda. In all this mess, we must not lose site of the basics of living. We mustn't forget what keeps us living—truly living. Once we regain our dignity, perhaps we will merge as one and move forward in a beautiful movement unlike any other in history. Rather than a downward spiral, we'll form a poetic ascension.

To do so, Love must lead the way. We must love freedom. We must love independence. We must love family. We must love friends. We must love neighbors. We must love the Earth. We must love community. We must love Nature. Then and only then, shall we progress. Then and only then, shall we evolve.

Healing Herbs and Natural Medicine

The medical and pharmaceutical industries are a classic example of the smearing of Mother Nature. Hundreds, if not thousands of various plants offer the same healing properties as all these little blue pills to cure all our ills. Yet we continue to spend billions each year on prescription drugs.

One of the critical ways in which we must alter our minds is regarding how we think of medicine. We accept a little blue pill to cure all our ills, yet we are hesitant to think a plant might cure the same ill. We accept surgery as a logical solution to disease, but healthy food and exercise are overlooked. We accept undergoing CAT scans or radiation treatment that require an extra mortgage on our homes, yet Reiki or other forms of energy healing are dismissed as ridiculous hoaxes.

I've seen and felt various natural methods heal the human body. Personally, I've used devil's claw root to help my grandfather's arthritis. I've applied raw garlic to clear a tear duct infection in my father's eye within three days when countless trips to his doctor (along with lots of money and unnecessary toxic pills) had proved ineffective. I've used dandelion tea to cure my own fevers, and boiled onion juice to cure my baby's colic. I've rubbed peppermint on his belly to cure stomach aches, used oregano oil to get rid of warts, and applied comfrey to a sprained wrist (which healed in two weeks, not the diagnosed six weeks). Nature has the answers, not Man. Perhaps to acknowledge this is still our greatest challenge. Whether it is through pride, ego, or blocked emotion, we refuse to accept we are not Mother Nature's master. We mustn't look at her as our master either but rather our Mother and our teacher.

Healthy herbs, fruits, and vegetables are the greatest allies we have for attaining a healthy life, along with daily exercise, stretching, meditating, and stress-free thoughts. Essential oils are expensive, but by purchasing a handful of oils an entire family can ease pain and sickness for several months, if not years. I recommend lavender, frankincense, myrrh, thieves, lemongrass, oregano, and peppermint or spearmint. These oils help deal with a wide variety of illnesses. Personally, I recommend the oils from Young Living in Utah. Their oils are biodynamic and seem to have a greater influence on my body.

By utilizing Nature's cures, we're tapping into that Oneness flowing throughout this world. Relying solely on pills constructed by man in a laboratory will not balance our body, mind, and spirit. Polluting our bodies with more toxic pills disturbs our vitality and weakens our immune system. Hundreds of herbs, oils, and crystals are used in healing and strengthening one's body against illness and disease. I highly recommend the books suggested at the end of this chapter for reference to these alternative healing methods. Listed below are simply a few natural products known to have cured certain ailments:

Ailment	Herb	Essential Oil
Arthritis (muscles, bones)	devil's claw (root), yucca (root)	pine, lemongrass, spruce, lavender, basil, oregano
Asthma (allergies)	blessed thistle, pleurisy, skullcap	lavender, lemon, rose, frankincense, peppermint
Circulatory (blood, heart)	golden seal, blessed thistle, safflower	lemon, lemongrass, longevity, thieves
Cough (ear, nose, throat)	alfalfa, eucalyptus, peppermint	goldenrod, Peace and Calming, thieves
Digestion (stomach, intestines)	dandelion, peppermint, basil, spearmint, lemon	basil, peppermint, ginger,
Headaches (head, eyes)	skullcap, violet, lavender	Clarity, basil, lavender, thieves, spearmint
Immunity (fatigue, sickness)	dandelion, feverfew, garlic, oregano	frankincense, myrrh, thieves
Nervous system (stabilizing emotion)	chamomile, vervain, lavender	lavender, rose, valor, Peace and Calming

Relaxation (reducing stress)	lavender, valerian, vervain	lavender, frankincense, joy, rose, valor
Reproductive (sexual organs)	black cohosh, saw palmetto	lavender, St. John's wort, Peace and Calming
Respiratory (chest, lungs)	basil, thyme, garlic, blessed thistle	oregano, spearmint, thieves, pine

Certain herbal remedies require the use of different parts of the plant, whether the root, flower, or the entire plant. Some plants can simply be grown in your home, such as lavender and chamomile to promote a calm and relaxing environment. Many herbs make a powerful tea, while some (such as comfrey) should not be taken internally. Others do best outdoors in your garden or even grown in the wild. When uncertain about the variety of a plant, do not ingest it as some wild plants can be toxic to the human body. Most oils can be placed directly on the affected part of the body or over the respective chakra. For example, for headaches lavender could be placed on the third eye chakra between the eyes.

Down to the Nitty-Gritty

I'm well aware nobody is getting out of this alive—we've all got to die at some point along the horizon. But, what we do between our first and last breath determines who we are in the next life. This I truly believe. Not all share this belief, and that is okay. I do not pretend to be a Christian or religious on any level. A not-so-old saying goes, "A religious life is for those afraid of going to hell. A spiritual life is for those who've already been there." And after growing up on a dryland cotton farm in the prairie-like desert that is West Texas, the concept of hell sounds like a refreshing change of pace.

We've wasted much of our energies through many generations coercing our own particular religion of choice on everyone else around, whether that be our family, friends, neighbors, or those we perceive to be our enemies. The vast majority of Christians or Muslims are really no different from one another in the notion that they think everyone else should believe what they believe. These expectations only encourage confrontation. In realizing the fact most religions proclaim we are near "the end of time", one might argue by basing our existence on our unwavering religious principles we are conveniently permitting, if not encouraging, the destruction of Mother Nature as we all profit from such plundering.

We're so busy burning bridges with religion, so intent on building walls between our church clubs, we've lost the concept of unconditional love. We are still huddled masses of souls yearning to breathe free. We've grown so tired and weary of our own games, many haven't the strength to stand up and confess such an awakening is needed. But it is.

As we inch closer to the December 21, 2012, date at which the Mayans stopped measuring time, I feel it is more of a cosmic transformation we will experience. Not some Hollywood-depicted or biblical Armageddon, but a shift of consciousness that has been long overdue. Perhaps our spirits, our true selves will overcome our egos. Perhaps our souls will preside over our minds. Perhaps we'll experience a spiritual orgasm. Perhaps nothing at all. I will not pretend to know exactly what will take place in the future, but I know what I feel inside. We are about to embark upon a truly remarkable revolution powered by our true selves rather than our egos. What happens around us will alter our lives without question, but if our minds and spirits are prepared beforehand then we will not fear the transformation.

Our body forms are vehicular temples we allow to carry and protect what is truly vital. These forms are here to serve our purpose in this Life, but they will not be necessary once our work here is complete. Why not use them to our advantage? Why not allow our muscles and bones and ligaments and cartilage and flesh to carry out the intention of our spirits, to fulfill the duty of our souls? Why would we allow our bodies to imprison our souls when we are capable of utilizing every part of our being? Let us not continue to be slaves to a master we truly despise. Let us not worship the very things we know are of no significance on the Other Side. We must begin to put aside our irresponsible ways, our childlike tendencies to value money over Love, or material possessions over natural resources. We must stand strong, and we must stand together.

An appreciation of Nature is an appreciation of the Self. Refusing to accept the damage we cause Nature is a refusal to accept the damage we cause our Self. Surely, at one point or perhaps several you have asked, "What am I doing here? What is my purpose?" We've all gone through our moments of existential masturbation. What did you come up with? How are we justifying our existence? Simply by producing another generation of confused humans? By making as much money as possible? By submissive reactions to a corrupt government? By rising to social or political power, and using that power strictly for your own good? What then? What shall we say this Life really is all about?

I like to think we are here to love and be loved, to overcome our fears, to rise above ourselves for the greater good. That is to say, we have all been scattered like ash into the wind and seas, drifting and floating to all corners of the universe. At one moment or through a series of experiences, we are to reconnect with one another, learning from this poignant ride in the form of a tragic comedy. We were all once connected. Bill Maher made a brilliant documentary entitled *Religulous*, which painted the broad portraits of the major religions and our various attempts at reaching heaven in the next life. It was both fascinating and funny. He questions religion's intention and our dubious quest to follow each respective religion's teachings unyieldingly. And I must agree as I've checked religion at the proverbial door, no longer considering myself a Christian but merely a flesh and bone spirit. For lack of a better term, perhaps I'm spiritual. And people (including Bill Maher) often ask, "Well, what does 'being spiritual' mean?" To me, it means searching for the meaning of the soul and our existence on this planet in this life; and trying to not only verify the recognition of our soul, but also that our existence is connected to everything else. Or maybe, just maybe it is a life in which we recognize all the delusions and refuse to accept this is how we should live simply because that's what we were taught as a child or it is what everyone else is doing.

We are trying to make sense out of all this. Some days it is harder than others. Some days, nothing matters. Others, everything matters. Fight it. Love it. Hate it. Embrace every last moment. Ignore it altogether. It shouldn't be a mirror of what others make or say it is, but rather what we will it to be.

Resources

BOOKS

Essential Oils Pocket Reference by Essential Science Publishing
Field Guide to Edible Wild Plants by David Foster and Bradford Angier
From the White House to the Hoosegow by Gerald McCathern
How to Live a Self-Sufficient Life by John Seymour
Plan B4.0: Mobilizing to Save Civilization by Lester Brown
Reinventing Collapse by Dmitri Orlov
SAS Survival Handbook: How to Survive in the Wild, In Any Climate, on Land or at Sea by John Wiseman
The Encyclopedia of Country Living by Carla Emery
The Essential Crystal Handbook by Simon and Sue Lilly
The Little Herb Encyclopedia by Jack Ritchason, N.D.
The Long Emergency by James Howard Kunstler
U.S. Army Survival, Evasion and Recovery by the U.S. Department of Defense
What's the Matter With Kansas? How Conservatives Won the Heart of America by Thomas Frank
When Technology Fails by Mathew Stein

WEBSITES
backwoodshome.com
cluborlov.blogspot.com
earthcomegablock.com
earthship.org
equipped.org
farmandranchfreedom.org
greenhomebuilding.com
infowars.com
localharvest.org
nffc.net/
sonofafarmer.com
survival-center.com
transitionculture.org
transitiontowns.org
urbanhomestead.org
whentechnologyfails.com
wilderness-survival.net
wildsurvival.com

VIDEOS
Garbage Warrior
Religulous
The Garden
The Power of Community: How Cuba Survived Peak Oil
What's the Matter With Kansas?

Chapter 7

REAPING WHAT WE'VE SOWN
Being Part of the Whole

*There would be no advantage
to be gained by sowing a field of wheat
if the harvest did not return more than was sown.*
NAPOLEON HILL

*Here in this body are the sacred rivers,
here are the sun and moon,
as well as all the pilgrimage places.
I have not encountered another temple
as blissful as my own body.*
SARAHA

Harvest Time Is Here

For several years I roamed the Earth without a home in search of more. Throughout my travels I explored, looking for a better way to do things, a better way to live, because I was certain what I'd witnessed was not the pattern to follow. I had glimpses of unharnessed joy in the dusty wooden pubs of England, in the cliff-carved villages of Italy, along the vineyards of Greece, in the Alps of Switzerland, in the Englischer Garten in Munich, down the cobblestone streets of Prague, in curvy reflections of Barcelona, in coffee shops of Amsterdam, in polished marble of Rome and Athens, and upon the rooftops of Morocco. In countless city squares and patio cafés, I saw the smiling eyes of strangers wanting nothing more than laughter and love and freedom to fill their days and nights. I have witnessed the same here in America. Just not as frequently as I should. I finally realized the answers would never be found in one city, country, or continent, but rather in that piece of us that is connected to one another and everything else. We, both farmers and humanity as a whole, are capable of so much more.

Often life is as much anticipation as it is action. This is an undeniable truth. For what is action without planning? This is not to say that instinct and intuition are to be forgotten. They are equally vital. But mental blueprints must be written upon the wrinkles of our brain before muscles take action. Work without thought is merely laborious toil, encouraging poverty, cynicism, and old age. However, hard work inspired by efficient thought is indeed the greatest revolution any individual may experience in this body form.

Confucius said, "If you think in terms of a year, plant a seed; if in terms of ten years, plant trees; if in terms of 100 years, teach the people." What exactly have we been teaching in agriculture the past 50 years? What lessons have we refused to learn or accept? Should we improve the soil and conserve our resources to ensure a healthy balance in Nature? Or should we just try to make as much money as we can this year? Seems like a tough one, doesn't it? Yet for the majority, which of the two has been chosen consistently year after year this past century?

We demand immediate results and seldom, if ever, contemplate the long-term effects of wasteful and careless acts. All the money in the world will not save us from our incessant greed and fruitless desires. All the oil beneath our feet cannot conceal our insecurities. All the wonderful inventions modern technology has to offer cannot cover up the destruction we've caused. The true measurement of who we are can be viewed in our children's remaining resources.

Apocalyptic predictions are becoming more and more popular each passing month. The days we are now living can be ambiguous and depressing. Our near future appears uncertain and our distant future bleak. Yet, crying out that "The end is near!" or "Jesus is coming!", or whatever doomsday phrase tickles your fancy, will only delay us from organizing, restructuring, transitioning, and rethinking ahead, defying the strenuous nature of such an unprecedented workload of reform. Perhaps that is why we secretly desire an Apocalypse—we merely want to avoid years of unknown struggle and strife. Something our not-so-distant ancestors accepted as just another day. Life will no longer be easy—not in the way we have grown accustomed to for 70 years. Now, we must all roll up our sleeves, strap on our work boots, sharpen our skills, hone our senses, and retune our minds back to the Earth, back to what is pure, wholesome, and natural, back to basic survival skills. It's very sad that, because we've taken so many vital resources for granted, unnecessary die-offs have begun. We can't change the past, but we can sure as hell mold the future.

It would be a shameful waste if we never evolve past our current standard of short-term thinking and self-absorbed, materialistic manner of living. We are excessive carnivores hell-bent on filling our bellies as quickly and cheaply as possible, all the while spending the vast majority of our days trying to make as much money as possible or as is necessary to make life comfortably numb. We constantly deny ourselves access to the most wonderful places of imagination, self-expression, and creation, while we focus the majority of our thoughts on destruction, ridicule, and the naive notion of conformity. We are much better than this. When will that recognition be strong enough to motivate us into action against the saddened state of tyranny we currently face?

Fortunately, some are well aware of our critical situation. We are the ones who must come together, uniting in purpose. We haven't the time to stand courteously on the front porch, hat in hand, ringing the bell or knocking politely at the door. Now is time to kick the damn door down, and be the change of presence we need. Yes, we will face tireless opposition and the influence of corruption, but we must not be weakened by its gutless persuasion. We must let a new energy flow from within—gaining glimpses of our true meaning, releasing old patterns of fear, and expressing the courage of Oneness.

Our Gift to Future Generations

At this point in time everything we say has been said before. It is simply a different arrangement of words to help convey whichever emotion, idea, or purpose we wish to get across to someone else. Still, we must continue to arrange these words so that the message is clear enough for multitudes to understand.

I had a phone conversation with a fellow young farmer one night, and somehow we got onto the subject of deserts. He said, "All I've been hearing about for years is that the desert is moving east out here. I'm in it, and it is headed your way, I guess."

I agreed, saying how I'd noticed the changes in the topsoil in the ten years I was away from the farm. We also talked about the desertification of China.

"Well, maybe we'll make our money now. Our kids can deal with that instead of us," he chuckled.

Surprised by his remark, I insisted, "I'm not comfortable handing off something like that to my kids. We need to do what we can to correct it while we're here."

He changed the subject, "Well, that's a depressing subject. I don't want to get down about that after we just had a good rain."

And I'll agree most of this is depressing to think about. But it is just as inspiring to do something about it. So long as we do nothing, depression is inevitable. But with proper action, the positive outweighs the negative. We shouldn't ignore a problem, only to pass it on to the next generation. Rather we should do anything and everything we can to better the situation.

From my childhood I remember a hymn we sang in church that went, "This world is not my home, I'm just a passing through. Our treasures are laid up somewhere beyond the blue." Perhaps this world is not our permanent home, but it is the home our children, grandchildren, and future generations must endure. Why not leave them with something greater than what we had? Why not do any and every last thing we can to make sure it is better than we found it? One of my favorite Native American sayings is from Chief Seattle, who said, "We do not inherit the Earth from our ancestors, we borrow it from our children." My question to you as fathers, mothers, grandfathers, and grandmothers is: What is your legacy? What will you leave behind? If we adopt this mentality in all that we do, no doubt our children will be thankful. Let us be the ones who change Life for the better. Let us open our minds and hearts so that it is our soul shining through. Before my son turned two years old, I would constantly tell him, "Be creative, not destructive." Yes, I'm aware that "boys will be boys", but I want to instill in him the importance of Nature. We must rewire the circuits of our minds and we must not allow our previous destructive methods to survive another generation. The tasks from here on should be simple for not only our vocation but our entire species: heal the Earth, nourish humanity, and protect Nature just as we protect our family, friends, and selves.

As concerned as we are with the presentation of our fields and yards on the surface, we think nothing of destroying what we can't see. We'll spray poison in our fields, our yards, our homes, and wonder why we feel sick and have to go to the doctor three or four times a year—if not more. We wonder why cancer consumes many of our loved ones. We wonder why our water is no longer drinkable. We wonder why all the creeks and rivers no longer run. We wonder why all these incurable diseases pile one on another. It is because we are creating the diseases with our own unclean acts and reckless activities. It is difficult to be the cure when you are the disease. We're contaminating our nest. We've become mindless machines. But we can change. We can enlighten ourselves if we just stop and think about what we're doing and why.

We must alter our perspective on what our crops symbolize and represent to us. We must become stewards, not producers. We can't simply look across a beautiful field of cotton, corn, soybeans, or wheat, and boast, "Aw, look at all that money!" So long as that is our attitude, agriculture has little to no chance of making it as a healthy, sustainable livelihood. Perhaps we could rather look across those same fields, smile and say, "Look at all that life. Look at all that beauty and energy." Then, we have a chance. Our satisfaction in a job well done should come from us being focused more on how much we give back to the Earth out of respect and love rather than how much we take away from her due to bitterness and self-indulgence.

The lesson of Easter Island should have been enough to make our species rethink our way of doing things. Perhaps what took place there wasn't quite recent enough. Easter Island is known for its gigantic stone head statues (about 600 altogether) situated along grassy hills looking over the Pacific Ocean. The 150-square-mile island was once home to 7,000 natives in the early 1700s. Apparently their warfare and competition for who could build the biggest and most statues were more important than their environment. The transportation of the 20-foot-high statues required numerous large tree trunks to roll along the earth, carrying each respective statue. They also used the trees to build homes, shelter, and canoes for travel. Once covered in lush forest and vegetation, the island was slowly transformed into a barren grassy nub before the 20th century. Their competitive nature and shortsightedness led to the destruction of their resources and consequently their entire society. Today, there are no natives remaining on the island, and what trees grew back are few and far between.

Whether we realize it or not, we are experiencing the same meltdown in our society and in particular with agriculture. As we deplete our resources and continue to damage fragile ecosystems, few options will remain for us to restore our topsoil and encourage healthy plant production. As the reality of Peak Oil slaps us harder in the face each day, the methods used to produce and transport goods will change faster than we can keep up with. Agriculture is the lightning rod in all this. Without food and water, we are nothing. It is imperative we begin experimenting and implementing healthier organic methods to give our species a fighting chance of survival in the near future. There remain many options for us to build something far greater than we currently have. Curt Ellis, co-producer of *King Corn*, admitted he didn't have all the answers either, yet he provided a fitting guideline for how to measure our farming operations in the near future:

> There's no one recipe for "good farming", but I think there are a few questions that are worth asking about any operation. Is it growing food that's healthy for the people who are going to eat it and the land it's grown on? Is it making that high-quality, sustainable food available to consumers at all income levels? Is it operating in a way that respects the dignity of the workers on the farm and in the processing sector? Is it respecting the lives of animals involved in the system as livestock and impacted by it as wildlife living nearby? Is it operating at a scale that keeps the family and community engaged? My guess is if you can answer yes to all those questions, you've got a good farm—and a great life—on your hands.

Let us abandon the addictions to chemicals and toxins in our soil, air, and water. Let us minimize our uses of petroleum and over-priced machinery. Let us protect our seed supplies. Let us heal the Earth by rotating our crops and planting native grasses and trees. Let us provide a healthy food chain for all walks of Life to enjoy. We may not solve all the problems we've created, but we can sure as hell try.

We must tackle the challenge of restoring our soil and immediately begin practicing methods leading us away from our addiction to chemicals. Do I use chemicals in our current farming operation? Yes. But we are continuing to make strides, relying less and less on chemicals while eliminating commercial fertilizers and pesticides. It is my goal to one day never purchase a single ounce of chemicals. It will be challenging and many changes must be tackled, but it is certainly attainable in the near future.

The long-term risk to not only our health but our future existence far exceeds the temporary reward of monetary gain or wealth. Money is the greatest illusion we must peer past if we are ever to grasp the beauty of living freely. Breaking free of such chains is necessary for a much more fulfilling Life.

The Road Ahead

Let us not paint a scene of hopelessness, but rather develop a means to create acute awareness of the problems we've caused and their dire consequences if we refuse to change. Let us be inspired and awaken so that we may begin a new path in agriculture and living, setting a standard based upon a harmonious relationship with Nature and preserving our natural resources. The focus should be on the quality of Life, not the quantity of dollars.

This is a map of reality. Here is our present location and our potential destinations lie over the next hill. These times we are experiencing and living should not be viewed so dire or catastrophic. Yes, perception is reality. So long as we suck our thumbs in a fetal position, hiding in the basement's darkness, then we improve nothing and change nothing. Whether this is an orchestrated collapse by the Powers That Be or simply Mother Earth and Reality providing us with a much overdue magnificent douche, our fears must be transcended into strength. Our anger must be transcended into determination. Our words must be transformed into action. No more talk. Just hard work.

For quite a spell, I viewed the future as grim. But I realized something—I have the power to change the future. We all do. Moaning and worrying accomplishes nothing. In fact, it denies us the achievement of greatness. Positive thought breeds positive action. Let us rise above the greedy nature of multi-national corporations, the corruptness in big government, and all the vicious idealism that has brought us to our knees. Let us wisely exert our way into another style of living—a living that does not depend

242

on fabricated falsehoods regarding freedom. Money is not power. Money is a cleverly disguised form of shackles and chains for most of us. It is an illusion we must rid ourselves of if we ever dream to evolve into complete beings and rise above this ominous fog.

I'm the product of a wide range of cultures who hoped a vastly improved life existed somewhere beyond the horizon. Some were absolutely astounded by what they found. Some were disappointed. On my best and worst days, I'm a little of both. Our reality today is far different than that of a century or two ago. Now, there are no more horizons. No more undiscovered territory. Like it or not, this is it. The only undiscovered territory lies in the caverns of our minds where there exists an ability to understand the concept of Now. Even in the darkest shadows, we can live in harmony with an undeniable appreciation that results in being perfectly content with where we are, who we are, and what we do. How much of what is reality now will remain so in the near future? Considering our current path, how much closer are we to the ending than the beginning? Careful, because that next step is extremely important in the continuation of our dance.

We no longer can afford the luxury of saying, "Yes, but I have to make a living." Very soon, that attitude alone will not only limit but extinguish us. There is no margin for the persistence of error. There are no scapegoats available for such a vast sacrifice. We are the only ones to blame for our failures, just as we are the only ones to look toward for support. Only we have the power to decide what will become of our lives and perhaps all of Life as we know it. It is my plea, my prayer, and my hope that not only all farmers but all people feel these words in the depths of their souls. My pride is vanquished so that I may request this. Is yours too great to ignore it?

The latest and greatest poison in the form of herbicide, pesticide, or whatever -icide is not the answer to our problems. We must be students willing to learn from Nature, from the past, and the daily signs above, below, and beside us. It is up to us as individuals to learn, absorb our surroundings, and seek answers that empower Nature, not inhibit her. If we do this, I am confident we'll be amazed at the results.

Now more than ever "global weirding" is overwhelming much of our entire Planet. Growing seasons may very well become shorter, as both winters and summers intensify more than the norm. While governments use this as yet another way to tax citizens, and corporations jockey into profiting position, we must look past this to the real problem—that we continue to overwhelm the Earth with toxic formulas and excessive habits. Being at the top of the food chain does not quarantine us from annihilation once the other links are ripped apart. Apart from being a matter of survival, this is an ethical issue. Any other hot topic such as gay marriage, border patrol, or abortion inspires most "religious" people to mount their moral high horse, armed with an arsenal of ethics, dressed to the theatrical "t", complete with red crosses painted across reinforced chests. Yet when the very fabric of Life is threatened, where are our knights in shining armor? Where have all our heroes fled? Are they too busy hiding fragile egos? At what point will true leadership emerge?

My fellow liberators, *we* are those knights in shining armor. *We* are those heroes. *We* are intended to be such leaders. Not government. Not corporate America. Not some prophetic savior descending from the Heavens. Not some alien Mother Ship landing to take us away to our perfectly identical sister planet. Not some miraculous invention in a garage. Not some heralded discovery in a laboratory. Not some comic-strip superhero. It is up to you and me—*us*. We the people. If not us, if not now...well, then we are all really in trouble. There is no hope. There is no future—only our failure to deal with the reality of our dire situation. The solution to the problem is for us to recognize the problem, change our course, heal the Earth, and heal ourselves by reconnecting our inner being to the Spirit of Nature. All true revolutions are begun and won by common people with a common goal based upon the principles of freedom. This one will be no different. But it will be more necessary than ever before.

These times are not for us to ignore the signs we witness. *Now* is the time to change, to transform internally so that this beauty may be appreciated by those who will follow us. Now is the time we must come together and acknowledge our purpose for living *this* life in *this* body. To delay reacting to or to ignore our challenges will be our worst and most fatal regret. Let us not be the ones who will look back in penitence, but let us be the ones posterity will look back at with great admiration of our strength to unify, and praise our ability to act as One with Love.

Everything is One here. The rocks, trees, rivers, oceans, birds, coyotes, lizards, deer, birds, horses, cows, goats, pigs, sheep, rabbits, people, worms, armadillos, and especially the soil—all One. The mountains are the skeletal system, the bones of this magnificent organism. The rivers are the blood flow pulsing through veins and arteries to major organs—lakes, seas, and oceans. The trees are the lungs, allowing all things to breathe in and out each day. The animals are the nervous system, keeping the mind alert to what is about to occur. Insects represent the immune system, healing by destroying what needs to be removed for a healthy body to survive. The grass is the Earth's flesh, protecting her from the unforgiving elements. The soil is the digestive system, restoring Mother Earth with much needed energy. The Earth may not be our permanent dwelling place, but she is our Mother. She is our legacy. As humans (particularly farmers), we are the caretakers— the walking and talking collective consciousness of Mother Earth. We are the Holy Spirit wearing clothes and driving cars. Yet, it is a task we seem most unwilling to accept or, at the very least, attempt to verify. Why would we dare deny or ignore this blessed undertaking? Instead, we've chosen the part of Ego over Consciousness. This continues to be the main source of our downfall.

As human beings, we should be the fully aware collective conscience—the mind's eye of this wonderful planet. As farmers, we should be guardian angels protecting the flesh and bone Holy Grail that is our soil. Instead, we've sold out. We've exchanged home-grown methods for disparaging schemes because it is easier to do what we're told rather than adhere to what we feel deep inside us. Now is the time for all of us to realize what must be done, what must change, and to begin that process today. Not tomorrow. Today! The problems existing now were not solely created by inept government and greedy corporations. These problems were also created by a lack of resistance by all people. Yes, the problems exist. No, it is not too late to do something about it.

Everything is connected. That bond is what keeps this planet dancing round in poetic choreography. That connection is what keeps us all alive. What we do to the Earth, we do to ourselves. If we are capable of destruction, we are most certainly capable of healing. We are an extremely privileged species, not omnipotent masters. Once we realize this, the healing process will begin. If we insist on our current disconnection then we are most certainly expendable, and our purpose as a species is lost in a crowd of confusions and misinterpretations. Only when we listen, truly listen to the Earth will we know how intertwined we are within the web of life. We are merely one fragile thread in the web, not the spider itself.

Somewhere within all of us awaits the greatest of intentions. It is a desire we know must be fulfilled to make sense of not only the invention of our very species but also the concept of evolution as a whole. This awareness is not so much a fulfilling of one's destiny, but simply a means by which our minds might fully understand what our hearts and spirits are desperately yearning to explain. This message which beats within our chests is the same song sung by the river's flow, the mountain's summit, the prairie's wind, and the desert's cry.

We should be shepherds, not sheep herders. A good friend of mine once explained the difference between the two. Sheep follow the shepherd. The sheep herder follows the sheep. We are merely part of the whole, my fellow liberators. Not the whole thing. Without the rest, we are nothing. If we are so anxious to be masters, let us only master ourselves. The rest will take care of itself. We are limited only by our imaginations and lack of desire to see those images through with hard work.

246

My wife and I took a trip in the spring of 2008 and ventured into the abyss that is the Carlsbad Caverns. Such a magical place. Such a divine experience immersing one's self deep into the Earth below the roots of all trees and plants, underneath the planet's flesh. After hours of exploring, we paused at a place called "On the Cross" to rest and meditate. It is the center where four major areas meet as one in the heart of the caverns. Closing my eyes, I focused intensely on the Earth and our connection as One. These words came to me...

> *You are here to feel my heart beating. You are here to listen to my words. Love me as I love you. Care for me as I care for you. Without this love, without respect for one another, neither of us will remain nor survive the other. Let us continue our dance together. Let our hearts beat as one. Let our hearts beat as one.*

Let us dance as we've never danced before. Let our respect and love for all things grow. Let our dreams reach for the sun. Let our minds melt into our souls. Then and only then will we have truly lived. Then and only then will our lives have truly been exactly what they were intended to be. Perhaps all of this sounds like some crazy dream. Maybe it is, but at least the seeds are planted firmly in your mind. Whether they lay dormant beneath the surface or break free and reach for the sun is entirely up to each and every steward. So go on now and do with them what you will.

About the Author

Eric Herm was raised on a cotton farm near Ackerly, Texas. He graduated from Abilene Christian University with a degree in broadcast journalism. After working in sports television broadcasting, he traveled extensively. Having broadened his mind, Herm eventually returned to Texas to work the land that has been in his family for almost 100 years. Startled by the changes he saw in the land, he began to change practices on his own farm and to speak out against the ravages caused by commercial agriculture. Eric lives on the farm with his wife, Alison, and their two sons.

Please visit Eric's website, www.sonofafarmer.com, for more information.